Rethinking Collaborative Learning

# Rethinking Collaborative Learning

Edited by

Richard Joiner, Karen Littleton, Dorothy Faulkner
and Dorothy Miell

FREE ASSOCIATION BOOKS / LONDON / NEW YORK

First published in Great Britain 2000 by
Free Association Books
57 Warren Street
London W1T 5NR

ISBN 1 85343 513 9 hbk; 1 85343 514 7 pbk

A CIP record for this book is available from the British Library

Designed, typeset and produced for
Free Association Books by Chase Publishing Services

Printed in the European Union

# Contents

## Part IV  Identity, Motivation and Affect

## Part V  Making Space for Collaborative Learning

# Preface

In recent years new translations and interpretations of the work of L.S. Vygotsky and the emergence of new sociocultural accounts of development and learning have generated considerable research activity by developmental psychologists and educational researchers on the relationship between the social and cognitive dimensions of learning. In recognition of this, a workshop was organised by the Social Dynamics in Development and Learning Research Group at the Open University in October 1998 with the aim of bringing together researchers with these particular interests. During the workshop a number of themes emerged. One that kept recurring over the two days was reconceptualising the nature and quality of collaborative activity. Following this workshop, we decided to produce a book of edited chapters on this issue from the workshop participants and from other researchers working in this area across the world. Before going on to give a brief summary of the book, I would like to thank all the contributors for providing an interesting collection of chapters and I hope they think all the 'creative tension' was worth it.

The book has been organised into five parts: (i) development; (ii) mediation; (iii) adult support and guidance; (iv) identity, motivation and affect, and (v) making space for collaborative learning. These different parts reflect some of the emergent themes from the workshop. The first part focuses on issues of development and collaborative learning. The place of the development of individual skills and competencies is an issue not often considered in research on collaborative learning. Sharon Ding and Emma Flynn (Chapter 1) consider the relationship between the development of children's collaborative skills and the development of more general cognitive skills. They describe research which has investigated children's behaviour in various collaborative tasks, drawing parallels between the development of this ability and the development of skills in the areas of intersubjectivity, planning, communication and inhibition skills. They argue that the mastery of these skills underpins the ability to successfully engage in complex collaborative activity. David Messer and Karen Pine (Chapter 2) report research that is based on Karmiloff-Smith's (1992) Representational Redescription model of cognitive development. Karmiloff-Smith puts forward the idea that cognitive development involves the progression through a number of developmental levels from implicit non-verbalised processes to explicit verbal knowledge. For Messer and Pine the interesting aspect of this model is that there is one level of development at which children seem to focus on internal representations and fail to take account of external information either from the social or physical environment, suggesting that at certain levels of development children will not benefit as much from collaborative activity than at other levels. Messer and Pine then report three studies which suggest that the beneficial effects of collaboration are mediated by the developmental level of the child.

The second part of the book contains chapters concerned with mediation. Mediation is an important concept in Sociocultural theory and refers to the fact that we do not interact directly with reality, but through psychological and technical tools. The first chapter in this section examines the role of technical tools in mediating collaborative activity. Richard Joiner and his colleagues (Chapter 3) found that the introduction of a computer changed the nature and quality of collaborative activity and also changed what the children learn from that activity. The next two chapters examine the role of musical interaction in mediating collaborative activity. Louise Morgan and her colleagues (Chapter 4) report three studies that investigated the role of verbal and musical interaction across three different musical tasks. They found that there was a strong and positive relationship between musical interaction and the quality of the groups' musical compositions for all three tasks, but there was only a positive relationship between verbal interaction in one of the tasks. Raymond MacDonald and Dorothy Miell (Chapter 5) also investigate the role of verbal and musical interactions, while comparing friends and non-friends on a creative musical task. They analyse the talk in terms of transactive discussion which is characterised by the exploration and integration of ideas. Raymond MacDonald and Dorothy Miell also develop a method of transactive music analysis where children explore and integrate ideas expressed through music. They found that the most successful collaborations were those between friends and that these interactions were characterised by high levels of transactive musical communication and transactive verbal communication.

The third part of the book looks at the role of adult guidance and support in productive collaborative activity. Research suggests that successful and productive collaboration between children is not guaranteed and requires organisation and preparation. Christine Howe and her colleagues (Chapter 6) examine how to integrate peer collaboration and adult guidance in the context of science learning. They report two studies which show that it is possible to integrate adult guidance and peer collaboration. Andrew Tolmie and his colleagues (Chapter 7) also examine whether it is possible to integrate adult guidance and peer collaboration in the context of children's pedestrian skills training. They conducted a number of studies where they compared peer collaboration, adult guidance and a combination of the two and found that children benefited the most when there was a combination of adult guidance and peer collaboration. Rupert Wegerif (Chapter 8) looks at the role of adult guidance in a different way by examining the benefits of training children to use exploratory talk when working in groups. He presents a dialogical model of reasoning which views meaning, not as logical structures but as created out of the interaction between different voices and different meanings. Dialogical reasoning can be modelled by a set of groundrules. He identifies three different sets of these groundrules, cumulative, disputational and exploratory. Previous research has shown that productive collaborative learning is best modelled by exploratory talk. He then reports two studies where he trains children to employ exploratory talk and finds that children who are taught to collaborate using exploratory talk gain both in terms of curriculum learning and on a general measure of reasoning.

The fourth part of the book looks at the aspects of the social situation, which have not received sufficient attention in the literature on collaborative learning. These chapters point to the limitations of a purely cognitive account of collaborative learning. Patricia Murphy (Chapter 9) examines the role of social identities, in particular gender identity and the process of negotiation in social interaction. Murphy discusses how gender identities mediate the interpretation, negotiation and meaning of educational tasks. Charles Crook (Chapter 10) argues that motivation or agency is a concept which is lacking from research on collaborative learning. Collaboration is something which sometimes people will seek out and sometimes they will avoid. He argues that we have to adopt an ecological perspective to understand which circumstances will lead people to work together and which circumstances will lead them to work alone. An ecological perspective situates collaboration in the environment and emphasises the systemic nature of social interaction. Crook then presents two studies. The first examines how the design of physical space and virtual space can support informal collaboration, and the second examines the use of resources that mediate collaborative activity. Margarita Azmitia (Chapter 11) examines how considering the affective process in social interaction can broaden our understanding of collaborative cognitive development. She makes a number of very interesting proposals concerning the role of negative affect and frustration in collaborative cognitive development. These negative emotions can lead to time-outs from collaboration which can sometimes have a beneficial effect because they allow individuals to work out ideas and manage their emotions.

The fifth part contains chapters that have evaluated the design of new spaces for collaborative activity. A range of new information and communications technologies have led to the design of these new spaces and the following chapters evaluate their use in a range of different learning contexts. Vivienne Light and her colleagues (Chapter 12) look at the way in which computer-mediated communication (CMC) can be designed to support a more communal learning experience in a campus-based university. They report three studies which evaluate a form of CMC called 'Skywriting'. Light and her colleagues conclude from these studies that skywriting changes the students' relationships to each other and to the tutor; learning was less private and their sense of belonging to community was enhanced. Eileen Scanlon and her colleagues (Chapter 13) present two case studies that evaluate the use of video and audio links in two collaborative learning environments: one in science and one in statistics. From both of these case studies they found that the use of audio and video links enhanced problem solving. Pascale Marro Clément and Anne-Nelly Perret-Clermont (Chapter 14) evaluate a project which was designed to provide adult education in information and communications technology to a linguistically and geographically remote region of Switzerland. The interesting aspect of this study was the way the design of the project was re-negotiated between the designers of the initial project and the inhabitants of this region in a way which is not observed in research concerned with children's collaborative learning.

Karen Littleton in the final chapter provides an overview of the book. The contributors all start from the premise that the research agenda on the process of collaborative learning has been rather narrow in focus. Karen Littleton uses the voices of the contributors to summarise the key themes and issues arising from the chapters, presenting an overview of the ways in which the contributors invite us to rethink collaborative learning. It is clear that in rethinking collaborative learning a new and exciting research agenda emerges.

*Richard Joiner*
Bath University

# Part I
# Development

# 1
# Collaborative Learning: An Underlying Skills Approach

*Sharon Ding and Emma Flynn*

## Introduction

The aim of this chapter is to consider the relationship between the development of children's collaborative abilities and some of their more general cognitive skills. We describe research which has investigated children's behaviour in various collaborative tasks, drawing parallels between the development of this ability and the development of skills in the areas of intersubjectivity, planning, communication and inhibition skills. We argue that mastery of these skills underpins the ability to successfully engage in complex collaborative activity.

There now exists a strong body of knowledge which documents the benefits of collaborative learning for subsequent individual cognitive gains (Rogoff 1990, Howe et al. 1995). This work has been carried out in both Piagetian and Vygotskian traditions. Although social influences on development are not central to Piaget's theory, he did state that cognitive development depends on social contexts as well as the physical environment. 'Social life is a necessary condition for the development of logic. We thus believe that social life transforms the individual's very nature' (Piaget 1928, p. 239). Neo-Piagetian researchers followed through this strand of thought, focusing on the effects of cognitive conflict in social learning situations. Research has shown that when a child has his or her views challenged by another child who holds an alternative perspective, the children in the dyad are forced to compare their differing viewpoints. This results in each child decentreing from their own beliefs, leading to a deeper understanding of the problem (Doise and Mugny 1984).

Social interaction is a central tenet in Vygotskian theory. He argued that it is impossible to understand individual cognition in isolation from the cultural context in which the child is situated. Interaction with a more able other introduces children to social structures and tools which have developed over time, and which enable individual development. A child learns first by interaction on the social plane, and then internalises this knowledge on to the psychological plane (Vygotsky 1981).

This growing body of psychological knowledge has been complemented in recent years by a change in classroom pedagogy. Emphasis has moved away from a total commitment to a competitive environment; instead, children are being introduced to learning situations in which they are encouraged and often required to work together on a joint task (Foot et al. 1990, Rogoff 1990). Research is suggesting that co-operative as opposed to competitive environments are leading to increases in children's academic achievements (Slavin 1995). Similarly, current assessment policy includes measurements of children's social development from the age of 4 years, highlighting the importance of early interaction (Department of Education 1998).

This bringing together of research and practice is resulting in a powerful body of opinion concerning the benefits of social interaction for cognitive development. There is now a consensus that in certain circumstances, children can benefit from collaborative interactions. Much research has been carried out which focuses on the outcome of the interaction. Studies have looked at the composition of the learning dyads; for example, by pre-testing children on their understanding of scientific phenomena and using the results of this pre-testing to form the dyads (Howe 1993). Glachan and Light (1982) looked at the effect of the structuring of the task on learning gains. They found that structured tasks led to increased outcomes for some children, whereas children working collaboratively in unstructured environments did not benefit from the experience.

Other work is more ambivalent with respect to the advantages of social interaction for learning. Gauvain and Rogoff (1989), for example, found that some children who worked together on an errand-planning task performed no better than children who worked alone, when later carrying out the task independently. One way of investigating this disparity is to look at the processes within the different collaborative situations. It could well be that very different events are taking place in different situations, which will have a profound effect on the quality of the interaction. In order to unpack the differences in collaborative learning situations we can look at the mechanisms which might underlie them. What are the relevant skills which individuals bring to the interactive learning process? In other words, we are suggesting a change in focus from looking at the effects of collaboration on individual learning gains, to look at the effect of individual skills on the collaborative interaction. This is comparable with work carried out by Dunn et al. (1996) with pre-school children, looking at verbal competence in an everyday environment, so considering the effect of language skills on sociocognitive development. By investigating the processes within the interaction at such a micro level one can begin to understand what elements produce the outcome. If the skills which facilitate effective collaboration can be pinpointed then strategies can be used to encourage the use and development of these behaviours.

The following sections will sketch some of the work which has been undertaken on the early development of collaborative learning ability, describe some of the skills which we believe underlie successful collaboration, and then end by discussing some of the problems concerned with this type of analysis.

## The Development of Collaborative Skills

Use of the term 'collaborative learning' within the literature has varied greatly. Foot et al. (1990) used the umbrella term 'peer-based learning' to describe all the types of social interaction for which cognitive growth and/or learning is viewed as the desired outcome. Within this term he includes asymmetrical relationships, which will involve some element of tutoring, and symmetrical ones, which are characterised by equality, both in terms of age, stage of cognitive development and equivalence of knowledge or skill in the task to be carried out (Phelps and Damon 1991). This chapter makes the assumption that the skills which underlie these different types of collaboration are likely to be common across the different types.

### Early Evidence of Interaction

There is a strong body of literature which documents social interactions between young infants and their primary care-givers (Schaffer et al. 1977). There is no doubt that babies do engage in social behaviour, and it seems reasonable to suggest that this will have a positive effect on cognitive growth. Of course, this behaviour is not necessarily intentional on the part of the infants. Schaffer (1989) talks in terms of a pseudo-dialogue, in which the adult achieves conversational smoothness by inserting his or her contributions into the infant's pauses. Thus the adult allows the child to set the pace by careful monitoring and an accommodation to the less-skilled partner, thereby being the active agent in maintaining the interaction. Researchers such as Trevarthen (1977) have argued for a much more active role being played by the infant, where the adult follows the infant's lead by responding to actions or imitating expressions. Trevarthen holds that, by the age of 8 or 9 months, infants have achieved secondary intersubjectivity. Having passed through the primary stage where they have a recognition that the world is shared with others, they move on to create joint activity by focusing on other objects. It would seem that care-givers make use of this to increase infants' knowledge of the world, so building on the interactive situation. Working within a Vygotskian framework, therefore, we can see the beginnings of collaborative learning at a very young age, albeit with more able others taking a proactive tutoring role.

Whilst research into collaborative learning has been most frequently carried out with school-aged children, there are a few examples of work with younger age groups. These are not conclusive, however, as they present results which vary greatly in the degree to which the participants have collaborated successfully. As one might expect, there is also a great deal of diversity in the learning situations in which these young children have been placed.

Verba (1994) observed three different age groups of young children (13–17-month-olds, 18 months to 2-year-olds, 2–4-year-olds) in their usual day-care settings. The children were provided with a variety of different play objects such as containers, beads and blocks. These were placed on a low table, and the participants were left to engage in spontaneous play for 20–30 minutes. Verba describes three modes of sociocognitive functioning in the three groups of children, with strong similarities between groups:

*Observation-elaboration*: Here one child observes another and suggests an idea for action. Both children then act almost simultaneously, giving them the opportunity to view their own actions being carried out by another. This opportunity to distance oneself from action is viewed as crucial to the abstraction process, considered by Piaget to be one of the most important mechanisms for cognitive growth. All groups showed similar patterns of observation-elaboration, but the older children were more capable of complex co-ordination between their actions.

*Co-construction*: At this level a common objective arises when one child starts to take part in another's activity. This provides the necessary frame within which mutual adjustment is possible. Meanings are shared by inferential processes, and some understanding of intentions is achieved by smiling, gesturing and vocalising. Again, patterns of co-construction were similar across the age ranges, however, older children had longer and more involved interactions.

*Guided activity*: In this activity one child acts as 'knower' and assists another child in reaching a goal which s/he has previously achieved. Here there is no individual action, nor a shared goal, but the 'knower' infers the goal and prompts the 'learner' to carry out some activity. A rudimentary form of tutoring was observed with this young age group, though it was usually an explicit prompt or an action facilitation, which contrasts with more subtle guidance which has been observed in research with slightly older children (Cooper 1980).

Verba argues that the three modes of interactive functioning described above form a continuum from the individual to the social pole in cognitive elaboration. The learner moves from controlling his or her own action plan to being guided by a more knowledgeable other. Nonetheless, they are all dependent on interpersonal co-ordinations, enabling children to gain new perspectives on their actions. The data do provide evidence that, at least in some circumstances, there is an early emergence of sociocognitive formats which enable young children to co-ordinate their actions with those of others. It could well be that the development of other cognitive and social skills make more complex interaction possible.

Recent work by Ashley and Tomasello (1998) has found similar results when looking at the collaborative skills of slightly older children in a more goal-directed task. They investigated the collaborative problem solving of pairs of children aged 24, 30, 36 and 42 months. The dyads were introduced to a physical task which required them to co-ordinate their actions in order to obtain a reward. Once each of the partners had become proficient, they were paired with a naive partner and given the opportunity to teach the task to them. The 24-month-old children did not learn how to gain the reward, even when given adult assistance. The 30- and 36-month-olds rarely needed adult intervention in order to be successful, but they were slow to master the task and rarely co-ordinated their actions. Also, they seldom tutored their naive partners, though they could often recognise that a new partner had not encountered the problem previously. The 36-month-olds made more adjustments for their new partners, and so this interaction was more successful. In contrast to the younger age groups, the behaviour of the 42-month-olds was qualitatively different. It was characterised by a comparatively high number of both co-ordinated attempted solutions and specific communicative directives. They were also the only age group who 'taught' their partners by using demonstrations. These differences resulted in success being achieved in approximately half the time that it took the younger children to complete the task.

These results are in contrast to those obtained by Brownell and Carriger (1990). They discovered that $2^1/_2$-year-olds were able to co-operate in a problem-solving task in order to gain a reward. However, all the apparatus manipulation in this task was carried out by one child, whilst the other waited for the reward to become available so that he or she could collect it. Thus, whilst actions had to be co-ordinated so that they occurred in the correct order, only one child had engaged in complex manipulation, and the temporal co-ordination of the actions was not as difficult as in the Ashley and Tomasello task.

Ashley and Tomasello explain their results by comparing the level of perspective-taking ability of the different age groups of children. They contest that the 42-month-olds were able to understand that their partner had a different perspective on the problem from their own; they had some knowledge of what that perspective was and some views about how to change it. The 30- and 36-month-olds, whilst showing some signs of appreciating the different perspective of their partner, still needed to develop a clearer view of what that perspective might be, and what to do in order to effect change. This could explain the potential conflict with the results reported by Brownell and Carriger (1990). Success in this situation did not depend on a deep understanding of another's perspective, but rather on an understanding of the consequences of a course of action.

Informal observations by the present authors of children's collaboration in playground games also adds evidence for the ability of young children to collaborate. Children aged 3–4 are very successful in their performance during playground games which require complex interaction with a partner or partners. However, children are very familiar with the explicit rules and rituals which govern these types of games, and it may well be that some of the 'cognitive load' which would normally be necessary for successful collaboration is carried in these rules, so significantly simplifying the task. Nonethless, those of us who are familiar with a nursery playground may recognise that when a child's own needs are in conflict with those of the group, collaboration breaks down quickly, and often an adult needs to be present to co-ordinate the game in these types of situations.

Other research has considered children's collaborative ability on more specific classroom-style tasks. Azmitia (1988) looked at social interaction within a block-building task. She paired 4–5-year-old children and found that they were more likely to advance in cognitive skills than peers who had worked alone. However, when the interactions were examined there was very little discussion, and it seems that the most likely learning strategy was that of observation. Although this demonstrates an awareness that another child may know more than you do yourself, it does not necessarily show a knowledge of the content of another's perspective.

A comprehensive study which has illustrated the changes in the quality of collaborative interactions which lead to effective tutoring was carried out by Wood et al. (1995). They taught a 3D puzzle to children aged 3, 5 and 7 years and then required them to tutor a same-aged peer. They analysed the tutoring in terms of the child's abilities to tutor contingently; that is, the tutor's ability to support learning by giving an appropriate level of help in light of the learner's last action. If the last action by the learner was correct, then a contingent tutor should give less support in the next interaction, whereas failure should result in a higher level of support. As might be expected, the different age groups showed an increase in this ability. The 3-year-olds showed little evidence of contingent teaching, whereas the 5-year-olds had begun to display more contingency. In the 7-year-old group, the level of contingent teaching was high.

The behaviour of the learners in the study also displayed interesting age differences. All three groups were eventually able to learn the task, but it took the youngest children much longer and they had many more periods of trial and error, seeming to learn mainly from a laborious process with many mistakes. Previous work with this task showed that the nature of learning in the 5-year-olds relied mainly on observation, rather than being related to the degree of contingency displayed by their tutor. The 7-year-olds, in contrast, were able to take advantage of the tutoring they received in order to learn how to carry out the task successfully.

The studies reviewed above show an interesting development in terms of the type of collaboration in which the children engage. This has been outlined theoretically by Tomasello et al. (1993). They describe an initial phase of collaboration which is largely carried out by the process of imitation. Here, children copy the actions of others, and by doing this can achieve task success, but this may not involve any real sense of intentionality. It is rather a matter of a child copying the actions of another, and success occurring through that action. The second phase is that of observation. Children know that another can achieve a goal more successfully than they can, and so they observe that other child's behaviour so that they can learn from it. The final phase involves true collaboration where both children understand that they need to co-ordinate their actions and their perspectives in order to obtain success. Thus what we refer to in a general sense as collaborative learning is in fact an umbrella term for a progression of intersocial activities, which could rely more and more heavily on complex cognitive skills. When we consider the changes which occur between the ages of 2 and 7, it would be surprising if children did not take advantage of their developing skills to improve their interactions with others. For example, the frontal lobe continues to develop during early childhood leading to an increase in the ability to regulate one's behaviour. Also the enculturation of children into formal schooling is also likely to bring new skills, such as the ability to follow formal rules, which can be utilised. By the age of 7 years, when children appear to be able to collaborate effectively, they have an exemplary cognitive toolkit of skills at their disposal to facilitate this activity. An investigation of the nature of collaboration with a view to unpacking some of the constituent skills will enable us to propose some of these likely 'tools'. We have referred several times above to the development of perspective taking, or intersubjectivity, and it seems obvious that this will be an ability which is crucial for fully successful collaboration. The next section will discuss research which has been undertaken in this area, which begins to investigate the link between intersubjectivity and collaborative learning. However, there are also other candidates which seem likely contenders to underpin effective collaboration and so we go on to outline similar possible links in the areas of communication, planning and inhibition.

## Underpinning Cognitive Skills

### Intersubjectivity

As previously discussed, there is evidence that young infants show some signs of intersubjectivity, a recognition that the world is shared with others and that these others can share in joint attention. The topic of intersubjectivity has had a long history. Piaget's work referred to the necessity for the child to decentre and take on a perspective other than his or her own in order for cognitive development to occur (Piaget 1923). Children's ability to take on the perspective of others has been investigated more recently within the 'Theory of Mind' literature. This research is too extensive to review in any detail here. However, there now appears a consensus that a child begins to have insight into another's mind, and to be able to use this insight at around the age of 4 years. This means that the child understands that the knowledge that he or she possesses is different from the knowledge that another person possesses, and this understanding can be used to predict how that person will behave. A more sophisticated recursive understanding, where children understand that someone else may have an incorrect belief about another person's 'state of mind', emerges at 6–7 years (Perner and Wimmer 1985).

The ability to be able to reason about the knowledge which a collaborator possesses would seem to be a crucial skill which underpins successful collaboration. Without this, it would be extremely difficult for either member of a dyad or group to learn by collaboration, rather than by observation. These ideas were proposed by Tomasello et al. (1993) in their cultural learning paper. They claimed that children would not be able to collaborate effectively before the age of 6–7 years as they did not have the conceptual skills; that is, recursive perspective taking, to support such interaction. They argued that in order to teach effectively; that is, contingently, one would have to have an idea of the knowledge and lack of knowledge possessed by one's collaborator. This viewpoint was also discussed by Wood et al. (1995). In Tomasello et al.'s (1993) paper, they commented that it did not seem coincidental that the age differences, with 7-year-olds surpassing 5-year-olds, that appeared in their participants contingent tutoring abilities, were in parallel to the stages of development of mentalising skills. From this work theoretical predictions were made concerning the relationship between a child's mentalising skills and his or her ability to tutor. In order to be able to teach contingently the tutor must reflect between his or her own knowledge and that of the tutee, and be able to plan actions from this reflection. Additionally, the children must understand that they may each hold differing beliefs about each other's knowledge; that is, an even more sophisticated ability which incorporates the capacity to handle recursive belief patterns.

Similar claims have been made concerning children and their ability to participate in pretend play with a peer (Tan-Niam 1998). Tan-Niam worked with $4^{1}/_{2}$-year-old children and found a relationship between a child's theory-of-mind status and the quality of his or her play. Pairs of children where one child had displayed theory-of-mind ability as measured on a false-belief task had a better quality of social interaction than pairs where neither child had been successful on the theory-of-mind tests. This quality of interaction was measured in terms of sharing meaning and play facilitation skills. This shared understanding of the tasks, together with the joint attention displayed, are elements of collaboration which can be observed and which illustrate the use of intersubjectivity.

We have recently carried out some research which also addresses the issue of theory of mind and its role in effective collaboration (O'Malley et al. forthcoming). We looked at 6-year-old children, because previous research had demonstrated that at this age children were beginning to teach contingently. The children were tested on their theory-of-mind ability using two tests which tapped into their ability to use and understand embedded mental states. One test was a standard second-order test designed by Perner in 1985 ('the ice-cream story'), and the second was adapted from the 'surprise puppy story' devised by Sullivan et al. (1994). Using the results of these tests, dyads were created in order to compare the tutoring ability of children with differing theory-of-mind statuses. We found that those tutors who had been successful in the theory-of-mind tests were more contingent tutors than those who had failed the tests. This result is important, as it is the first study which has carried out a direct comparison to investigate the existence of the link between theory-of-mind and collaborative learning. It does not appear surprising that the acquisition of collaborative skills could be underpinned by intersubjectivity skills. In order to collaborate effectively one must have a shared understanding of the task and goals.

## Communication

In order to participate successfully in collaborative learning, children must be able to understand their partner's point of view, and also to understand the difference between their own understanding and that of their partners. As well as an understanding of another's perspective, children have to be able to communicate their knowledge and their needs to each other. Without this ability it would be very difficult for any shared understanding to develop.

One of the important factors in communication which is particularly crucial for collaborative learning is the ability to give unambiguous messages, and to understand when messages you have been given are ambiguous and not beneficial in obtaining the goal. This ability has been studied for the last 20 years or so as part of the referential communication paradigm. The purpose of this research is to investigate the development of speaking and listening skills (Lloyd 1994). A successful speaker will be able to produce statements which uniquely describe a particular object or event; a successful listener will be able to distinguish between statements which uniquely describe a particular object or event, and those which do not. Furthermore, when ambiguous messages are given, a successful listener will be able to decide on the appropriate additional information to ask for in order to disambiguate the message. The principal findings described in this literature demonstrate that speaker skills develop before those of successful listening. School-aged children usually have no difficulty in giving adequate descriptions. They may give more information than is required, though this is not thought to prevent any real barrier for successful collaborative learning. Listening ability develops much more slowly during the early school years – 4–5-year-olds often respond to the message they are supposed to be attending to before the speaker has actually finished delivering it. Lloyd and Beveridge (1981) argue that this is because young children do not understand that successful communication requires that listeners attend and respond to the information they are being given. Hence, they are very passive listeners, and are not aware of the interdependence of the activity.

Further evidence of young children's lack of understanding of the role of the message comes from work carried out by Robinson and Robinson (1976). When an ambiguous message was given, such that the listener was unable to select the correct object, 5–7-year-old children always blamed the listener, rather than appreciating that the message which had been given was inadequate. The ability to detect ambiguity, together with an understanding of what information is missing, continues to develop during the primary school years (Patterson et al. 1981).

Again, when we review the development of communicative competence, we see developmental change which runs in parallel to goal-directed, complex collaborative learning. This, taken in conjunction with our analysis of the necessary components of collaborative learning, suggests that those children who are successful collaborators will also be successful communicators.

Work on the communicative ability of children has demonstrated that a substantial minority of children do not possess the communicative competence needed to play a successful role in collaborative learning situations (Brown et al. 1984). However, there is also evidence that participation in appropriate collaborative training activities can help communicative skills to develop (Lamb et al. 1995). The activities involve the children being encouraged to seek clarification and confirmation when giving and receiving messages. Extended experience with these tasks resulted in better communicative behaviour and more successful collaboration.

Although full referential communicative competence does not develop until well into the primary school years, there is evidence that much younger children are capable of bringing to bear their communicative abilities on the collaborative situation. Shantz and Gelman (1973) found evidence of downward speech accommodation amongst 4-year-olds when interacting with 2-year-olds, thereby showing some understanding of the differential needs of their collaborator. In a similar vein, Cooper (1980) tested pairs of children aged $3^1/_2$ and $4^1/_2$ years on their ability to co-operatively solve a balance-beam problem. The older children used more directive language than the younger ones, resulting in more successful co-ordination of behaviour.

## Planning

Planning is the process of looking ahead to devise actions aimed at achieving a goal and monitoring the effectiveness of the actions for reaching the goals as the plan is executed. In the type of collaborative learning situations we have been considering, where the children have to engage in a set of co-ordinated joint activities, this ability to hold in mind a plan and work towards that plan will help to achieve a successful outcome. This is because the means by which the goal can be attained can be held in mind and worked towards. Evidence suggests that although children's planning begins as early as the first year (Piaget 1969), with development children's planning becomes more effective and makes greater use of foresight when advanced planning is warranted (Gardner and Rogoff 1983).

English (1992) investigated the ability of children aged 4–9 years to plan ahead when solving a set of combinatorial problems. She discovered that the 4–6-year-old children very rarely demonstrated any problem-solving strategies which involved planning. Instead, their behaviour was largely trial-and-error. From the age of 7 years, the children began to favour the more sophisticated planning strategies, with a strong preference being exhibited in the behaviours of the 8- and 9-year-olds. This resulted in a more efficient and more reliable means of solving the problem. Additionally, the more successful older children also engaged in comprehensive monitoring of their problem solving.

In a study designed to look at the effects of collaborative working on children's planning abilities, Gauvain and Rogoff (1989) compared the planning abilities of 5- and 9-year-old children on a task which required them to 'buy' several items located in different aisles on a map of a grocery store, whilst covering the shortest distance possible. Although the effects found for collaborative planning were somewhat inconclusive, they found that the older children were much more likely to plan their actions as they negotiated their way around the map. In contrast, the 5-year-olds tended to react in a more haphazard fashion, moving around the map in response to a selection of items chosen by preference, rather than with a view to the optimum route length. The older children also scanned a wider area of the map more extensively before beginning the task.

The studies described above demonstrate a gradually developing ability to plan effectively in order to achieve a goal, and again the developmental path mirrors the change in collaborative abilities we see as children become older.

## Inhibition

In a complex learning environment, children must inhibit their own behaviour if both members of the dyad are to be able to play a full and active part in the collaborative situation. In a teaching situation, a tutor who is being effective must be able to monitor his or her learner, and engage in a new path through the task if the one he or she is teaching is proving unsuccessful. A child intent on monitoring his or her own pathway through the task will not be able to do this. Also, a learner may engage in a different action from the one which the tutor was attempting to initialise. However, innovating a new strategy may result in success, rather than failure. To facilitate this change in route the tutor must disengage from his or her own activity, and inhibit his or her own initial responses. Then the tutor will be able to evaluate the actions of the learner in terms of potential for success, rather than in terms of the similarity to the tutor's own planned actions.

Wood et al. (1995) found that there was a major change for task responsibility from 5–7-years. The older tutors passed more of the task over to their learner for completion, whereas younger tutors completed more of the task themselves. The 7-year-olds tended to replace doing with telling, illustrated by the explicit instructions they gave at the beginning of the task. Some 5-year-olds also gave instructions, but then acted on these themselves rather than allowing their learner to do so. This is a direct example of the relationship which exists between successful collaborative learning and the ability to inhibit one's own activity.

The above overview has outlined some of the cognitive skills which we feel may well underpin the ability to collaborate successfully. The complexity of findings in this area and an analysis of collaborative learning point to the existence of some necessary underpinning skills. We are currently undertaking a study (O'Malley et al. forthcoming) which directly investigates the relationship between these underlying skills and the ability to collaborate effectively.

## The Way Ahead

The literature reviewed above has begun an analysis of some of the cognitive skills which might underpin successful collaborative learning. In order to develop a comprehensive view of this complex area, it is necessary to consider some further factors which we suggest will also affect the interaction.

Apart from the general skills we have outlined there are other clusters of competencies which will also affect the ability to participate effectively in a collaborative learning situation. A comprehensive description of underlying skills will need to look carefully at the domain expertise of both collaborative partners, their general intelligence, and also their knowledge of what it is to collaborate, to name but a few. When we consider these, together with social factors such as gender and friendship pairings, we can see that the desire for investigations which look for interdependencies between skills is an ambitious one.

Our discussion has centred on the two partners in the collaborative situation and the abilities they bring to it. Another important aspect concerns the type of tasks in which the children engage. Most of the current literature has investigated collaborative situations in the contexts of tasks which are largely about skill acquisition. Participants have been asked to build 3D jigsaws, for example (Wood et al. 1995), or to manipulate apparatus in order to obtain a reward (Ashley and Tomasello 1998). Exceptions include Howe's work (Howe et al. 1995), looking at the effect of pre-existing views on conceptual change in science. Whilst it seems likely that many of the skills we have outlined above will apply to both skills-based and conceptual tasks, a full investigation needs to look at both types of tasks, as there may also be some important differences.

We have discussed the skills above in isolation from each other. However, in reality they are extremely likely to be interdependent. Children who have a well-developed theory of mind, for example, may well also have good executive functioning skills, an area which has recently attracted a large increase in research activity (Russell et al. 1991, Hughes 1998, Flynn et al. 1999). Indeed, it would be surprising if this were not the case. One of the tasks for the future, then, is to investigate the existence of, and possibly develop models which can explain, this interdependency and allow us to see whether any of the skills are primary. In order to do this, we will need to undertake large-scale studies which enable the use of sophisticated statistical modelling techniques.

The direction of effect between successful collaborative learning and the underlying skills may not be straightforward. We have argued that the possession of certain cognitive abilities will contribute to a successful learning situation. However, researchers such as Gauvain and Rogoff (1989) have suggested that the experience of working in a collaborative situation encourages the development of metacognitive abilities such as planning. Hartup (1985), in a similar vein, argues that problem-solving situations where decision making is shared provide opportunities for the development of metacognitive strategies. We do not wish to claim that this is not so, and do not see such research as incompatible with our views. Indeed, the most fruitful way forward may well be to adopt a longitudinal approach, whereby we investigate the development of successful collaborative learning and the associated underlying skills in parallel.

## References

Ashley, J. and Tomasello, M. (1998). 'Co-operative problem-solving and teaching in pre-schoolers'. *Social Development*, 7(2), 143–63.

Azmitia, M. (1988). 'Peer interaction and problem solving: when two heads are better than one?' *Child Development*, 59, 87–96.

Brown, G., Anderson, A., Shillcock, R. and Yule, G. (1984). *Teaching Talk*. New York: Cambridge University Press.

Brownell, C.A. and Carriger, M.S. (1990). 'Changes in co-operation and self–other differentiation during the second year'. *Child Development*, 61, 1164–74.

Cooper, C.R. (1980). 'Development of collaborative problem solving among pre-school children'. *Developmental Psychology*, 16(5), 433–40.

Department of Education (1998). *Baseline Assessment for Primary Schools*, Circular Number 6/98.

Doise, W. and Mugny, G. (1984). *The Social Development of the Intellect*. Oxford: Pergamon Press.

Dunn, J., Creps, C. and Brown, J. (1996). 'Children's family relationships between two and five: developmental changes and individual differences'. *Social Development*, 5(3), 230–50.

English, L. (1992). 'Children's use of domain-specific knowledge and domain-general strategies in novel problem solving'. *British Journal of Educational Psychology*, 62, 203–16.

Flynn, E., O'Malley, C. and Wood, D. (1999). 'Executive functioning and theory of mind: a meta-representational debate'. Paper presented at the British Psychological Society Developmental Section Conference, University of Nottingham, UK.

Foot, H.C., Morgan, M.J. and Shute, R.H. (eds) (1990). *Children Helping Children*. Chichester: John Wiley and Son Ltd.

Gardner, W. and Rogoff, B. (1983). 'The development of flexibility in children's improvisational and advanced planning'. Paper presented at the 91st annual convention of the American Psychological Association, Anaheim, CA.

Gauvain, M. and Rogoff, B. (1989). 'Collaborative problem solving and children's planning skills'. *Developmental Psychology*, 25, 139–51.

Glachan, M. and Light, P. (1982). 'Peer interaction and learning: can two wrongs make a right?' In G. Butterworth and P. Light (eds) *Social Cognition: Studies in the development of understanding* (pp. 238–62). Chicago, IL: University of Chicago Press.

Hartup, W. (1985). 'Relationships and their significance in cognitive development'. In R. Hinde and A. Perret-Clarmont (eds) *Relationships and Cognitive Development* (pp. 67–82). Oxford: Oxford University Press.

Howe, C. (ed.) (1993). 'Peer interaction and knowledge acquisition' [Special Issue]. *Social Development*, 2(3).

Howe, C.J., Tolmie, A., Greer, K. and Mackenzie, M. (1995). 'Peer collaboration and conceptual growth in physics: task influences on children's understanding of heating and cooling'. *Cognition and Instruction*, 13, 483–503.

Hughes, C. (1998). 'Finding your marbles: does pre-schoolers' strategic behaviour predict later understanding of mind?' *Developmental Psychology*, 34(6), 326–39.

Lamb, S., Wood, D., Leyden, G. and Bibby, P. (1995). *Children with Learning Difficulties: A profile of abilities and implications for intervention*. (Technical Report No. 23). Nottingham, UK: ESRC Centre for research in development, instruction and training, University of Nottingham.

Lloyd, P. (1994). 'Referential communication: assessment and intervention'. *Topics in Language Disorders*, 14(3), 55–69.

Lloyd, P. and Beveridge, M.C. (1981). *Information and Meaning in Child Communication*. London: Academic Press.

O'Malley, C., Ding, S., Flynn, E. and Wood, D. (forthcoming). *The Development of Peer Tutoring Skills*. Nottingham, UK: ESRC Centre for research in development, instruction and training, University of Nottingham.

Patterson, C., O'Brien, C., Kister, M., Carter, D. and Kotsonis, M. (1981). 'Development of comprehension monitoring as a function of context'. *Developmental Psychology*, 17, 379–89.

Perner, J. and Wimmer, H. (1985). '"John thinks that Mary thinks that ..." Attribution of second-order beliefs by 5 to 10 year-old children'. *Journal of Experimental Child Psychology*, 39, 437–71.

Phelps, E. and Damon, W. (1991). 'Peer collaboration as a context for cognitive growth'. In S. Straus (Series ed.) and L. Tolchinsky Landsmann (Vol. ed.) *Human Development: Vol. 4. Culture schooling and psychological development* (pp. 171–83). Norwood, NJ: Ablex.

Piaget, J. (1923). *The Language and Thought of the Child*. London: Routledge and Keagen Paul, 1959.

Piaget, J. (1928). *Judgement and Reasoning in the Child*. New York: Harcourt, Brace.

Piaget, J. (1969). *The Child's Conception of Time*. New York: Basic Books.

Robinson, E.J. and Robinson, W.P. (1976). 'The young child's understanding of communication'. *Developmental Psychology*, 12, 328–33.

Rogoff, B. (1990). *Apprenticeship in Thinking*. New York: Oxford University Press.

Russell, J., Mauthner, N., Sharpe, S. and Tidswell, T. (1991). 'The "windows task" as a measure of strategic deception in pre-schoolers and autistic subjects'. *British Journal of Developmental Psychology*, 9, 331–49.

Schaffer, H.R. (1989). 'Language development in context'. In S. von Tetzcnner, L.S. Siegel and L. Smith (eds) *The Social and Cognitive Aspects of Normal and Atypical Language Development.* New York: Springer Verlag.

Schaffer, H.R., Collis, G.M. and Parsons, G. (1977). 'Vocal interchange and visual regard in verbal and pre-verbal children'. In H.R. Schaffer (ed.) *Studies in Mother–Infant Interaction* (pp. 291–324). London: Academic Press.

Shantz, M. and Gelman, R. (1973). 'The development of communication skills: modification of speech of young children as a function of listener'. *Monographs of the Society for Research in Children Development,* 38, 152.

Slavin, R.E. (1995). *Cooperative Learning* (2nd edition). Boston, MA: Allyn and Bacon.

Sullivan, K., Zaitchik, D. and Tager-Flusberg, H. (1994). 'Pre-schoolers can attribute second-order beliefs'. *Developmental Psychology,* 30(3), 395–402.

Tan-Niam, C. (1998). 'Social interaction and theory of mind in children's pretend play'. Unpublished doctoral thesis, University of Nottingham, UK.

Tomasello, M., Kruger, A. and Ratner, H. (1993). 'Cultural learning'. *Behavioral and Brain Sciences,* 16, 495–552.

Trevarthen, C. (1977). 'Descriptive analyses of infant communicative behaviour'. In H.R. Schaffer (ed.) *Studies in Mother–Infant Interaction* (pp. 227–70). London: Academic Press.

Verba, M. (1994). 'The beginnings of collaboration in peer interaction'. *Human Development,* 37, 125–39.

Vygotsky, L.S. (1981). 'The genesis of higher mental functions'. In J.V. Wertsch (ed.) *The Concept of Activity in Soviet Psychology* (pp. 144–88). Armonk, NY: Sharpe.

Wood, D., Wood, H., Ainsworth, S. and O'Malley, C. (1995). 'On becoming a tutor: toward an ontogenic model'. *Cognition and Instructions,* 4, 565–81.

# 2
# Is Collaborative Learning Influenced by Children's Representations?

*David J. Messer and Karen J. Pine*

In this chapter we argue that there is a need to consider collaborative learning and the effects of collaborative learning in relation to the level of children's cognitive representations. Much of the research about collaborative learning focuses either on cognitive or social processes, it is comparatively rare for bi-directional influences to be considered. For example, many of the chapters in this volume emphasise the way that talk and social interaction can provide a basis of more advanced understanding. In this and other research, children's collaboration is often investigated in order to describe the social processes that occur or an examination is made of the way that these social processes influence cognitive abilities. We wish to argue that a further issue needs to be considered, the way that cognitive level can influence the benefits that children derive from collaboration, and the way that verbalisation may be a key process in children's cognitive development. Most of the research we discuss is concerned with peer interaction as a form of collaboration, but adult–pupil collaborative learning is also discussed where it is important to consider wider perspectives.

Previous research into collaborative learning and peer interaction has generally produced findings of benefits (for example, Blaye et al. 1991) or neutral effects (for example, Littleton et al. 1992) rather than negative effects. A number of investigations have taken place in an effort to identify key variables that assist collaborative learning and a number of dimensions have been found to be associated with positive outcomes (see Doise and Mugny 1984). However, there is still uncertainty about which dimensions are sufficient and which dimensions are necessary for the facilitation of learning. It also remains an open question as to why some children benefit from the collaborative learning experience whilst others do not. We argue that part of the reason for this uncertainty is because insufficient attention has been paid to the level of children's representations when they take part in collaborative learning.

The research described in this chapter is concerned with children's abilities in relation to balancing a beam on a fulcrum (see Figure 2.1). To balance these beams children need to move them across the fulcrum to identify the balance point. It is worth emphasising that this task is very different from that employed by Siegler (1976), and we have had indications that the two tasks do not closely map on to one another. One of the starting points for our research was Karmiloff-Smith's (1992) Representational Redescription (RR) model of cognitive development. This puts forward the idea that cognitive development is a progression from implicit non-verbalisable processes to explicit verbalisable knowledge. For us, one very attractive feature of the model was the idea that this progression involves a number of different levels, so that cognitive development is a more complex progression than suggested by a dichotomy between implicit and explicit knowledge (see Berry and Broadbent 1988, Reber 1993). Another attractive feature of the model is the idea that there is one level of development at which children (and adults) seem to focus on internal representations and as a result can fail to take account of external information, feedback and arguments. This aspect of the model was helpful in explaining the lack of benefit of computer-aided feedback in some of our previous research (Messer et al. 1996a). It is worth emphasising that Karmiloff-Smith's discussion of the RR model has been largely restricted to non-social processes. Consequently, the research that we describe involves extending the RR model to a broader area of functioning. Furthermore, it is interesting to contrast the RR model with Vygotskian perspectives which focus on the way that the internalisation of social events and processes provides a basis for cognitive development. The RR model does not reject such ideas, but it does suppose that children's ability to utilise information will be influenced by their level of cognitive representations. As a result, it is supposed that at some levels of representation social processes may be less influential than at other levels.

The RR model has four representational levels in the progression from Implicit to Explicit Knowledge. Our work used these levels as a starting point for research, however, over the years the precise way that we have classified children's performance has changed and become more elaborate. The research into these processes suggests that there may be as many as seven levels which can be identified in beam-balancing tasks (Peters et al. 1999, Pine and Messer 1999). However, for the purpose of this chapter we will concentrate on four levels which we believe provide useful distinctions between different types of ability. These levels are given in Table 2.1.

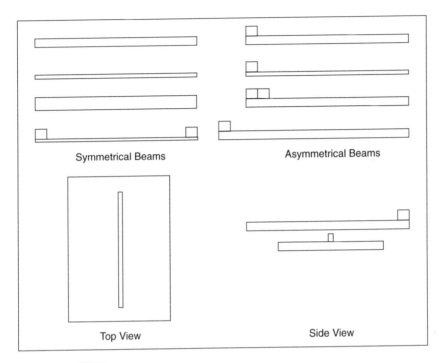

Source: Peters (2000).

*Figure 2.1* Examples of beams presented to children and the wooden fulcrum across which the beams were balanced

*Table 2.1* Levels of representation in relation to a balance beam task

|  | Successful with Symmetrical beams | Successful with Asymmetrical beams | Explains weight/distance |
|---|---|---|---|
| Implicit | YES | YES | NO |
| Abstraction Verbal | YES | NO | NO |
| Abstraction Non-Verbal | YES | NO | YES |
| Verbal Explicit | YES | YES | YES |

The Implicit level occurs when children are successful in balancing most of the beams on the fulcrum, but are not able to explain the basis of their success in terms of weight or distance. Thus, they seem to have procedures to accomplish the task, but cannot put into words the way that the task is accomplished. Sometimes children at this level when asked how they balanced a beam will say they don't know or mimic the movements that they used. Children at the Abstraction Non-Verbal level act as if beams usually balance at their geometric centre; as a result these children are able to balance symmetrical beams which have the same weight on either side, but have difficulties balancing asymmetrical beams which have different weights on either side of the balance point. This level corresponds to the E1 level of the RR model. According to the RR model, children at the Abstraction Non-Verbal level have difficulty incorporating external information into their existing representations and as a result, their representations are more difficult to change. We have also identified children who perform the task in a similar manner to those at Abstraction Non-Verbal level, but unlike them are able to say that the beams balance in the middle (this level is not described in the RR model). This we term the Abstraction Verbal Level. At the fourth level, children once again are successful in balancing most of the beams, but can also give an explanation in terms of weight and/or distance (level E3 in the RR model). It is important to emphasise that these levels do not correspond to Piagetian-like stages, so an individual child might be at one level for balancing and another level for using notation.

## The Level of Representation: Coding and Validity

It has proved to be relatively easy to code the majority of children according to the levels of representation that we have identified by examining their success and their explanations. If children are able to balance the majority of symmetrical beams but fail to balance the majority of asymmetrical beams, then they are assigned to the Abstraction Non-Verbal or Abstraction Verbal levels. The latter distinction is made according to whether or not children are able to give some explanation of their strategy. For the remaining children classification is largely determined by whether or not they can provide verbal explanations about their successes (and occasional failures). If they cannot explain these processes in terms of the effects of weight and/or distance then they are assigned to the Implicit level. If children can explain the effects of weight and/or distance then they are assigned to the Explicit level.

It should be apparent that the major difference between the Implicit and Explicit levels depends on whether or not a child can explain his or her success in balancing the beams. Given the reluctance of many children to articulate their ideas, it is possible to argue that such a difference is little more than a matter of verbal ability or confidence. Thus, it is reassuring that a comparison of the verbal ability of children at different levels as assessed by the BPVS (British Pictorial Vocabulary Scale) failed to find significant differences according to their level of representation (Pine, 1997). Another piece of evidence that supports our description of the representational levels comes from a study that collected data from children every day, over a five-day period. In 88% of the cases children progressed to a higher level, and there were no instances of children jumping directly from the Implicit to Explicit levels. Thus, the ordering of the levels appeared to correspond to the developmental progression made by children, and the progression from the Implicit to Explicit level did not appear to be simply due to confidence in explaining the process of balancing, but appeared to involve intermediate cognitive representations. In addition, other findings indicate that the levels involve different forms of representations as assessed by the children's ability to choose correct pictures of a beam at its balance point, to make predictions about whether a beam can be balanced, and the relation between predictions and actual performance (Pine and Messer, under review). Further findings which support the RR model concern the difficulty that children at the Abstraction levels have in learning from external information. For example, computer-based feedback significantly assisted children at the Implicit level, but failed to be of significant assistance to children at the Abstraction levels (the two Abstraction levels were combined in these experiments – Messer et al. 1996b). Nor have the benefits of collaborative learning been found to be particularly clear or marked for children at the Abstraction levels (Messer et al. 1993).

## Studies of Collaboration: Helping Children Learn about Balancing

Three of our experiments are reviewed in this section. All three experiments concern processes that are relevant to peer interaction and balancing. The first study (Pine and Messer 1998) investigated whether peer interaction assists children's progress with balancing; the second study compared the effectiveness of observation and children's self-explanations in relation to learning about balancing (Pine and Messer 2000), and the third study compared peer interaction with other forms of intervention (Murphy and Messer 2000). One theme present in this work is that children at the Abstraction Non-Verbal level have greater difficulty than children at other levels in benefiting from collaborative experiences.

The three studies involve a similar design. The children take part in a pretest where they are asked to try to balance between four and eight beams (depending on the study) on a fulcrum and are asked why the beams do or do not balance. They then take part in an intervention session, and finally there is a post-test. The children in our studies are usually aged between 4 and 9 years, and the complete duration of all the sessions is typically between 15 and 30 minutes. Despite the comparatively short duration of the sessions, it is possible for progress to occur from pre- to post-test. This design has allowed us to investigate the effect of various influences on collaborative learning when children have different levels of representation, something that would be difficult in a more naturalistic investigation.

## The Effects of Discussion

The aim of this study was to investigate whether discussion with peers would be of assistance to children at the different representational levels, even to those who were at the Abstraction Non-Verbal level. As has already been mentioned, these latter children are believed by Karmiloff-Smith to fail to utilise external information during learning opportunities. This is because these children are supposed to have a representation about balancing which guides their actions (that is, attempting to balance objects at their geometric centre), but which they cannot access for verbal explanations. Such a mix of abilities makes it is especially interesting to investigate the effects of peer discussion on their performance and to determine whether it can overcome such characteristics.

It is also of interest to investigate the performance of children at the Implicit level. These children tend to be successful in balancing both asymmetrical and symmetrical beams; however, they cannot explain their actions supposedly because they have no coherent representation to access and use for verbal explanations. Karmiloff-Smith suggests that their success occurs because the children use trial and error procedures together with proprioceptive feedback to eventually balance a beam. She also claims that the experiences of success and failure are not integrated together by the child, so that future attempts at a task are not guided by past experiences. Recent research by Peters (2000) questions these claims; however, the descriptions made by Karmiloff-Smith capture important characteristics of the attempts made by children at this level. Whatever the nature of the underlying cognitive processes associated with this level, an interesting question is whether or not these children can benefit from peer discussion when they do not have the ability to describe and explain their own success. A further issue that was addressed in this investigation was whether there were greater benefits in groups which contained children of mixed representational levels than in groups which contained children of the same levels. There has been a longstanding interest in this issue and most findings point to the benefits of mixed groups (for example, Doise and Mugny 1984), and we expected similar findings.

In the investigation, 103 children completed all the sessions (56 boys and 47 girls) and they were aged between 5 years 2 months, and 7 years 1 month. All the children took part in an individual pre-test to identify their level of representation (for full details of the methods used, see Pine and Messer 1998). They were then assigned to one of 26 groups of four children who were either all at the Same level of representation (either Implicit or

Abstraction Non-Verbal levels; there were insufficient numbers of children at other levels), or the groups contained at least three children who were at different levels of representation. These groups were then randomly allocated to either a Discussion or No Discussion condition on a constrained random basis to ensure equal numbers of each type of group in each type of condition.

In both the Discussion and No Discussion conditions, the groups were taken to an empty classroom and presented with the beams that they had been given in the pre-test, together with a sheet of paper with drawings of each of the beams. After checking that the children could identify the beams from the drawings, the experimenter asked the children to decide for themselves whether the beam could be balanced by writing 'Y' for yes or 'N' for no, and help was given to younger children who might not understand this notation. The children in the No Discussion group returned to their classroom after they had completed this part of the experiment. The children in the Discussion group remained in the classroom and were asked by the experimenter to 'talk about each of these beams in turn and discuss whether or not you thought it they could be balanced' and that they should try to reach agreement amongst themselves. When this was done the children were to write 'Y' or 'N' beside another set of drawings of the beams. The experimenter gave neutral prompts if the group had difficulty in initiating discussion. These sessions were videotaped. Three days later the children took part in a post-test that was similar to the pre-test.

A two-way analysis of variance revealed a main effect of Discussion, no significant effect of group composition, and a significant interaction between these two variables. Further analysis indicated that Discussion was more effective in Mixed than in the Same-level groups. Analyses of video recordings were conducted to compare the type of discussion that took place in the two types of group, this revealed no significant difference in the total number of task-relevant utterances. However, there were significantly more counter-arguments in the Mixed rather than the Same groups (mean of 9.7 and 2.8, respectively). These were utterances that challenged or contradicted the other person's utterance that preceded it.

An examination of pre- to post-test progress according to the representational level of the children was also conducted. Of the 40 children at the Implicit level at pre-test, 32% had improved by the post-test. Of these Implicit-level children, 77% of those who improved were in the Discussion groups and only 33% were in the No Discussion groups. Of the Implicit level children who did not improve, 37% were in the Discussion groups and 63% in the No Discussion groups. An analysis using Chi-square revealed that children at the Implicit level were significantly more likely to improve if they were in a Discussion group.

At the Abstraction Non-Verbal level, 41% of children improved between the pre- and the post-test, but there was a different pattern of findings. Of the children who improved, 57% had been in Discussion groups and 43% were in No Discussion groups. Of the children who did not improve, 41% were in Discussion groups and 59% were in No Discussion groups. This pattern of findings was not significantly different from that expected by chance.

Thus, the analyses revealed that there was an overall effect of Discussion and that children in the Mixed Discussion groups seemed to benefit most from this experience. This is consistent with findings about the positive effects of children being involved in discussions with those who have different views to themselves (Doise and Mugny 1984, Azmitia 1988, Howe et al. 1992). What is especially interesting about these findings is that this positive effect appeared to be confined to children at the Implicit level, and was not present in the children at the Abstraction Non-Verbal level. This supports Karmiloff-Smith's claims that children at this level have difficulty in making use of external information and is consistent with previous research about the ineffectiveness of computer-based feedback with children at this level (that is, non-social information – Messer et al. 1996b). Taken together, these findings support our argument that the effects of peer interaction may be mediated both by the social experiences of the child and by the child's level of cognitive representation. Thus, it is possible that some of the previous failures to find positive effects of peer interaction may be because of the children being at a level of representation similar to the Abstraction Non-Verbal level.

## The Effects of Explaining and Observing

The process of collaboration and peer interaction involves both the exposure to the ideas of others and also individuals having to articulate their own ideas. Much of the interest in collaborative learning has focused on the former dimension. However, it also is possible that the process of having to explain how something happened could help children understand and succeed at a task. This is an especially interesting possibility in relation to children at the Abstraction Non-Verbal level as these children are not able to describe their strategy and tend to ignore external information.

To investigate this issue an experiment using a pre-test, intervention, post-test design was conducted (Pine and Messer 2000). In one intervention condition children were told by the experimenter: 'Now I am going to balance some beams and I would like *you to watch carefully* how I do it, then you can have another turn at balancing them.' This was termed the Observe Only condition (OO). In the Observe and Explain condition (OE), the instructions were similar except that children were asked to '*watch care-*

*fully and try to tell me how each one balances* on the bar. Then you can have another turn at balancing them.' The OE condition follows some of the principles identified in the work of Chi (Chi et al. 1989, 1994). In neither condition did the child attempt to balance the beam. Of the 140 children who were given a pre-test, 127 completed the study (some children were not present for all assessment sessions; some could not be classified (9%), and some were at the highest Explicit level (26%)).

A Chi-square analysis of the whole sample revealed that 70% in the OE condition improved between pre- and post-test, whereas only 50% improved in the OO condition ($p < 0.05$). Asking children to produce an explanation thus helped their performance on this task – an interesting effect in itself. Further analyses were conducted to investigate whether this effect occurred in children at the Abstraction Non-Verbal and Abstraction Verbal levels, as these two groups contained enough children for the statistical analyses.

At the Abstraction Non-Verbal level, 37% of children improved between pre- and post-test, and 88% of children at the Abstraction Verbal level improved between pre- and post-test. However, this overall effect is due to a contrasting pattern of improvement at the two levels. At the Abstraction Non-Verbal level, 67% of children in the OE condition improved between pre- and post-test, whereas only 14% improved in the OO condition; this effect was significant. In contrast, at the Abstraction Verbal level there was no significant difference in these figures: 93% of children improved in the OE condition and 82% in the OO condition, and this was a non-significant effect. This indicates that explaining was particularly effective with children at the Abstraction Non-Verbal level.

The findings about the sample as a whole suggest that it is more effective to ask children to explain a process that they observe rather than simply asking them to observe the process, an effect that has been identified in previous research (for example, Chi et al. 1994, Siegler 1995). More detailed analyses on children at the abstraction levels revealed an interesting contrast in their receptiveness to information. A much higher percentage of children improved at the Abstraction Verbal level than at the Abstraction Non-Verbal level, suggesting differences between these levels in their general ability to make use of information provided by external sources. We suspect that this difference between the two levels is because children at the Abstraction Verbal level can assimilate new information from a variety of sources because they already have their representations accessible in a verbal code. In contrast, the children at the Abstraction Non-Verbal level may not be able to use a verbal code for their representations, and this makes it much more difficult for them to assimilate new information.

The difference in receptiveness between levels was coupled with a difference in the effectiveness of the two forms of intervention. At the

Abstraction Non-Verbal level, the OE condition was significantly more effective than the OO condition, whereas at the Abstraction Verbal level there were no significant differences between the two conditions. This is consistent with our expectations that asking children at the Abstraction Non-Verbal level to explain processes they observe provides a useful way to help these children to improve their abilities. The demands of accessing information and putting it into verbal form may very well enable children to begin changing their representations when there is information which contrasts with their ideas.

These findings have a number of implications for using peer interaction and collaboration as a means of supporting children's learning. First of all, they suggest that exposure to appropriate models is not sufficient to bring about cognitive advances. What may be required are procedures that encourage children to try to access their representations about phenomena, especially when the children have inappropriate representations that do not correspond to the phenomena being observed. Second, the findings point to the possibility that the benefits from collaboration are not only caused by the exposure to different opinions (as suggested by the previous study), but also, for some children, by having to explain and justify their own strategies and predictions. This is consistent with studies that have found that constraining children to reach an agreement is helpful to their learning (Howe et al. 1992).

## The Effects of Peer Interaction, Scaffolding and Working Alone

The third experiment we report concerns whether children can benefit from an intervention session where they attempt to balance everyday objects on a fulcrum (Murphy and Messer 2000). The purpose of this study was to compare the effectiveness of three forms of intervention: a tutorial using scaffolding, peer interaction and a condition where the children worked alone on a task. The difference between this study and most previous ones is that although the intervention session concerned the same domain, there was no direct correspondence between the material in the intervention session and that in the pre- and post-tests. Children were assessed in the pre- and post-test with beams that had been used in previous experiments (see Figure 2.1), but everyday objects were employed during the intervention session. In this study, 122 children took part, aged between 5 years 2 months, and 7 years 4 months.

In the adult scaffolding condition the experimenter provided a tutorial about balancing which was linked to the children's level of understanding and involved a progressive reduction in explanations and an increasing use of prompts and hints (see Wood et al. 1976). The peer interaction condition for the children was similar to that used in the first experiment we have described in this chapter (Pine and Messer 1998), except that the children had a turn at balancing the beams after they had reached a consensus, and the discussion could continue after this event. Children in the work-alone condition were simply given the everyday objects to play with and were told that they could see if the objects balanced.

An examination of the pre- to post-test improvement of the whole sample indicated that scaffolding was the most effective condition with 76% of the children improving between pre- and post-test ($p < 0.05$). In the work-alone condition, 58% of children improved, and 50% in the peer-interaction condition improved, but these increases were not significant. Analyses were subsequently conducted to see whether these effects were also present for children at the different representational levels. Three groups of children were investigated: those at the Implicit, Abstraction Non-Verbal and Abstraction Verbal levels. The findings from these analyses are given in Table 2.2, which shows that scaffolding was the most effective intervention with children at the Implicit level and the only form of intervention at this level which resulted in a significant pre- to post-test improvement for children ($p < 0.01$). Our previous experiment showed a positive effect of peer interaction with children at the Implicit level. However, the present study involved children having to be able to transfer knowledge from the intervention task to the different materials used in the post-test; this is likely to be a more difficult process and is likely to be the reason why peer interaction was not significantly effective.

*Table 2.2* The number of children in the Implicit, Abstraction Non-Verbal and Abstraction Verbal levels who advanced or did not advance from pre- to post-test

| Level | Total | Advance | No Advance |
|---|---|---|---|
| *Implicit* | 52 | | |
| Scaffold | 16 | 14 | 2* |
| Group | 15 | 9 | 6 |
| Control | 21 | 11 | 10 |
| | | | |
| *Abstraction Non-Verbal* | 34 | | |
| Scaffold | 11 | 7 | 4 |
| Group | 12 | 4 | 8 |
| Control | 11 | 11 | 0† |
| | | | |
| *Abstraction Verbal* | 29 | | |
| Scaffold | 10 | 7 | 3 |
| Group | 11 | 6 | 5 |
| Control | 8 | 2 | 6 |

*Significant at < 0.01.
†Significant at < 0.0005.
Source: Murphy and Messer (2000).

To our surprise, for children at the Abstraction Non-Verbal level, the most effective form of intervention was to leave them to work by themselves. This effect was very strong as all children in this condition improved between pre- and post-test. Children at this level in the other intervention conditions did not show significant pre- to post-test gains. There was no intervention condition which produced a significant improvement for children at the Abstraction Verbal level; 70% of children in the scaffolding condition improved, but the effect failed to reach significance.

These findings suggest that peer interaction was not a particularly effective way of promoting learning when children have to acquire information from other children and transfer it to another task. In some ways this is surprising as one might think that peer interaction would promote more flexible thinking and prepare children for new experiences. Clearly it would be useful to discover whether similar difficulties exist with peer interaction in other domains, and whether peer interaction could be structured in ways which promote the transfer of knowledge. Taking the sample as a whole, scaffolding was an effective form of intervention, and significantly so for children at the Implicit level. These children may very well benefit from a structured approach that helps them to understand the way that their success is based on processes involving weight and distance. The success of the children at the Abstraction Non-Verbal level when left to work by themselves is counter to many previous findings about the effectiveness of peer interaction. However, the success is consistent with some of Karmiloff-Smith's ideas about representational redescription. She characterises the cognitive development of children at this level as being based on success and on a process of internal cognitive reorganisation. Previous findings suggest that children find balancing everyday objects easier than the beams we employ (Pine 1997), and this success when coupled with the contrast between the two sets of beams could have contributed to the restructuring of children's representations at this level. In addition, the discrepancy may have made children consciously access their existing representations about balancing and thereby facilitate cognitive change. Azmitia (Chapter 11, this volume) discusses a related phenomenon, the importance of time out during the process of collaboration. The arguments that she and we put forward suggest that, in the enthusiasm that has developed for collaborative learning, there may have been an underestimation of the gains from solitary activities at certain points in the learning process.

The study thus raises questions about the general effectiveness of collaborative processes in providing a basis for the learning of general principles. It also highlights the possibility that working alone on a task may be an effective way to help the progress of children who are at a level of cognitive development where change is internally rather than externally provoked. The study extends the number of variables which need to be considered in relation to understanding the effectiveness of collaborative learning, but does offer the promise of a more effective explanation of the success and failure of this process.

## General Discussion

The three investigations that we have described all suggest that the level of children's representations influence the type of benefit that children can gain from collaborative learning. The first study indicated that children at the Implicit level benefited from taking part in a discussion about balancing. In contrast, children at the Abstraction Non-Verbal level did not gain significant benefit from this experience. Consequently, the information provided by peers in their discussions about balancing did not appear to be sufficient to help children at the Abstraction Non-Verbal level to improve their ability. The second study identified a method that helped the learning of children at the Abstraction Non-Verbal level and pointed to a reason for the lack of effectiveness of peer discussion with children at this level. Significantly more children at the Abstraction Non-Verbal level improved if they had to explain how the beams were balanced compared to only having to observe the beams being balanced. This relatively minor difference between the two conditions resulted in an appreciable difference in the percentage of children who showed a pre- to post-test improvement. Together the results suggest that children at the Abstraction Non-Verbal level may fail to benefit from peer discussion because they have difficulty explaining their own ideas, and it is also possible that they avoid fully explaining their own ideas when interacting with peers. The third experiment indicated that peer interaction may be less effective than adult scaffolding when children have to transfer knowledge acquired during an intervention session to a related problem which involves different objects. The surprising feature of this experiment was that working alone during the 'intervention condition' proved to be a very effective way to help their cognitive development at the Abstraction Non-Verbal level.

Findings from these three experiments can be explained by supposing that children at the Abstraction Non-Verbal level are less able than children at other levels to make use of external information. This idea was put forward by Karmiloff-Smith (1992) in her discussion of the RR model, and it has been supported by a number of experimental studies (for example, Messer et al. 1996b). Thus, it seems likely that the difficulties that Abstraction Non-Verbal children have in making use of information results in them failing to make appreciable gains from collaborative learning. However, putting children at the Abstraction Non-Verbal level in a situation where they have to attempt to access their representations and produce verbal explanations appears to help them to restructure and develop their ideas.

An issue of concern is the wider implications of these and related findings. Karmiloff-Smith set out the RR model as a general description of cognitive development and drew together research from a number of different domains to support her model. In thinking about her model process, it has become apparent to us that an Implicit level may not be the appropriate description of performance and thinking for some domains. For balancing and some other tasks it is possible for children to be successful by a process of trial and error, and to be successful without having access to their representations. However, for many problems this process of trial and error is unlikely to result in success (for example, the tower of Hanoi). Thus, the combination of success and an inability to explain this success may be limited to some domains such as the one that we have investigated. Even so, it is possible that children may initially attempt to solve many types of problems without having a particularly good strategy for doing so; they may also have difficulty explaining their strategy, and in some sense they would still be considered to have Implicit representations. Further research is needed to investigate the characteristics of this initial level, and to discover the form of representations that occur across a range of problems and tasks.

It is also worth commenting on the way that the Abstraction Non-Verbal level is related to other phenomena that have similarities to this form of thinking. The discussions about naive theories of science often seem to refer to a level of understanding which is difficult to change and which is sometimes (but not always) difficult for the person to explain (Kuhn 1989, Schauble 1996). Furthermore, there are other interesting parallels between this cognitive level and the attitudes or prejudices that people may have. For example, there are similarities between the Abstraction Non-Verbal level and self-serving biases in attitudes, since both can be difficult to change, both can involve the rejection of counter-evidence, and both can involve representations and reasoning which are not fully accessible to the individual (Klaczynski and Narasimham 1998; also see discussions of attitude formation in relation to health). Furthermore, it is interesting to note that many forms of therapy that attempt to address inappropriate behaviours and beliefs involve the therapist helping the client to both access and re-represent events and beliefs. All this is to draw attention to interesting parallels between different forms of cognitive functioning which involve related processes, and to the way that collaborative social processes need to be carefully structured to enable people to move beyond certain cognitive levels.

There are thus interesting questions about the general nature of children's and adults' levels of cognition and the accessibility of their representations. What we wish to emphasise is that these representational levels may influence the individual's ability both to discuss the phenomenon and to make use of the discussion of others. As a result, collaboration and peer interaction may not have *uniform* influences across all individuals; instead, their effectiveness may depend on the level of an individual's representation. We believe that an appreciation of these complexities will help to develop a fuller understanding of the process of collaborative learning.

## References

Azmitia, M. (1988). 'Peer interaction and problem solving: when are two heads better than one?' *Child Development*, 59, 87–96.

Berry, D. and Broadbent, D. (1988). 'Interactive tasks and the implicit-explicit distinction'. *British Journal of Psychology*, 79, 251–72.

Blaye, A., Light, P., Joiner, R. and Sheldon, S. (1991). 'Collaboration as a facilitator of planning and problem solving on a computer based task'. *British Journal of Developmental Psychology*, 9, 471–83.

Chi, M.T.H., Bassok, M., Lewis, M., Reimann, O. and Glaser, R. (1989). 'Self-explanations: how students study and use examples in learning to solve problems'. *Cognitive Science*, 13, 145–82.

Chi, M.T.H., de Leeuw, N., Chiu, M. and LaVancher, C. (1994). 'Eliciting self explanations improves understanding'. *Cognitive Science*, 18, 439-477.

Doise, W. and Mugny, G. (1984). *The Social Development of the Intellect*. Oxford: Pergamon Press.

Howe, C., Tolmie, A. and Rodgers, C. (1992). 'The acquisition of conceptual knowledge in science by primary school children: group interaction and the understanding of motion down an incline'. *British Journal of Developmental Psychology*, 10, 113–30.

Karmiloff-Smith, A. (1992). *Beyond Modularity: A developmental perspective on cognitive science*. Cambridge, MA: MIT Press.

Klaczynski, P.A. and Narasimham, G. (1998). 'Development of scientific reasoning biases: cognitive versus ego-protective explanations'. *Developmental Psychology*, 34(1), 175–87.

Kuhn, D. (1989). 'Children and adults as intuitive scientists'. *Psychological Review*, 96(4), 674–89.

Littleton, K., Light, P., Joiner R., Messer, D. and Barnes P. (1992). 'Pairing and gender effects in computer based learning'. *European Journal of Psychology of Education*, 7(4), 1–14.

Messer, D.J., Joiner, R., Loveridge, N., Light, P. and Littleton, K. (1993). 'Influences on the effectiveness of peer interaction: children's level of cognitive development and the relative ability of partners'. *Social Development*, 2(3), 279–94.

Messer, D.J., Mohamedali, H.H. and Fletcher, B.C. (1996a). 'Using computers to help pupils tell the time, is feedback necessary?' *Educational Psychology*, 16, 281–96.

Messer, D.J., Norgate, S., Joiner, R., Littleton, K. and Light, P. (1996b). 'Development without learning?' *Educational Psychology*, 16(1), 5–19.

Murphy, N. and Messer, D. (2000). 'Differential benefits from scaffolding and children working alone'. *Educational Psychology*, 20(1), 17–32.

Peters, L. (2000). 'Children's early learning about object balancing: behavioural and connectionist studies'. Unpublished doctoral thesis, University of Hertfordshire, Hatfield, UK.

Peters, L., Messer, D., Smith, P. and Davey, N. (1999). 'An investigation into Karmiloff-Smith's RR model: the effects of structured tuition'. *British Journal of Developmental Psychology*, 17, 277–92.

Pine, K. (1997). 'Implicit and explicit representations in children's learning'. Unpublished doctoral thesis, University of Hertfordshire, Hatfield, UK.

Pine, K.J. and Messer, D.J. (1998). 'Group collaboration effects and the explicitness of children's knowledge'. *Cognitive Development*, 13, 109–26.

Pine, K.J. and Messer, D.J. (1999). 'What children do and what children know: looking beyond success using Karmiloff-Smith's RR framework'. *New Ideas in Psychology*, 17, 17–30.

Pine, K.J. and Messer, D.J. (2000). 'The effects of explaining another's actions on children's implicit theories of balance'. *Cognition and Instruction*, 18(1), 37–54.

Pine, K.J. and Messer, D.J. (under review). 'The development of representations as children learn about balancing'.

Reber, A.S. (1993). *Implicit Learning and Tacit Knowledge: An essay on the cognitive unconscious*. New York: Oxford University Press.

Schauble, L. (1996). 'The development of scientific reasoning in knowledge rich contexts'. *Developmental Psychology*, 32(1), 102–19.

Siegler, R.S. (1976). 'Three aspects of cognitive development'. *Cognitive Psychology*, 8, 441–520.

Siegler, R.S. (1995). 'How does change occur: a microgenetic study of number conservation'. *Cognitive Psychology*, 28, 225–73.

Wood, D., Bruner, J.S. and Ross, G. (1976). 'The role of tutoring in problem solving'. *Journal of Child Psychiatry and Psychology*, 17, 89–100.

# Part II
# Mediation

# 3

# Peer Interaction and the Effect of Task Presentation on the Acquisition of Scientific Reasoning

*Richard Joiner, Dorothy Faulkner, Karen Littleton, Dorothy Miell and Linda Thompson*

## Introduction

Mediation is a central concept in Sociocultural theory. It refers to the fact that we do not interact directly with reality but indirectly through psychological and technical tools. Examples of technical tools are rulers, watches, calculators or computers. Examples of psychological tools are graphs, number systems, mnemonic strategies and language, the latter being the universal psychological tool. It is a cultural tool because it is created and shared by members of a cultural community. It is the universal psychological tool because it is used to think with and facilitates the acquisition of other psychological tools.

Vygotsky (1981) identified two major properties of tools. The first was that tools by their very nature are social. Technical tools are products of Sociocultural history, and are neither invented nor discovered by a solitary individual. Psychological tools are social in the sense that they have their origins in social interaction (Vygotsky 1978). They first appear in shared activity between people and are then internalised by children who use them in their own cognitive activity. This is what Vygotsky referred to as the general genetic law of development: 'any higher mental function necessarily goes through an external stage in its development because it is initially a social function' (Vygotsky 1981, p. 161).

The second property of both psychological and technical tools identified by Vygotsky was that their introduction into an activity qualitatively changes the nature of that activity. Vygotsky (1978) describes how memory is transformed with the introduction of mnemonic strategies, such as tying a knot in a handkerchief or writing. Werstch (1995) describes how the introduction of fibreglass poles changed the nature of the pole-vaulting. In the 1960s pole-vaulters started to use fibreglass poles. Previously, pole-vaulters used the pole and their momentum to carry them over the bar; with the introduction of fibreglass poles, the athletes could bend the poles almost to 90 degrees at take-off and use the pole to catapult themselves over the bar. Using this technique led to dramatic increases in the pole-vault record and to controversy concerning whether pole-vaulting using a fibreglass pole was still in fact pole-vaulting.

Computers are very powerful and flexible technical tools, which have been used for some time now in schools to support learning. Although originally intended to support individualised instruction, they are now used increasingly to support children working in groups on some shared activity. According to Sociocultural theory, the introduction of computers into joint activity should radically change the nature of that activity (Crook 1994, Säljö 1996, 1999); and because Sociocultural theory argues that learning is the internalisation of joint activity, any transformation of activity should affect learning. However, there have been very few studies that have investigated whether the introduction of computers changes the nature of joint activity, and even fewer which have investigated whether these changes have any effects on learning. Keogh et al. (2000) have started to investigate this issue by comparing the nature of the talk and joint activity observed in same- or mixed-gender pairs of children engaged in an identical language problem-solving task (involving the assembly of a poem from a jumbled collection of phrases) presented either on or off the computer. Their findings highlight the impact that the presence of the computer has on the activity of the mixed-gender pairs: boys dominate the task when it is presented on the machine, whereas the activity is distributed more equally between the pair members when the task is off computer. Fitzpatrick and Hardman (2000) reported similar findings. They examined the interaction style of 7–9-year-old children working in either mixed- or same-gender pairs on a computer task and a non-computer task. They found that collaboration broke down in the mixed-gender pairs with the boys in the mixed-gender pairs dominating the interaction in the computer task, whilst the girls in the mixed-gender pairs dominated the interaction in the non-computer task.

Other researchers have reported findings, mainly from observational studies, which suggest that the introduction of the computer does change the nature of collaborative activity and that these changes could be beneficial. Classroom-based observational studies have shown that the computer could act as an effective motivator for group work (Cummings 1982) and has the potential to support collaboration on joint projects (Hawkins et al. 1982). Newman et al. (1989) showed how the introduction of a Local Area Network and a shared database supported the management and co-ordination of group work in science investigations. Teasley and Roschelle (1993) reported a case study of a pair of 15-year-old children using a computer simulation, called the Envisioning Machine, to learn about the Newtonian concepts of velocity and acceleration. From their observations, they identified three ways in which the computer could act as a resource for mediating collaborative learning. First, it can provide a means for disambiguating language. They found that the children did not have the technical vocabulary to talk about motion and they used the computer display for establishing shared references. Second, the computer could resolve impasses. When students had different opinions they used the Envisioning Machine to try out ideas to see which one worked. Third, the computer could constrain interpretations. The Envisioning Machine was designed to invite and constrain the students' interpretations.

In this chapter we report a study which compared pairs of children working around a computer with pairs of children working around physical apparatus on the same scientific-reasoning task. We hope to show that the introduction of a computer qualitatively changes the nature of the joint activity and that it has an effect on the development of children's understanding of scientific reasoning.

## Method

In this study, 96 children (48 girls and 48 boys) took part, aged between 9 and 10 years old. The study had two conditions: a computer condition where the children worked in pairs with a computer simulation of the task, and a physical apparatus condition where they worked in pairs with physical apparatus (that is, chemicals and pipettes). We designed the study so that it had four sessions: a pre-test, an interaction session, an immediate post-test and a delayed post-test. The children were given an individual pre-test to assess their scientific-reasoning ability using a combinatorial reasoning task developed by Kuhn and Ho (1980). They worked in same-sex pairs and were randomly allocated to either the computer condition or the physical condition.

Approximately two weeks later in the interaction session the children tackled either a computer version or a physical version of Inhelder and Piaget's (1958) chemical combinations task, a task used to investigate the development of children's scientific reasoning. At the start of the session the children were given a demonstration of either the computer or the physical task, depending on which condition they had been allocated to. They were shown that the five different colourless liquid chemicals could be mixed together with the 'mixer' and that some combinations created a reaction which turned the liquid yellow. They were then asked to work together to find out which chemical or chemicals were needed to turn the liquid yellow when the mixing liquid was added. The children in the physical condition were asked to record the tests they carried out on a record sheet supplied, whilst in the computer condition the computer automatically kept a record of these tests. The children were only given 20 minutes to find out which chemical or chemicals turned the mixture yellow when mixed with the mixer. Two weeks after the interaction session the children were given an individual post-test, and three months later they were given an individual delayed post-test. Both the post-tests measured combinatorial reasoning and were isomorphs of the pre-test.

## Performance in the Interaction Session

First we compared the performance of the pairs in the interaction session. We found a number of differences in joint performances between the pairs who worked in the computer environment compared to the pairs who worked with the physical apparatus (see Table 3.1).

*Table 3.1* Performance in the interaction session for study 2

|  | Computer (n = 24) | | Physical (n = 24) | |
|---|---|---|---|---|
|  | M* | SD‡ | M* | SD‡ |
| Time (seconds) | 563 | 308 | 1181 | 55 |
| Number of combinations tested | 17 | 13 | 11 | 3 |

*Mean
‡Standard deviation

### Combinations Tested

Pairs working in the computer environment tested significantly more chemical combinations than children working in the physical apparatus environment ($F(1,46) = 6.2$, $p < 0.05$). Children in the computer condition carried out on average 17 tests compared to an average of 10.9 tests in the physical.

### Time Taken

Children in the computer condition took nearly half as long as children in the physical condition ($F(1,46) = 91.2$, $p < 0.05$). As can be seen from Table 3.1, most of the children in the physical condition took the full 1200 seconds to complete the task, whereas the children in the computer condition took on average 561 seconds.

## Problem Solution

The problem solutions were classified into three categories: (i) *completely correct* – combination B + E plus mixer; (ii) *partially correct* – any combination of three or four out of the five chemicals containing both B and E and single chemical answers giving B or E in combination with the mixer, and (iii) *incorrect* – any combination not containing B and E; answers which gave all five chemicals; single chemical solutions that were neither B nor E.

Using these three categories we found that children using the computer simulation performed better in the interaction session than children using the physical apparatus (Chi-square = 7.3, Df = 2, $p < 0.05$). In the computer condition, 13 out of 24 pairs (54%) gave a completely correct answer, compared with only 4 pairs (19%) in the physical condition (see Table 3.2). However, 13 out of 21 pairs (62%) in the physical condition arrived at a partially correct solution. The number of pairs giving incorrect solutions was approximately equal in the two conditions (see Table 3.2).

*Table 3.2* Distribution of types of solution

| (Number of Pairs) | Computer (n = 24) | Physical (n = 21) |
|---|---|---|
| Correct | 13 | 4 |
| Partially correct | 6 | 13 |
| Incorrect | 5 | 4 |

So, pairs in the computer condition tested more combinations, took less time to complete the task and had better-quality solutions than pairs working with physical apparatus.

## Analysis of the Talk During the Interaction

Next we looked for differences between the two conditions in terms of the talk between the pairs while solving the chemical combinations task. Again we found a number of striking differences between the two conditions.

### Type of Talk

We initially classified the talk between the children into four broad categories. These categories were based on the work of Bennett and Dunne (1992):

1. *Task related* – utterances relating to the cognitive aspects of the task (that is, selecting chemical combinations to test, identifying the answer, making predictions, and observations).
2. *Social* – utterances used to manage social aspects of the interaction (for example, turn taking and role allocation).

3. *Procedural* – utterances which referred to some aspect of the practical situation (for example, how to use the keyboard and mouse, features of the computer display, using the apparatus and chemicals in the physical condition).
4. *Off-task (extraneous)* – all utterances not assigned to any of the above categories.

Using these four broad categories we found a number of differences between the conditions (see Table 3.3). The children in the computer condition made proportionally more task-related utterances ($F(1,88)$ = 10.8, $p < 0.05$) and social utterances ($F(1,86) = 26.6$, $p < 0.05$), but less procedural ($F(1,88) = 30.2$, $p < 0.05$) and off-task utterances ($F(1,88) = 11.5$, $p < 0.05$), compared with the children in the physical condition.

*Table 3.3* Type of utterance expressed as a percentage of the total number of utterances

| Percentage of utterances/pair | Computer (n = 48) | | Physical (n = 42) | |
|---|---|---|---|---|
| | M* | SD‡ | M* | SD‡ |
| Task related | 85.2 | 10.3 | 77.7 | 11.6 |
| Social | 5.8 | 5.7 | 1.0 | 1.8 |
| Procedural | 8.5 | 7.0 | 18.9 | 10.8 |
| Off-task | 0.5 | 1.4 | 2.3 | 3.4 |

*Mean
‡Standard deviation

## Transactive Analysis

After examining the different categories of talk the children used during the interaction session, we next compared the two conditions in terms of the proportion of transactive discussion evident during the interaction session. Transactive discussion has been found to be positively related to children's development of moral reasoning (Kruger 1992), to the development of children's scientific reasoning (Montgomery and Azmitia 1993) and to the quality of children's music compositions (Macdonald and Miell, Chapter 5 this volume, Miell and MacDonald forthcoming). Based on the work of Kruger (1992), transacts were defined as utterances that operated on a partner's prior reasoning (other-oriented) or that significantly clarified a child's own prior reasoning (self-oriented). The unit of analysis was an utterance and each utterance was first classified according to whether it was transactive or non-transactive. Next, three specific types of transacts were coded: transactive statements (self-oriented or other-oriented), transactive questions (self-oriented or other-oriented) and transactive responses (self-oriented or other-oriented).

(i) *Transactive statements* were defined as spontaneously produced critiques, refinements, extensions or significant paraphrases of ideas. Operations on the partner's ideas were labelled as other-oriented. Spontaneously produced clarifications of a child's own ideas were coded as self-oriented.

(ii) *Transactive questions* were defined as spontaneously produced requests for clarifications, justification, or elaboration of the partner's ideas. Operations on a partner's idea were labelled other-oriented. Requests for evaluative feedback regarding a child's own ideas were labelled self-oriented transactive questions.

(iii) *Transactive responses* were defined as clarifications, justifications or elaboration of one's ideas given in answer to a transactive question. They included critiques, refinements, extensions or significant paraphrases of the partner's ideas given in response to a transactive question. Other-oriented responses elaborated on the partner's ideas; those that elaborated on a child's own ideas were classified as self-oriented. Response transacts were given only directly following a transactive question.

We then compared the proportion of transactive discussion in the computer condition with the proportion of transactive discussion in the physical condition, and found substantial differences between the two conditions (see Table 3.4). Children in the computer condition used proportionally more other-oriented transacts ($F(1,88) = 15.4$, $p < 0.05$) and proportionally more other-oriented transactive statements ($F(1,88) = 42.9$, $p < 0.05$) than children in the physical condition.

Table 3.4  Other-oriented transacts expressed as a percentage of total number of utterances

| (Percentage of other-oriented transacts) | Computer (n = 48) | | Physical (n = 42) | |
|---|---|---|---|---|
| | M* | SD‡ | M* | SD‡ |
| Statements | 26.5 | 18.5 | 7.3 | 4.3 |
| Questions | 7.0 | 10.1 | 6.6 | 5.1 |
| Responses | 4.4 | 7.8 | 4.4 | 4.1 |
| Total transacts | 42.2 | 32.5 | 21.8 | 9.3 |

*Mean
‡Standard deviation

In sum, the children in the computer condition used proportionally more task-related utterances and social utterances and less procedural and off-task utterances compared with the children in the physical apparatus condition. They also made proportionally more transactive utterances than children in the physical apparatus condition.

## Examples of Children's Scientific Reasoning

Although the previous analyses indicate that there were large differences in the talk between pairs working in the computer environment and pairs working in the physical environment, they do not show the qualitative differences between the two conditions. Four extracts will be reported below which will hopefully show how qualitatively different the types of interaction were between the two conditions.

### Computer Condition

The first example is from a pair of girls in the computer condition and shows the kind of reasoning carried out by children in this condition. Natasha was classified at level 3 on the pre-test and Kathryn was classified at level 1.

| | | |
|---|---|---|
| 1 | K: | How about we do all of them but miss out the A? |
| 2 | N: | So then that means if it doesn't come up yellow you need the A to make it yellow probably<br>[*Test Chemical Combination BCDE*] |
| 3 | K: | Yeah it is |
| 4 | N: | Yeah it is yellow |
| 5 | K: | So you don't need the A that much |
| 6 | N: | You don't need the A. A isn't one of the colours that actually make it. Try missing out the B |
| 7 | K: | Yeah miss out the B |
| 8 | N: | Miss out the B 'cos that might be an important one and then miss out the E afterwards<br>[*Test Chemical Combination ACDE*] |
| 9 | K: | No |
| 10 | N: | No so you need the B what about not including the E<br>[*Test Chemical Combination ABCD*] |
| 11 | K: | No |
| 12 | N: | Colourless. So you need the B and E what about leaving out |
| 13 | K: | We need the D probably 'cos look colourless without the D that has the A in so |
| 14 | N: | So you don't need the A but you need the B and the E don't you? What about missing out the D this time but having the B and E in<br>[*Test Chemical Combination ABCE*] |

15   K:   Yeah
16   N:   Yeah that's yellow so you don't need the D then
17   K:   Yes you don't need the D

This example shows how children in this condition solved the problem. This pair, like all the pairs in this condition and the physical condition, does not systematically test every possible combination. They test a combination of chemicals with one chemical missing. If the resultant mixture turns yellow then they reason that the missing chemical is not part of the solution. If the resultant liquid is colourless they reason that the missing chemical is part of the solution.

Example 2 shows another strategy employed by children in this condition, and is an extract from a pair of boys who were using the computer simulation. Chris and Dean were both classified at level 0 on the pre-test.

1    C:   Try again
2    D:   No your turn now
3    D:   Because it's not them
          I think we should still try B
4    C:   D
5    D:   D B and then M
6    C:   B
7    D:   And then M
8    C:   No and E
9    D:   E M
10   C:   No
          [*Test Chemical Combination DBE*]
11   D:   We've done it
12   C:   I got it I got yellow
13   D:   It has to be D and B this time
14   C:   D B and E we tried
15   D:   D and B right
          so we go to OK
          and then we'll try D and B yeah?
16   C:   yeah
17   D:   Erm B and we'll see sort of thing and see if it was that
          [*Test Chemical Combination DB*]
18   D    No not really
19   C:   So let's try
20   D:   So the other chemicals have to have something to do with it
          No because we had E in the other one
21   C:   D mix so it must be

           [*Test Chemical Combination D*]
22    D:  Colourless
23    C:  It must be E and B or something

This pair employs a typical strategy commonly used by children in the computer condition. In line 13 they decide that the solution is the chemical combination BD and they test this by mixing chemical BD with the mixer. Unfortunately, they discover this combination is not the solution. This strategy was commonly observed in the computer condition but was rarely seen in the physical condition.

**Physical Apparatus Condition**

Example 3 shows a common strategy used by children in the physical condition, and is an extract from a pair of girls working with physical apparatus. Haley was classified at level 2 on the pre-test and Alice was classified at level 0 on the pre-test.

1    H:  A and what haven't we used much?
           A D and
2    A:  A D and E
3    H:  A D and E
           [*adds A D and E*]
           Okay
4    A:  A E
           and D
           I'll add M
           Probably be clear
5    H:  It might not be, Alice
6    A:  [*has trouble getting M out of bottle; H helps her*]

This pair decides which combination to test based on whether they have tested this combination before (see line 1). There is no hypothesis-led testing of chemicals commonly seen in pairs using the computer simulation.

    Not only were there differences between the conditions in terms of the strategies used, there were also differences in terms of the discussion of the evidence. Example 4 shows the children in the physical apparatus condition discussing whether a chemical combination has turned yellow. It is an extract from a pair of girls in the physical condition, Lauren and Avia, who were both classified at level 1 in the pre-test.

1    A:  E [*writing*]
2    L:  D

[*adds D to test tube*]

M

[*adds M to test tube*]

Now I've gotta mix

[*shakes the test tube*]

3   A:   Is it going yellow?

It's going yellow I think

4   L:   No that's not going yellow, it's the same

So no colour

Yeah it's going yellow

[*previous chemical combination tested*]

5   A:   Shall I cross it out now?

6   L:   Yeah

7   A:   I'll do B

[*add B to test tube*]

This one here?

[*test tube*]

Lines 3–5 show the  discussion about whether the combination of chemicals tested has turned the liquid yellow. This type of discussion was never observed in the computer condition, because the computer simulation instantly indicates whether the combinations tested have turned yellow or not. In the physical condition it can take a couple minutes for the chemical reaction to turn the mixture yellow. It was quite common for the children in this condition to discuss the colour of the resultant chemical mixture.

## Analysis of Learning

We examined how the effect of collaborative activity using a computer simulation or physical apparatus affected children's development of scientific reasoning. This analysis only involved children who were classified at level 0 and level 1 in the pre-test. The other children were excluded because they were scoring near the ceiling level on the pre-test. Immediate learning gains were analysed using pre- to post-test changes (see Table 3.5). Children in both conditions significantly improved between the pre-test and the post-test (computer, $t(35) = 5.3$, $p < 0.05$ : physical, $t(34) = 6.7$, $p < 0.05$), but there was no difference between the children in the two conditions in terms of their pre-test to post-test gain.

Long-term learning gains were analysed using pre- to delayed post-test changes. Children in both the conditions significantly improved between the pre-test and the delayed post-test (computer, $t(35) = 4.3$, $p < 0.05$: physical, $t(33) = 6.5$, $p < 0.05$). However, there was a significant difference between children using a computer simulation and the children working with physical apparatus in terms of their pre- to delayed post-test learning gains. Unexpectedly, the children using a computer simulation did not improve as much as children using the physical apparatus ($F(1,68) = 4.2$, $p < 0.05$).

*Table 3.5* Pre- to post-test and pre- to delayed post-test change scores for study 2.

| Change scores/child | Computer (n = 36) | | Physical (n = 34) | |
| --- | --- | --- | --- | --- |
| | M* | SD‡ | M* | SD‡ |
| Pre- to post-test change | 1.0 | 1.1 | 1.3 | 1.1 |
| Pre- to delayed post-test change | 0.8 | 1.1 | 1.4 | 1.2 |

*Mean
‡Standard deviation

## Discussion

The study investigated differences in the collaborative activity of children around a computer compared to children working around physical apparatus, and tried to relate those differences to learning outcome. The main finding of the study, supporting Sociocultural theory, was that the introduction of the computer transformed the activity. Children made proportionally more task-related talk and social talk when working around a computer than children who worked with the physical apparatus. Children in the computer condition also made proportionally less procedural talk and proportionally less off-task talk than children in the physical condition. There were also large differences in the quality and amount of transactive discussion between the two conditions. Children in the computer condition made proportionally more transactive utterances than children in the physical condition, and made more transactive statements than children in the physical condition. Children in the computer condition also produced better-quality solutions than children in the physical condition. More detailed analysis also revealed that these differences in talk were systematic of larger differences between the conditions in terms of the quality of the interaction. There were differences between the conditions in terms of the strategies the children used to decide which chemicals to test and in terms of the amount of discussion concerning the reaction of the chemicals. These findings support the Sociocultural view of development, which stresses the importance of tools for mediating activity. They also replicate the findings reported by Keogh et al. (2000) and Fitzpatrick and Hardman (2000), who also showed that the introduction of a computer transformed children's collaborative activity.

According to Vygotsky (1978) higher mental functions are internalised from joint activity. If the introduction of a computer transforms joint activity then this should, by implication, also affect children's learning. We found that children's learning was mediated by the type of tool they used. Unexpectedly, children who worked with the physical apparatus improved significantly more than children who worked around the computer. Teasley and Roschelle (1993), from their observational study of children working on the Envisioning Machine, had argued that working around a computer mediates collaborative learning, and the children in the study in this chapter who were in the computer condition had what appeared to be more productive interactions. They talked proportionally more about the task, less about the procedures and used less off-task talk than children working around the physical apparatus. They also engaged in substantially more transactive discussion, which has been found to be positively related to learning outcome (Kruger 1992, Montgomery and Azmitia 1993). But these types of interactions did not appear to have had a significant impact on the development of children's scientific reasoning, as measured by changes in children's combinatorial reasoning.

However, the pre- and post-tests were not designed to test improvement in children's ability at isolating variables in a multivariable experiment, an ability that is necessary to solve Piaget's chemical combinations problem. The analysis of children's talk and problem-solving strategies presented in this study shows that it was only children in the computer condition who were using the feedback record deductively to make and test predictions. This strongly suggests that the computer version of the chemical combinations task provides a more sophisticated environment for developing children's ability to isolate variables than the physical version. Our findings show that the computer mediated children's performance by providing clear and unambiguous information which allowed them to test their predictions in a systematic and rigorous manner. This type of support was not available to children in the physical condition and consequently they could only arrive at partial solutions to the problem. Thus it is possible that if we assessed children's ability to isolate variables, the children in the computer condition may have benefited more from the interaction than the children in the physical condition.

Another interesting aspect of this study is the way that the tasks in the two conditions were very different even though they were designed to be as similar as possible. This aspect of the study is clearly shown in the examples. Children in the physical condition discussed the evidence much more than children in the computer condition, because the nature of the evidence was very different. In the computer condition, the children tested the combinations and they instantly found out whether it was yellow or not. In the physical condition the evidence was not so clear-cut. It could take several minutes for the solution to turn yellow, and even when it did the reason may not have been because of the chemicals used, but because the chemicals were contaminated. The children in the physical condition were experiencing how to deal with the possibility of uncertain evidence, a skill which scientists have to use all the time. These two conditions are thus very different activities which provide children with very different learning experiences.

In conclusion, the main finding of the study was that the introduction of the computer transformed the nature and type of collaborative activity and also affected the development of children's scientific reasoning. For pairs working around the computer, there was proportionally more talk about the task and management of the task, proportionally less procedural and off-task talk, proportionally more transactive discussions, and better-quality solutions were produced than for children in the physical condition. However, pairs who worked with the physical apparatus improved significantly more in tests of scientific reasoning than pairs who worked with the computer. These findings support the Sociocultural perspective and show the importance of tools for mediating collaborative activity.

## References

Bennett, N. and Dunne, E. (1992). 'The nature and quality of talk in co-operative classroom groups'. *Learning and Instruction*, 1, 103–18.

Crook, C. (1994). *Computers and the Collaborative Experience of Learning*. London: Routledge.

Cummings, G. (1982). 'Small group discussions and the microcomputer'. *Journal of Computer Assisted Learning*, 1, 149–58.

Fitzpatrick, H. and Hardman, M. (2000). 'Mediated activity in the primary school classroom: girls, boys and computers'. *Learning and Instruction*, 10(5), 431–46.

Hawkins, J., Sheingold, K., Gearhart, M. and Berger, C. (1982). 'Microcomputers in schools: impact on the social life of elementary classrooms'. *Journal of Applied Developmental Psychology*, 3, 361–73.

Inhelder, B. and Piaget, J. (1958). *The Growth of Logical Thinking from Childhood to Adolescence*. New York: Basic Books.

Keogh, T., Barnes, P., Joiner, R. and Littleton, K. (2000). 'Gender, pair composition and computer versus paper presentations of an English language task'. *Educational Psychology*, 20(1), 33–44.

Kruger, A.-C. (1992). 'The effect of peer and adult–child transactive discussions on moral reasoning'. *Merrill-Palmer Quarterly*, 38, 191–211.

Kuhn, D. and Ho, V. (1980). 'Self directed activity and cognitive development'. *Journal of Applied Developmental Psychology*, 1 , 119–33.

Miell, D. and MacDonald, R.A.R. (forthcoming). 'Children's creative collaborations: the importance of friendship when working together on a musical composition.' *Social Development*.

Montgomery, R. and Azmitia, M. (1993). 'Friendship, transactive dialogues and the development of scientific reasoning'. *Social Development*, 2(3), 202–21.

Newman, D., Goldman, S.V., Brienne, D., Jackson, I. and Magzamen, S. (1989). 'Computer mediation of collaborative science investigations'. *Journal of Educational Computer Research*, 5, 151–66.

Säljö, R. (1996). 'Mental and physical artefacts in cognitive processes'. In H. Spada and P. Reiman (eds) *Learning in Humans and Machines* (pp. 83–96). Oxford: Pergamon.

Säljö, R. (1999). 'Mental and physical artefacts in cognitive processes'. In K. Littleton and P. Light (eds) *Learning with Computers: Analysing productive interaction* (pp. 144–61). London: Routledge.

Teasley, S.D. and Roschelle, J. (1993). 'Constructing a joint problem space the computer as a tool for sharing knowledge'. In S.P. Lajoie and S.J. Derry (eds) *Computers as Cognitive Tools* (pp. 229–58). Hillsdale, NJ: Lawrence Erlbaum.

Vygotsky, L.S. (1978). *Mind in Society: The development of higher sociological processes.* Cambridge, MA: Harvard University Press.

Vygotsky, L.S. (1981). 'The genesis of higher mental functions'. In J.V. Wertsch (ed.) *The Concept of Activity in Soviet Psychology* (pp. 134–43 ). Armonk, NY: Sharpe.

Werstch, J.V. (1995). 'The need for action in sociocultural research'. In J.V. Werstch, P. del Rio and A. Alvarez (eds) *Sociocultural Studies of Mind* (pp. 56–74). Cambridge: Cambridge University Press.

# 4

# Children's Collaborative Music Composition: Communication through Music

*Louise Morgan, David Hargreaves and Richard Joiner*

## Introduction

There is a considerable amount of research which concerns the beneficial effects of peer interaction on children's learning and development. However, very little of this research has investigated the effect of collaboration in creative situations, with the notable exception of Baker-Sennett et al.'s (1992) study of children's group activity in creating a play. The aim of this chapter is to examine peer collaboration in the context of creativity – specifically music composition – where children are not working towards an absolute end product or a correct answer, but rather towards the acceptance of one solution from a potentially infinite number of solutions. It is important to establish whether the processes necessary to achieve this differ significantly from the processes required to complete science-based tasks.

Previous research has shown that an important element of task activity in groups is the dialogue among group members (for example, Damon and Killen 1982, Berkowitz and Gibbs 1985, Forman and Cazden 1985, Mercer 1995, Rogoff 1998, Wegerif et al. 1999). The recurring theme is one of sharing ideas verbally, arguing through alternatives and providing justifications for accepted and rejected solutions. Essentially, the more of this talk, the greater the productivity of the group. However, this may be due to the types of tasks used in these studies; they have all necessitated verbal interaction and communication of ideas if the group is to succeed. None of the research has looked at tasks where another medium exists for communication of ideas, and this is where the study of musical collaboration can make a unique contribution.

For Chomsky (1990), 'The structure of language does not allow direct expression of our thoughts' (p. 146). We know far more than we can tell, in that the knowledge we possess is not always reducible to words. 'There are, indeed, things that cannot be put into words. They make themselves manifest' (Wittgenstein 1953, p. 151). Language has the limitation of *representing* what one thinks without necessarily *being* what one thinks. This relates to another of Wittgenstein's arguments: that we can never be entirely sure that we do in fact correctly understand precisely what is intended; that language is not simply a matter of transmitting intentions and knowledge.

It is proposed here that within the context of peer collaboration and children's music composition, another medium exists for representation of thoughts and presentation of ideas. Knowledge can be demonstrated as well as stated verbally, so children working in groups on music composition might establish a common understanding of the task by projecting their thoughts and ideas directly on to the musical instruments rather than verbalising them. In this way, their ideas will be apparent without words. The children may engage in some form of 'musical discourse'; that is, discourse *through* music rather than discourse *about* music. If one accepts Chomsky's ideas that language is imprecise and does not directly express thought, the expression of musical ideas through the music itself is surely more constructive than the expression of musical ideas through words.

In support of this, Mills (1991) states that, 'When composing, we often try out ideas by performing them, and make judgements about them as a result of listening' (p. 9). And:

> Music has its own meaning, not all of which can be expressed in words. When we talk about music, we comment only on parts of it. The whole is more than the sum of the parts. Thus a verbal description of a piece is never more than a pale copy of the original. Talking about music is valuable because it enables us to communicate some of our ideas. But it is never a substitute for the experience of music itself. (p. 49)

Music has been said to 'provide a unique framework with which humans can express ... the structure of their knowledge and social relations' (Sloboda 1985, p. 267).

Furthermore, the National Curriculum for England (2000) states: 'Music is a powerful, unique form of communication that can change the way pupils feel, think and act. It brings together intellect and feeling and enables personal expression, reflection and emotional development.' It is seen as an important mode of communication and understanding which has its own rules and conventions. For Gamble (1984), 'Composing ... is thinking in sound' (pp. 15–16). This suggests that if one can think in sound, one can communicate one's musical ideas in sound, and this idea is reiterated by Swanwick (1979), who claims that, 'Music seems to possess a remarkable ability to speak for itself. Our problem is to try to understand how this happens' (p. 15).

The principal aim of the research reported in this chapter is to explore the importance of verbal and musical interaction in relation to the productivity of the group across a number of different types of music composition task. Three studies are reported , which differ only in the nature of the task given to the children. Study 1 employed a representational composition task, which required the children to compose a piece of music to represent the events of a story . Study 2 involved a formal music composition task, and required the children to compose a piece of music that has a 'beginning, a middle and an end', and study 3 used an emotion-based task that asked the children to 'compose a piece of music that will make me happy'. (For a detailed discussion on these three types of task, see Barrett (1995) and Morgan et al. (1998).) The research also examined the effects of the gender composition of the group on both the collaborative composition process and on the quality of the work produced. This is beyond the scope of the present chapter, but for a detailed discussion of these findings, see Morgan et al. (1998).

## Study 1: 'A Trip to the Seaside' – A Representational Music Composition Task

In study 1, 88 children (46 girls and 42 boys) aged between 9 and 11 years were divided into 22 groups of four by their class teachers. The children were taken in groups of four to a quiet area of the school where four musical instruments were arranged on the floor in front of them: a glockenspiel, a cabasa, a triangle and a drum. The children were asked to sit down behind one of the musical instruments and asked to compose a piece of music to represent a story about a family's trip to the seaside. The story was read out loud to the children and a paper version of the story was left with them. The story is shown below.

Mum, Dad, Ben and Sarah are all in the car, travelling to the seaside. The children are very excited about their day out and chatter all the way. Dad parks the car and Mum unloads the picnic from the boot. Ben and Sarah take off their shoes and rush through the sand into the water. The children shriek as the icy water laps up against their ankles. Dad throws a ball to Ben, who drops it. A dog snatches the ball and runs with it along the beach. Dad chases the dog, grabs the ball back and throws it to Sarah. Mum tells the others that the picnic is ready, and the family tuck into sandwiches and cakes. After their lunch, the children play in the sea once more before Dad shouts that it is time to go. Everyone is very tired and

Ben and Sarah fall asleep in the back of the car. Mum yawns, and Dad switches on the radio to keep himself awake for the rest of the journey.

The story was written by the researcher and all the children had prior experience of this type of composition task. They were then asked to choose a musical instrument, and to work together to come up with a series of sounds or music to represent or illustrate the events of the story. The entire session was videotaped. The importance of their collaboration was emphasised and it was also stressed that all children should agree on the finished piece. The children were told that they would be allowed to work on the composition for 20 minutes before they would be asked to perform their finished piece for the video camera, to enable the researcher to show their class teacher their work.

A five-point rating scale was developed to assess the quality of the finished compositions and is presented in full below:

*Score 1*: All sound effects[1] are played, with no evidence of selection or discrimination. Sound effects are stereotyped. No evidence of decision making as to which sound should represent which event or action within the story. No apparent organisation.

*Score 2*: More selective with a sense of unity. One or two instruments have been chosen to represent certain elements of the story. The sound effects tend to focus on events, rather than actions, and are still very stereotyped. Little structural control and the impression of spontaneity without development of ideas.

*Score 3*: Further selection of events/actions and of instruments is apparent. Sounds become more appropriate and more inventive. Evidence of a structure to the finished piece. Compositions still rather predictable.

*Score 4*: *More* selective still. Less narrative. Clear beginning and ending.

*Score 5*: High level of selection and discrimination, of both the events/actions chosen and of the instruments. Clear beginning, middle and ending. A more abstract level than previously. Equal representation of events, actions, emotions, etc.

The essence of this scale was the extent to which the children displayed selectivity or discrimination of both the actions and events within the story, and of the instruments chosen to represent these. There were many actions and events within the story, which could be represented by an infinite number of musical sounds. The children had to select a variety of actions or events from the story and decide how to illustrate these with the available musical apparatus. In this way, groups of children who scored well on the rating scale were those who demonstrated a certain degree of musical thinking, apparent in this context through the selection and rejection of sounds. (For a further discussion of the issues surrounding the assessment of music, the development of the rating scale and details regarding the validity of this scale, see Morgan et al. (1998).) The compositions were rated by three independent raters and the scale was found to be reliable.

The verbal and musical interaction among the children was analysed. The total talk occurring among the children during the collaborative working period was divided into four categories: (i) task-directed talk, (ii) time spent reading the story aloud, (iii) off-task talk, and (iv) interaction with the researcher.

(i)  *Task-directed talk* was defined as any talk directed towards the successful completion of the task. This type of talk included the presentation of ideas and suggestions to other group members, the discussion of alternatives and the justifications of accepted and rejected solutions. Task-directed talk was therefore assumed to be indicative of attempts to share the social reality of the problem-solving situation.

(ii)  *Read* was defined as the time spent reading the story aloud. This was included because it comprised a large part of the child's talk time, and whilst it was task-directed by nature, it was not seen as actively sharing one's ideas with other group members.

(iii)  *Off-task talk* was defined as any talk not directed towards completion of the task, suggesting time out from actively working to complete the task.

(iv)  *Interaction with the researcher* was any time spent talking to the researcher, including questions of help.

Similarly, there were two sub-variables of total time playing the instruments: (i) task-directed play, and (ii) exploratory play.

(i)  *Task-directed play* was defined as play directed towards completion of the task and towards other members of the group. This definition included the presentation of ideas directly on the instruments, and was viewed as an alternative means of sharing the social reality.

(ii)  *Exploratory play* referred to the exploration of the sound materials, and was seen as being directed towards the individual, or 'playing for oneself'. This type of play was not seen as contributing to a mutual understanding of the task, and did not move the group closer towards establishing shared understanding or towards the completion of the task.

These categories of 'talk' and 'play' were based on those studied in previous peer-collaboration research, but were much broader. The aim of the present research was to examine whether communication among the children through music occurred; and if so, whether it was important for group productivity, and whether it somehow replaced verbal communication. Thus this broad level of analysis is justified in this context.

Significant relationships were found between the amount of task-directed talk ($r = 0.47$, $p < 0.05$) and task-directed play talk ($r = 0.44$, $p < 0.05$) and the group score. No relationship was found between exploratory play, off-task talk, interaction with the researcher, the time spent reading the story aloud and the group score. There was also a significant difference between the total amount of talk and the total amount of play ($t(87) = 2.30$, $p < 0.05$). Children talked (M = 155.6 seconds, SD = 131.28) more than they played (M = 116.8 seconds, SD = 70.60). The results suggest that there was a significant and positive relationship between task-directed play and group productivity. However, in this particular study, communication through music did not replace verbal interaction, as there was a significant and positive relationship between task-directed talk and group productivity. Furthermore, there was more total talk than total play during the collaborative period. This may be due to the nature of the task. The compositions in study 1 were direct representations of external events and the stimulus was highly verbal. It could be that in these types of representational tasks, the child's musical ideas are adequately expressed verbally. To explore this fully, it is necessary to examine a second type of task, which was the goal of study 2.

## Study 2: 'Compose a Piece of Music with a Beginning, a Middle and an End' – A Formal Music Composition Task

The music composition task in study 1 involved the direct representation of external events, and the stimulus was highly verbal. It was suggested that, with this type of task, the children's ideas might be adequately expressed verbally, as a relationship was found between both verbal and musical interaction and group productivity. In study 2, a formal music composition task was used, which required the children to compose a piece of music 'with a beginning, a middle and an end'. It is proposed that with a task of this kind, which requires the children to work directly with musical form and structure rather than representations, communication of ideas through music will have a significant relationship with group productivity and that verbal interaction will be both less prevalent and less important.

The 72 children (36 boys and 36 girls) in study 2 were aged between 9 and 11 years. Their class teachers randomly divided the children into 18 groups of four. In this study, the children were asked to work together to compose a piece of music that had a beginning, a middle and an end. This was a formal music composition task, which contained elements of structure and form, but was not directly representational like that in the previous study. Again, it was established beforehand that this was a task with which the children were familiar. The children were given the same musical instruments as for the previous study.

The compositions in study 2 were assessed using a validated series of rating scales. Hargreaves et al. (1996) devised a series of 14 bipolar constructs on the basis of teachers' comparative judgements of children's creative work. Ten evaluative 7-point scales were used and these were as follows: (i) evocative–unevocative, (ii) lively–dull, (iii) varied–unvaried, (iv) original–unoriginal, (v) effective–ineffective; (vi) interesting–uninteresting, (vii) ambitious–unambitious, (viii) flowing–disjointed, (ix) aesthetically pleasing–aesthetically unpleasing, and (x) technically skilful–technically unskilful. This method of assessment was chosen because Hargreaves et al.'s rating scales were directed towards capturing the essence of a continuous piece of music. The selectivity rating scale discussed above was inappropriate here because it focused specifically on one key element (the selection of sounds). A continuous piece of music is about much more than this one element, and Hargreaves et al.'s scales provide a much broader and more relevant assessment of the compositions in this instance. Three independent raters assessed each of the 18 compositions and highly significant correlations were obtained between each of the raters ratings, suggesting adequate reliability of the scores.

A factor analysis was carried out on the scales to assess whether the set of constructs was measuring just one underlying factor, as Hargreaves et al. discovered. One factor emerged which explained 77% of the total variance in the scores, which confirms the finding of Hargreaves et al. Like them, we suggest that this factor represents the overall effectiveness of the compositions. Factor scores were computed on this factor for each of the group compositions, so that 'group score' (the factor score awarded to each composition) can be thought of as a measure of its effectiveness. In this study, the process variables were task-directed talk, off-task talk, interaction with researcher, task-directed play and exploratory play, each of which was defined in the first study.

There was a significant and positive relationship between task-directed play and group factor score ($r = 0.47$, $p < 0.05$). No significant relationship was found between the amount of task-directed talk and the group factor score ($r = 0.33$, $p = $ ns). There was a significant difference between the total amount of talk and the total amount of play, $t(71) = 10.71$, $p < 0.05$. Children played ($M = 241.76$, $SD = 100.19$) more than they talked ($M = 76.63$, $SD = 71.99$). As in study 1, the findings support the hypothesis that there would be a significant relationship between the amount of task-directed play during the collaborative working period and group productivity. However, in contrast to the first study, no relationship was found between the amount of task-directed talk and the group score. This suggests that while group productivity was dependent on the communication of ideas among the children, this communication was non-verbal, or more specifically was communication through the musical instruments. Ideas were presented musically rather than verbally. This is further apparent in the finding of significantly less total talk than total play among the children during the collaborative working period. It is suggested that these findings were due to the nature of the task. To add further weight to these claims, it is important to examine a further alternative task, and this is the goal of study 3. In this study, the children were required to work on an emotion-based composition task; specifically they were asked to 'compose a piece of music that will make me happy'. This task differs from the representational and formal composition tasks studied above in that it concentrates the children on the expression of emotions.

## Study 3: 'Compose a Piece of Music that will Make Me Happy': An Emotion-based Music Composition Task

On the basis of the above findings, it is suggested that with an emotion-based music composition task, musical interaction will have a significant relationship with group productivity and that verbal interaction will be both less prevalent and less important. This task is similar to the above task, and different from the representational task, in that it does not involve the direct representation of external events. It was thought that the representational-type tasks may somehow encourage more verbal than musical interaction, whereas the formal and emotion-based tasks are concerned more with form and structure in music, and may therefore encourage a directly musical interaction among the children.

The 72 children (36 boys and 36 girls) in study 3 were randomly divided into 18 groups of four by their class teachers. The procedure used in study 3 was the same as the one used in the previous studies, except that the children were asked to compose a piece of music 'that will make me happy'. This composition task has no elements of structure and form and requires pure representation of emotion. The children were given the same musical instruments as for study 1. As in study 2, three independent raters assessed each of the 18 compositions using Hargreaves et al.'s (1996) bipolar constructs and highly significant correlations were suggesting adequate reliability of the scores. Also as in study 2, a factor analysis was carried out on the scales and again, this revealed that there was one underlying factor, this explaining 82.9% of the variance in the score. As Hargreaves et al. suggest, and in line with the findings of study 2, this factor could be measuring the overall effectiveness of the compositions. In light of this, factor scores were awarded to each of the compositions. Thus the 'group score' refers to the factor score awarded to the composition and can be thought of in terms of how effective the composition was. The process measures used in this study were task-directed talk, off-task talk, interaction with researcher, task-directed play and exploratory play, and these are defined as for study 1.

There was a significant relationship between the amount of task-directed play and the group score ($r = 0.55$, $p < 0.05$). No significant relationship was found between the amount of task-directed talk and the group score ($r = 0.14$, $p$ = ns). There was a significant difference between the total amount of talk and the total amount of play ($t(71) = 17.96$, $p < 0.05$). Children played (M = 394.35, SD = 163.70) more than they talked (M = 76.53, SD = 72.81). These results support the hypothesis that with an emotion-based music composition task, there would be a significant relationship between the amount of task-directed play during the collaborative working period and group productivity. Also as predicted, no relationship was found between the amount of task-directed talk and the group score. This suggests that while group productivity was dependent on the communication of ideas among the children, this communication was non-verbal, or specifically was communication through the musical instruments. Ideas were presented musically rather than verbally. This is further apparent in the finding of significantly less total talk than total play among the children during the collaborative working period. These findings are in line with those of study 2.

## General Discussion

The three studies of children's collaborative music composition presented in this chapter provide support for those who claim that communication among children in collaborating groups is crucial for group productivity (for example, Damon and Killen 1982, Berkowitz and Gibbs 1985, Forman and Cazden 1985, Mercer 1995, Rogoff 1998, Wegerif et al. 1999). However, the present research suggests that this communication need not always be verbal, but can also be musical. These findings are important because they show that children communicated their ideas through music across a range of music composition tasks.

In study 1, the children were given a representational composition task and it was found to be important that they talked to each other during the collaborative working period in addition to playing the instruments. There were significantly higher levels of talk than play, but both were important for the productivity of the group. In study 2, the children were given a formal music composition task, in which they were asked to produce a continuous piece of music as distinct from a series of sounds. The most important element of the task activity was found to be task-directed play; that is, the presentation of ideas through music rather than words. Verbal interaction did not have a significant relationship with group productivity and there was significantly more play than talk during the collaborative working period. To assess this further, study 3 was conducted with a third type of task, an emotion-based task. In this task, the children were asked to compose a piece of music that 'will make me happy'. Again, communication of ideas through the musical instruments was both apparent and important, and verbal interaction showed no clear relationship with group productivity. There were very low levels of verbal interaction and high levels of musical interaction.

In study 1, there was a positive relationship between talk and quality of composition. No such relationship was found in study 2 and study 3. However, no such positive relationship was found when children were given a formal compositional task (study 2) or an emotion-based composition task (study 3). One possible explanation for these different findings is the nature of the task. In study 2 and study 3 the children had to work directly with musical form and structure, and thus communication through music was more important. This explanation is only tentative, because each of the studies was carried out in a different school with different approaches to music education. More research is needed to establish which of the findings are due to the nature of the task, and which are due to the differences among the schools.

All three studies showed there was a significant and positive relationship between musical interaction, as measured by task-directed play, and the quality of the music compositions. The research in the present chapter used the broad category of task-directed play and showed in all three studies with different types of music composition task that communication through music does occur and is related to the quality of the composition. Chapter 5 examines in more detail the role of musical interaction in children's collaborative music composition.

No relationship was found between exploratory play and the quality of the music composition in any of the three studies. The exact nature and function of what was called exploratory play is still rather unclear. It was defined as an individualistic form of play, as opposed to play directed towards the group or towards completion of the task. It was essentially the exploration of the musical instruments. While this element of play is considered individualistic rather than co-operative, it did not have a negative relationship with group productivity as would be expected; rather, it showed no relationship with group productivity. It is therefore dangerous to assume that exploratory play is somehow detrimental; it may in fact be a vital part of task accomplishment, or may have some other role that the present analysis has not tapped into. It may be an important precursor to task-directed play, in which the child may be trying out ideas for him- or herself before feeling ready or able to share those ideas with the rest of the group. What begins its life as an exploration of ideas at the individual level may somehow make the transition to task-directed play at the group level. 'Group score' may not be the most effective means of assessing its importance (see Chapter 11, this volume, for a similar discussion on the role of individual reflection in collaborative activity).

A fundamental difficulty with the definition of exploratory play was that it did not distinguish between individualistic playing involving trying out ideas, and simply 'messing around' with the instruments. On a behavioural level, this distinction is problematic to make as it involves inferences of intention on the part of the child. While exploratory play did not show a clear relationship with group productivity, high levels of this behaviour were observed in all three studies, and so it would seem feasible to suggest that it must have some function. Is it improvisation, exploration of ideas, exploration of the instruments, or simply a time-wasting activity to avoid working on the task? It is important to study the elements which make up the category of exploratory play as it may consist of all of these.

Although all three studies showed that children can make use of musical interaction for the effective communication of ideas, many questions remain unanswered. Does musical interaction act *like* verbal interaction? That is, if the purpose of verbal interaction in collaborating groups is to present ideas and discuss their alternatives, how is this happening in music? To what extent are ideas presented musically and subsequently modified musically? Verbal interaction essentially involves reciprocity; to what extent does this occur in musical interaction? Does one person in the group dominate in his or her instrumental playing as sometimes occurs in verbal interaction? These issues require further investigation.

Given Allison's (1986) argument that problem solving in the arts requires the use of thought patterns different from those in science, it may have been expected that the children would work in a way that was different from the way they might approach a science-based task. However, composition is a form of problem solving, where a problem is set up and decisions are taken to solve the problem, which results in the satisfaction of having answered them (Salaman 1988). While it is accepted that there may be infinite solutions to this problem, the results of the present research suggest that the work needed to complete the task may involve similar processes to those observed in science-based tasks; that is, behaviourally, the same factors found to be responsible for productivity in science-based tasks account for productivity in music composition tasks – namely, the communication of ideas and the establishment of a shared social reality.

In summary, the present research has been concerned with children's collaborative music composition, with the principal aim of establishing which factors within groups of children are important for group productivity. Previous peer-collaboration research has suggested that the most important element of task activity in groups is the dialogue among group members. In this study, the importance of verbal communication was found to be dependent on the composition task. The present research also showed that this 'dialogue' could occur musically; that is, through the music itself rather than through words. Thus, talking about music composition is not always productive, and there is no substitute for the experience of the music itself.

## Note

1. The use of the term 'sound effects' is for descriptive clarity only. At no time at all was it suggested to the children that they work on producing a series of sound effects. For the children, the emphasis was put on the transformation of elements within the story into a musical medium.

## References

Allison, B. (1986). 'Some aspects of assessment in art and design education'. In M. Ross (ed.) *Assessment in Arts Education: A necessary discipline or a loss of happiness?* Oxford: Pergamon Press.

Baker-Sennett, J., Matusov, E. and Rogoff, B. (1992). 'Sociocultural processes of creative planning in children's playcrafting'. In P. Light and G. Butterworth (eds) *Context and Cognition: Ways of learning and knowing* (pp. 93–114). London: Harvester Wheatsheaf.

Barrett, M. (1995). 'Children's composing: what have we learnt?' In H. Lee and M. Barrett (eds), *Honing the Craft: Improving the quality of music education.* Proceedings of the 10th International Conference of the Australian Society for Music Education. Hobart: Artemis Publishing Consultants.

Berkowitz, M. and Gibbs, J.C. (1985). 'The process of moral conflict resolution and moral development'. In M.W. Berkowitz (ed.) *Peer Conflict and Psychological Growth* (pp. 71–84). San Francisco, CA: Jossey Bass.

Chomsky, N. (1990). 'Language and Mind'. In D.H. Mellor (ed.), *Ways of Communicating: The Darwin College Lectures.* Cambridge: Cambridge University Press.

Damon, W. and Killen, M. (1982). 'Peer interaction and the process of change in children's moral reasoning'. *Merrill-Palmer Quarterly*, 28, 347–67.

Forman, E. and Cazden, C. (1985). 'Exploring Vygotskian perspectives in education: the cognitive value of peer interaction'. In J.V. Werstch (ed.) *Culture Communication and Cognition* (pp. 323–47). Cambridge: Cambridge University Press.

Gamble, T. (1984). 'Imagination and understanding in the music curriculum'. *British Journal of Music Education*, 1(1), 7–25.

Hargreaves, D., Galton, M. and Robinson, S. (1996). 'Teachers' assessments of primary children's classwork in the creative arts'. *Educational Research*, 38(2), 199–211.

Mercer, N. (1995). *The Guided Construction of Knowledge: Talk amongst learners and teachers*. Clevedon: Multilingual Matters.

Mills, J. (1991). *Music in the Primary School* (Revised edition). Cambridge: Cambridge University Press.

Morgan. L., Hargreaves, D. and Joiner R. (1998). 'How do children make music? Composition in small groups'. *Early Childhood Connections*, 4(1), 15–21.

National Curriculum for Music (2000). *Curriculum Guidelines*. London: HMSO.

Rogoff, B. (1998). 'Cognition as a collaborative process'. In W. Damon, D. Kuhn and R.S. Siegler (eds) *Handbook of Child Psychology: Cognition, perception and language* (5th edition) (pp. 679–744). New York: Wiley.

Salaman, W. (1988). 'Personalities in world music education. No. 7 – John Paynter'. *International Journal of Music Education*, 12, 28–32.

Sloboda, J.A. (1985). *The Musical Mind*. Oxford: Clarendon Press.

Swanwick, K. (1979). *A Basis for Music Education*. Windsor: NFER.

Wegerif, R., Mercer, N. and Dawes, L. (1999). 'From social interaction to individual reasoning: an empirical investigation of a possible socio-cultural model of cognitive development'. *Learning and Instruction*, 9(6), 493–516.

Wittgenstein, L. (1953). *Philosophical Investigations* (translated by G.E.M. Anscombe). Oxford: Blackwell.

# 5
# Musical Conversations: Collaborating with a Friend on Creative Tasks

*Raymond MacDonald and Dorothy Miell*

## Introduction

It is important when considering the process and outcomes of collaborative learning to be sensitive to the nature of the task which children are asked to work on together. Although there is a large amount of literature investigating children's collaboration on science-based problems, which several of the chapters in this volume build on, few studies (with the notable exception of Morgan et al., Chapter 4 of this volume) have examined children's styles of work on open-ended creative tasks, where collaboration is in fact very commonly required in the classroom. In tasks such as creative writing or music making there is no correct answer or, often, much by way of an externally imposed structure to guide the children's work. Therefore, the children not only have to define for themselves what they see as the problem or task and their goals for what they believe will be a satisfactory outcome, but also have to structure their approach to the task and working style. The interactive processes through which such negotiations take place are thus important defining characteristics of these collaborations, and the present chapter examines a key social influence on the nature of such interactions – the relationship between the children involved – in order to uncover its role in affecting the quality of a collaborative interaction.

One of the most important factors affecting the quality of collaborative interactions seems to be the presence of reasoned dialogue, the exploration of the ideas of more than one person and the attempt to integrate these. These are the features identified as characteristic of 'transactive communication' (Berkowitz et al. 1980) and they can be seen in the amounts of explanations, justifications, clarifications, resolved conflicts and elaborations of ideas produced by children working together, with a greater incidence of each reflecting more mutual engagement. We suggest that there will be a greater likelihood of such transactive communication in the interaction between friends than between those with no prior history of a relationship because of friends' experience with taking each other's perspective and engaging in joint planning (Hartup 1996), and since they have a history of shared experiences and engage in more play and pretence together (Miell and Faulkner 1994). Teasley and Roschelle (1993) suggest that when children exchange knowledge, monitor each other's interpretations of this knowledge and repair misunderstandings or potential conflicts, their collaborations are more successful. This form of close monitoring and resolving of disagreements is characteristic of the interactions of friends (Garvey and Shantz 1992, Pellegrini et al. 1997) where the success of individual interactions becomes important since the children are emotionally invested in each other and in the progress of their relationship; indeed, it has been established that friends find it easier than non-friends to establish productive joint working activities (Tharp and Gallimore 1988).

The small amount of research which has been conducted on the effect of working with a friend rather than an acquaintance or stranger has, however, provided mixed evidence about the effects of friendship, with some studies (for example, Nelson and Aboud 1985) showing benefits and others (for example, Berndt et al. 1988) finding no differences between the cognitive gains made when working with friends or acquaintances. In a comprehensive study by Azmitia and Montgomery (1993), they suggest that these differences between previous findings might be partially due to differences in the nature of the task children were asked to perform, since in their study the advantage of working with a friend was only evident in the most difficult tasks. They found that friends were more likely to evaluate their own and their partner's proposed solutions and to engage in transactive dialogues, and that these strategies were particularly helpful for successful problem solving, thus giving the friends an advantage on more difficult problems.

Taking what Azmitia and Montgomery (1993) have suggested about the nature of the task, we wanted to explore the extent to which friendship might affect collaborative work in unstructured tasks, where there is not a problem as such to be solved, but instead where the children need to work together to create something new. As Rogoff (1990) suggests, the main task for the partners working together is to establish a shared social reality, using dialogue to put ideas together which would otherwise not have occurred to the person working alone. We would expect friends to be particularly adept at this, and thus more successful in creative tasks than children who do not know each other, since they are used to establishing and maintaining a shared social reality in their everyday relationship and are adept at generating and developing ideas together.

Despite a strong emphasis on collaborative working for musical activities in most schools, and on promoting creativity within current music education policy, little research has looked into the interaction that goes on between children during the creative musical processes they typically engage in (although see Morgan et al., Chapter 4 of this volume, for an important series of studies which have begun this process of investigation). It is not yet clear just what goes on in pairs and groups as they collaborate to create a piece of music and there have been many calls for further research on the processes involved in the typical composition and improvisation activities which are so central to the current music curriculum (for example, Hennessy and Cox 1999). In creative tasks, as in some other curriculum areas, there is evidence that teachers have concerns about teaching children how to collaborate effectively, and about teaching creative techniques for them to use in pair or group work (Byrne 1996). As a result, there is a need for more research which examines the creative process, especially as it typically occurs in collaborative classroom contexts, which can inform the development of more effective teaching strategies.

One area which appears to offer an interesting path for research in this area is to examine the characteristics and functions of the music played by children working together, in ways similar to those of the researchers who have developed extensive systems for investigating children's talk and who then draw links between this talk and the quality of the collaboration. Many authors have commented on the parallels that exist between musical and verbal communication (MacDonald et al. 1999). For example, Harrison and Pound (1996) suggest that musical dialogues are most successful when participants take account of each other's contributions, an idea which echoes that of transactive communication in the verbal domain. Since an important aim for music education is to encourage children to learn how to communicate thoughts and emotions through music, examining this communicative function of music offers a novel yet potentially important area for investigation. Morgan (1999, in a series of studies reported in Chapter 4 of this volume) has begun this process by demonstrating that children can communicate musically with each other as they compose, and that the nature of such communication has an effect on the outcome of their work as judged by independent assessors. An aim of the study reported here was to develop a more detailed system for coding the music played in such collaborative sessions in order to chart what the children produced and explore its communicative qualities and how these relate to both the corresponding verbal communication and the outcome of their collaborative work.

In summary, here are few projects that have investigated the process and outcomes of children's creative tasks, such as musical collaborations and, given the importance placed on these tasks by national curriculum priorities, it is vital that we develop our understanding of such activities. We suggest that in working collaboratively on creative tasks, the quality of the children's interaction is likely to be particularly important, and that, as a result, factors such as their relationship with each other and consequent level of shared knowledge will have a significant effect on the quality of their work. The rest of this chapter reports the findings of a study designed to address these issues. (Full details of the methods and analyses used and results obtained can be found in Miell and MacDonald, forthcoming).

## Method

The study was carried out using 40 Year-7 children (11–12-year-olds) in an English suburban middle school. The children were allocated to 20 experimental pairs, based on each pair being made up of one child with at least some experience of instrumental lessons (ranging from 6 to 72 months) and the other with no experience. Half of these pairs (ten) were made up of mutual friends from the same class (that is, children who had nominated each other as one of their three friends), and the other ten pairs were made up of children from different classes who had not nominated each other as a friend. As a result of wanting to explore friendship pairs, we were constrained to using same-sex pairs, as very few children nominated opposite-sex children as friends. Furthermore, many previous studies of collaborative learning had suggested that same-sex pairs work more successfully together than mixed-sex pairs. There were equal numbers of male and female pairs in the present study. Each pair was asked to compose and record a piece of music about the rain forest. They were given 15 minutes in which to do this.

All the sessions were first transcribed from the video and then coded by research assistants. The verbal communication coding was carried out following the scheme developed by Kruger (1992) from that suggested originally by Berkowitz et al. (1980). We also wanted to consider the nature of the musical communication between the children and the extent to which the children could build on each other's music, as well as on the ideas they discussed verbally. To investigate this we developed a musical coding scheme based on Berkowitz et al.'s and Kruger's notions of transactive and non-transactive communication (see Appendix 5.1 for all codes used).

An experienced school music teacher (not from the school used for data collection) listened to each of the final performances of the compositions which had been recorded on audiotape. She was asked to rate each composition on a series of rating scales developed by Hargreaves et al. (1996).

## Results

### The Effects of Friendship

In general, the analysis demonstrated a very differing pattern of communication between the friendship pairs in comparison with the non-friendship pairs. For example, when we look at the outcomes measures – the teacher evaluations of the children compositions – we see that there is a marked difference between the ratings of the friends' and the non-friends' compositions, with the friends obtaining a mean of 33.78 in comparison to the non-friends' mean of 10.65. These results demonstrate that the pairs of friends produced compositions that were rated overall as of a significantly better quality than the compositions produced by pairs of non-friends.

Having established that there were differences in the rated quality of the compositions produced by friend and non-friend pairs, the interactive processes (both verbal and musical) in the children's collaborations were examined in more detail. A similar effect for friendship was also in evidence when we looked at these process variables. As referred to above, all the musical and verbal interactions were coded and, after this coding process was completed, each child's total scores for their contributions in each of the verbal and musical coding categories were calculated (see Appendix 5.1 for categories). MANOVA analysis revealed that the friends produced more talk and more music overall than the non-friends. Looking at the pattern of talk and music across individual categories provides more detailed information on their characteristic styles. Table 5.1 provides a summary of the verbal categories on which there were significant effects.

*Table 5.1*  Significant interaction effect between friendship and level of experience on mean proportion of utterances in TSO and TQO categories

| | TSO*<br>as % of all talk | | TQO‡<br>as % of all talk | |
| --- | --- | --- | --- | --- |
| | M | SD | M | SD |
| Friend/experienced | 0.19 | 0.07 | 0.72 | 0.03 |
| Friend/non-experienced | 0.19 | 0.05 | 0.11 | 0.07 |
| Non-friend/experienced | 0.11 | 0.02 | 0.15 | 0.08 |
| Non-friend/non-experienced | 0.03 | 0.04 | 0.04 | 0.02 |

*Transactive statements based on partner's ideas (other-oriented).
‡Transactive questions asked about the partner's ideas (other-oriented).

As Table 5.1 highlights, the friends made proportionally more statements within key transactive categories than the non-friends. This indicates that the friends are communicating in a style that previous researchers have suggested is indicative of good collaboration (Berkowitz et al. 1980). It is also important to note that the non-friends produced a significantly higher proportion of utterances in only two non-transactive categories. They gave more simple agreements and unelaborated disagreements than the friendship pairs, ways of talking which are less useful in promoting a real exchange of views and therefore good collaborative work. Some of the key features of the typical pattern of interaction between friends can be seen in the following example, where there is a clear mutual focus of attention and a good deal of development of each other's ideas.

Jo:   I think we should start it ... I'll start by going [*plays motif*]
      *P – Proposal*
Ann:  and I'll start with a really ... I'll start with a low note, [*plays motif*] ok, got it
      *TSO – Transactive statement based on other's previous contribution*
      [*Ann and Jo play chimes*]
Ann:  you could play that a few times like ... just ... do it all the way through
      *TSO – Transactive statement based on other's previous contribution*
Jo:   all the way through?
      *TRO – Transactive response based on other's previous question*
Ann:  no, just like a bit ... [*plays*]
      *TSO – Transactive statement based on other's previous contribution*
Jo:   what note were you playing? [*goes over to keyboard*]
      *TQO – Transactive question based on other's previous contribution*
Ann:  C, the lowest one
      *TRO – Transactive response based on other's previous question*
      [*both play*]
Ann:  keep going
      *P – Propose*
Jo:   no, play ... slowly at first and then we can get faster
      *TSO – Transactive statement based on other's previous contribution*
      [*both play*]

Similar friendship effects were also seen in the analysis of the musical communication. Once again, communication between friends was characterised by greater use of transactive elements. They offered proportionally more transactive musical responses to their partner's questions or enquiries (MTRO) than the non-friends. The friends also played proportionally more motifs that were transactive musical elaborations of their partner's ideas (MTSO) than the non-friends. Thus, it appears that the friends seem more sensitive to the music being played by their partners and can more easily respond to the musical ideas being suggested in these contexts. Within the non-transactive categories, the friends played proportionally less music in the MS category (music directed to the self rather than the partner) than the non-friends. The friends also played proportionally less music in the MP category (musical propositions) than the non-friends. These findings support the idea that the friends seemed more responsive to their partner's ideas rather than just focusing on their own music. However, the friends played proportionally more music than the non-friends within one of the non-transactive categories (MR – repeating a previous motif). Although the MR category is designated a non-transactive form of music, this is one type of communication that has a rather different significance when comparing music to verbal interactions. Simply to repeat a previous verbal utterance without significant change or development rarely serves a constructive purpose in interaction. However, in the process of composition, it is useful, indeed necessary, to repeat phrases or key sections of a piece being prepared in order to practise them before combining each section into the whole for the final performance.

## The Effects of Experience

The analysis also revealed a main effect for the children's level of musical experience, suggesting that the children who had experience of instrumental training talked to their partners and played music in a different way to those who had no such training. This effect was primarily evident in the category of TSO talk (transactive statements developing the other's ideas), with experienced children observed to use such transactive statements more than non-experienced children. Experienced children also asked significantly more transactive questions based on the other's ideas. Here we see that experience may be producing, in some ways, a similar effect to the friendship effects described earlier. It may be that previous musical experience enables the children to communicate verbally in a more transactive manner. By way of contrast, the talk of the non-experienced children was categorised by a larger proportion of simple agreements, highlighting that a lack of musical experience may make it difficult to communicate in a transactive style when discussing the musical composition.

The effect of previous musical experience on the proportions of music produced is highlighted in three of the individual categories. Music that elaborated previous motifs or ideas transactively was more commonly found in the music played by children who had previous experience.

Experienced children produced proportionally more music in the transactive code MTSO (building musically on the ideas of the partner). Experienced children also played proportionally more music in the category MTRO (responding musically to questions posed by the partner) than the non-friends. In comparison, the non-experienced children produced proportionally more music than the experienced children in the category MS, assigned to musical motifs that were played to the self and were not developments of previous motifs. Thus it appears that previous musical experience enhanced a child's ability to communicate in a musically transactive style, perhaps giving a child confidence to express his or her thoughts and ideas through this separate channel of communication.

**Friendship and Experience Combined**

Analysis also revealed a significant interaction effect between experience and friendship. This suggested that the pattern of talk between pairs of friends and pairs of non-friends was differentially affected by their level of previous experience of musical training (see Table 5.2). Similar effects can be seen in the categories TSO (transactive statements building on the partner's ideas) and TQO (transactive questions about the other's ideas). Children without musical experience produced a smaller proportion of transactive statements (TSO) when they were working with someone they did not know than when they worked with a friend. They also asked proportionally fewer transactive questions (TQO) when they were with a non-friend than when they were with a friend.

*Table 5.2*   Significant interaction effect between friendship and gender on total number of transactive and non-transactive musical motifs

|  | M | SD |
| --- | --- | --- |
| Female friends transactive | 19.00 | 3.86 |
| Female friends non-transactive | 37.80 | 5.39 |
| Male friends transactive | 14.6 | 2.91 |
| Male friends non-transactive | 24.20 | 7.28 |
| Female non-friends transactive | 7.80 | 2.57 |
| Female non-friends non-transactive | 28.50 | 10.21 |
| Male non-friends transactive | 9.7 | 3.50 |
| Male non-friends non-transactive | 33.90 | 9.10 |

The musical coding system allowed us to chart the development of specific musical ideas and demonstrated the impact that transactive communication had upon the musical motifs proposed and developed. For example, the effects of friendship and experience can be seen in musical extracts taken from the interactions. The two-bar motif shown in Figure 5.1, from a pair of friends, was played by the experienced boy (Sean) as a musical proposition (MP) on a glockenspiel during the first four minutes of the composition session.

Figure 5.1  Played on glockenspiel

Over the next two minutes a number of verbal and musical transactive exchanges resulted in the musical idea being developed into a modified motif played on a keyboard (Figure 5.2). The exchanges which led to this new motif focused on how to rhythmically embellish the original phrase and how to represent certain features of the rainforest. They also involved pairing the developing motif with a number of percussion instruments in order to explore various musical possibilities. Another feature of the interactions involved discussions about how best to utilise the keyboard sounds and rhythms. These transactive musical and verbal exchanges all played a role in the motif being developed and played once again in a developed form by Sean.

Figure 5.2  Played on keyboard

This motif occurred in various similar forms throughout the compositional period and also appeared in the final recorded composition in the form shown below and played by the inexperienced boy (John) (Figure 5.3).

Figure 5.3  Played on keyboard

## Multiple Regression Analysis

The results presented above indicate that the friends working together generated proportionally more transactive talk and music and that they obtained higher scores for their final compositions than the non-friend pairs. A multiple regression analysis was conducted in order to test further the relationship between the characteristics of the verbal and musical interactions. The mean total number of transactive utterances predicted 25.2% of the variance between the teacher's scores. When the mean total number of transactive utterances is removed from the equation, the mean total of transactive musical motifs predicts 22.7% of the variance in the teacher's score. This suggests that it was the *total amount* of transactive communication, both verbal and musical, which was associated with the final score the children received for their composition, in such a way that the more transactive communication there was between the children, the higher the children's final score awarded by the teacher.

## Discussion

The results of this study underline the importance of considering social factors which affect the nature of the interactive process when examining the ways in which children collaborate on a task. The pattern of results suggest that the most successful collaborations (as judged by the teacher's evaluations of the compositions) were those between pairs of friends, and that these interactions were characterised by high levels of transactive communication in both the verbal and musical domains.

The results of the present study demonstrate that the communication between children is enhanced when they are working with their friends, and this is likely to be because their established shared knowledge and pattern of interacting allows them to anticipate each other's ideas, draw on experiences they have shared or previously discussed and work efficiently by allocating roles and tasks based on their established expertise and preferences. Non-friends have to establish a way of working with each other before they can begin to establish a shared view of what the task is and start to compare their views about it. In the type of open-ended, creative task that we have examined here, this makes for particular problems for the non-friends as they have no external structure or target end point to help them work together, but instead not only do they have to decide on roles and a plan of action themselves, but they also need to work at developing the shared social reality which Rogoff (1990) has shown helps children to produce creative solutions.

It would be an interesting empirical question to examine the ways in which non-friends build up to productive collaborations over time, and to explore whether the nature of the task (structured versus unstructured, for example) would affect this development. It would also be interesting to examine the effects of friendship on the working patterns of children at different ages, and/or at different stages in a particular friendship's development. Indeed, a recent study (Mitchell 1999) has shown that when children are given a much more structured musical task involving just one instrument (a keyboard), the friendship effect demonstrated in this study is replicated only in a younger age group (8-year-olds).

Looking in more detail at the differences between friends and non-friends, the friends' successful transactive communication was very oriented to each other, most commonly picking up and elaborating on each other's ideas rather than on their own. This is a form of reasoning which Kruger (1992) suggests is the most effective, and is one which is commonly seen as characteristic of the interaction of friends who are more aware of each other's needs and more eager and able to meet them (Gottman 1983, Hartup 1996). In the non-transactive realm, the friends were giving more information useful for developing the composition, rather than the less productive alternatives of simply repeating what the partner said, minimally agreeing or disagreeing with each other or playing music to themselves (as the non-friends did).

It is interesting to examine the interaction between level of friendship and experience on the children's verbal interaction, since this gives us some insight into why friendship might be having the facilitative effect it has on these interactions. It appears that being with a friend gave the inexperienced children the confidence to engage actively in the interaction, developing and questioning more of their partner's ideas, whereas when such children were working with a non-friend they did this significantly less. Experienced children showed no such differences between working with a friend and a non-friend in the number of transactive statements and questions building on their partner's ideas.

Working with a friend seems to have more than compensated for the children's lack of experience in terms of giving them the confidence to take an active role in the interaction. This is in keeping with the findings of previous research (Shantz and Hobart 1989) which suggests that friends have a greater trust in each other and are more willing to take risks in interaction together – by revealing their ideas to each other and challenging each other. In the present study we have seen some evidence of this, with the inexperienced children working with a non-friend being significantly less inclined to develop and elaborate the other child's ideas – a reticence overcome by working with a friend. This is important for music education, as the music curriculum is committed to fostering an active role for the child as 'performer, composer and auditor/critic' (Hewitt

1995). As a result, building the child's confidence to 'have a go' becomes a vital part of the education process (O'Donnell et al. 1999). Anything which helps a child to build up his or her confidence in taking part in musical activities such as composing and performing is therefore useful, and the results of this study would suggest that allowing children to work together in pairs or groups based on supportive relationships would indeed be helpful – particularly to those children who lack experience.

The present study has extended our understanding of collaborative working in the field of creative tasks. In particular it has provided more detail about the nature of musical communication possible between collaborators, following the groundbreaking work of Morgan (reported in Chapter 4 of this volume) which established that children could use music as a channel of productive communication. The study has not only high-lighted the importance of transactive communication for successful collaborations in musical tasks, but has also extended this in two ways: (i) by establishing a link between the level of friendship and amount of trans-active communication typically used by children, and (ii) by showing that transactive communication is possible in channels other than talk – in this case, through the music children play with each other.

## Appendix 5.1: List of Codes and Operational Definitions

### Codes used for Speech

The first five are for simple non-transactive turns:

| Code | Description |
| --- | --- |
| P | When the child proposes something – asserts/suggests it. For example, 'Let's use the drum'; 'I can make a good lion noise' |
| R | When the child reiterates something – repeats without substantial alteration. For example, *Child A*: 'When does the snake come in?' [*Child B*: 'Um … '] *Child A*: 'When do we hear the snake?' |
| I | When the child provides information about something. For example, 'You can only just hear the sound' |
| A | When the child expresses explicit agreement about something. For example, 'Oh yeah, right' |
| D | When the child expresses explicit disagreement about something. For example, 'No, that's C, D not C, E' |

The remaining six codes are for transactive turns:

| Code | Description |
| --- | --- |
| TS | Transactive statements are spontaneously produced critiques, refinements, extensions or significant paraphrases of ideas. Operations on the other's ideas (TSO) are labelled 'other-oriented' (*Child A*: 'Key 18 gives us an insect noise'; *Child B*: 'That doesn't sound like insects, it's more like a big animal!'). |

Spontaneously produced clarifications of the child's own ideas are coded as 'self-oriented' (TSS) (*Child A*: 'I'll play 18' [*Child B*: 'OK'] *Child A*: 'Wait a minute, not 18, it should be 8')

TQ   Transactive questions are spontaneously produced requests for clarification, justification or elaboration. Requests for elaboration of the partner's ideas are labelled 'other-oriented' (TQO) (*Child A*: 'Make the tree felling noise again'; *Child B*: 'How did we do that – did we press key 20?'), and requests for evaluative feedback on the child's own ideas are coded 'self-oriented' (TQS) (*Child A*: 'We want something that sounds smoother' [plays on keyboard]; *Child A*: 'What about that?')

TR   Transactive responses are clarifications, justifications or elaboration of ideas given in answer to a TQ. Responses that elaborate on the partner's ideas are 'other-oriented' and coded TRO (*Child A*: 'We could use that – what's that called?'; *Child B*: 'Um … bells … yes, try that, that could be what we need'), and those that elaborate on own ideas are 'self-oriented' and coded TRS (*Child A*: 'Now we need to make rain' [plays on xylophone]; *Child A*: 'That works … yes, tinkly rain noises')

(NB: We had originally included a further non-transactive verbal code, for 'off-task chat', to include any utterances which were not concerned with the task in hand. However, we observed so few of these utterances (a total of 9 utterances across all sessions), that we decided not to include them in the analysis.)

## Codes used for Music

| Code | Description |
|------|-------------|
| MS | When a child appears to be playing for him- or herself and is not engaged with/oriented to the partner, the motif is coded MS |
| MP | When a new musical motif is played for the first time |
| MR | When a child reiterates a motif without substantial alteration |
| MTS | Spontaneously produced musical refinements, extensions or elaborations of previously played motifs. Where the previous motif was played by the child, this is coded MTSS; where it was previously played by the partner, it is coded MTSO. |
| MTR | Musical responses and elaborations of earlier (verbal) questions or enquiries. Where the question was asked by the child, this is coded MTRS; where it was asked by the partner, it is coded MTRO. |

# References

Azmitia, M. and Montgomery, R. (1993). 'Friendship, transactive dialogues, and the development of scientific reasoning'. *Social Development*, 2(3), 202–21.

Berkowitz, M.W., Gibbs, J.C. and Broughton, J. (1980). 'The relation of moral judgement disparity to developmental effects of peer dialogue'. *Merrill-Palmer Quarterly*, 26, 341–57.

Berndt, T.J., Perry, T.B. and Miller, K.E. (1988). 'Friends' and classmates' interactions on academic tasks'. *Journal of Educational Psychology*, 80, 506–13.

Byrne, C. (1996). 'The use of pattern and echo in developing the creative abilities of secondary school pupils'. *British Journal of Music Education*, 13, 143–54.

Garvey, C. and Shantz, C.U. (1992). 'Conflict talk: approaches adversary discourse'. In C.U. Shantz and W. Hartup (eds) *Conflict in Childhood and Adolescent Development* (pp. 93–121). New York: Cambridge University Press.

Gottman, J. (1983). 'How children become friends'. *Monographs of the Society for Research in Child Development*, 48(3).

Hargreaves, D.J., Galton, M.J. and Robinson, S. (1996). 'Teachers' assessments of primary children's classwork in the creative arts'. *Educational Research*, 38(2), 199–211.

Harrison, C. and Pound, L. (1996). 'Talking music: empowering children as musical communicators'. *British Journal of Music Education*, 13(3).

Hartup, W.W. (1996). 'The company they keep: friendships and their developmental significance'. *Child Development*, 67, 1–13.

Hennessy, S. and Cox, G. (1999). 'The learner's environment within schools'. Paper presented at the Mapping Music Education research in the UK conference, Roehampton Institute, London, October.

Hewitt, A. (1995). 'A review of the role of activity-based learning experiences in the music curriculum, and their current implementation in the standard grade music course in Scotland'. *British Journal of Music Education*, 12(3).

Kruger, A.C. (1992). 'The effect of peer- and adult-child transactive discussions on moral reasoning'. *Merrill-Palmer Quarterly*, 38, 191–211.

MacDonald, R.A.R., Davies, J.B. and O'Donnell, P.J. (1999). 'Structured music workshops for individuals with learning difficulties: an empirical investigation'. *Journal of Applied Research in Intellectual Disabilities*, 12(3), 225–39.

Miell, D. and Faulkner, D. (1994). 'Children's working relationships'. Paper presented at the Biennial International Conference on Personal Relationships, Groningen, Netherlands, July.

Miell, D. and MacDonald, R.A.R. (forthcoming). 'Children's creative collaborations: the importance of friendship when working together on a musical composition'. *Social Development*.

Mitchell, L. (1999). 'Children composing in the classroom'. Unpublished Masters of Research Methods thesis, University of Strathclyde.

Morgan L. (1999). 'Children's collaborative music composition'. Unpublished doctoral thesis, University of Leicester, UK.

Nelson, J. and Aboud, F. (1985). 'The resolution of social conflict between friends'. *Child Development*, 56, 1009–17.

O'Donnell, P.J., MacDonald, R.A.R. and Davies, J.B. (1999). 'Video analysis of the effects of structured music workshops for individuals with leading difficulties', In D. Erdonmez and R.R. Pratt (eds) *Music Therapy and Music Medicine: Expanding horizons* (pp. 219–28). Saint Louis, MN: MMB Music.

Pellegrini, A.D., Galda, L. and Flor, D. (1997). 'Relationships, individual differences, and children's use of literate language'. *British Journal of Educational Psychology*, 67, 139–52.

Rogoff, B. (1990). *Apprenticeship in Thinking: Cognitive development in social context.* Oxford: Oxford University Press.

Shantz, C.U. and Hobart, C.J. (1989). 'Social conflict and development: Peers and siblings'. In T. J. Berndt and G.W. Ladd (eds) *Peer Relationships in Child Development* (pp. 71–94). New York: John Wiley and Sons.

Teasley, S.D. and Roschelle, J. (1993). 'Constructing a joint problem space: the computer as a tool for sharing knowledge'. In S.P. Lajoie and S.J. Derry (eds) *Computers as Cognitive Tools* (pp. 229–58). Hillsdale, NJ: Lawrence Erlbaum.

Tharp, R. and Gallimore, R. (1988). *Rousing Minds to Life.* New York: Cambridge University Press.

# Part III
# Adult Support and Guidance

# 6
## Co-ordinating Support for Conceptual and Procedural Learning in Science

*Christine Howe, Val Duchak-Tanner and Andy Tolmie*

### Introduction

The starting place for the issues to be discussed in this chapter is a popular approach to science education. The approach involves engaging children with controversies regarding physical or biological concepts, introducing them to experimental procedures as tools for resolving these controversies, and encouraging them to draw conclusions from what use of the procedures shows. The conclusions may be drawn immediately after the experimental activity or there may be an interval for reflection, but either way they are expected to show enhanced conceptual grasp. The approach's popularity stems from an apparent consistency with two themes that are stressed within the National Curriculum for England and Wales (Department for Education 1995) and the 5–14 Programme for Scotland (Scottish Office Education Department 1993). These themes are that children should learn about investigative methods whilst boosting their conceptual knowledge, and that they should gain insights into how professional science proceeds. This is not to say that consistency with the themes has been universally accepted: Wellington (1998), for one, is highly sceptical. Rather, it is to claim that because many educationalists have been persuaded, the approach is a fact of life within science classrooms, and thus a key question is how to maximise its potential.

At first sight, the answer seems straightforward: the approach should be delivered with the support of both peer collaboration and expert tutoring. Peer collaboration is not simply an obvious context for exposing a range of positions, and therefore for presenting physical and biological concepts as potentially controversial. It has also been shown to have a positive impact upon conceptual growth in science, with the benefits being a direct consequence of the articulating and debating of positions. Experimental research by ourselves and our colleagues has provided supportive evidence (see Howe et al. 1990, 1992a, 1992b, 1995a, 1995b, Tolmie et al. 1993), but the point has also been endorsed in standard classroom settings (by, for example, Nussbaum and Novick 1981, Osborne and Freyberg 1985, Thorley and Treagust 1987). As for expert tutoring, it has emerged as a crucial factor in the mastery of many procedural skills (see Damon and Phelps 1989, Rogoff 1990), and as demonstrated by our own research (Tolmie and Howe 1994, Howe and Tolmie 1998a) the experimental procedures of science are no exception.

Nevertheless, whilst the need to combine peer collaboration with expert tutoring seems incontrovertible, the manner in which combination should be achieved is far from transparent. Moreover, to make matters worse, research in developmental psychology suggests potential incompatibility between the two forms of support. Piaget (1932) theorised that the exposing and debating of positions during peer collaboration (whose significance he anticipated) can be undermined when authority figures such as parents and teachers participate. Recent empirical research (for example, Kruger 1992, Tolmie et al. 1993) suggests that, at the very least, Piaget's views must be taken seriously. Yet expert tutoring seems to depend upon input from authorities. In addition, work summarised by Damon and Phelps (1989) and Rogoff (1990) indicates that tutoring should follow the principles that Vygotskians have established for the crossing of 'zones of proximal development' (see Vygotsky 1978). As Crook (1994) points out, these principles appear to require carefully tailored and individualised attention, and would therefore seem hard to reconcile with openly contrasting positions between collaborating peers.

The implication is, then, that if peer collaboration is to be combined with expert tutoring, as the favoured approach to science education requires, a method of task organisation is needed that will pre-empt the potential difficulties. The remainder of the chapter will focus on research that we have conducted which provides clear indications of what the method should involve. The next section discusses work which indicates that one crucial ingredient may be the achievement of *consensus* between collaborating peers. The sections that follow outline two recent studies which provide systematic evidence on the role of consensus and which document its central importance. Finally, the chapter's concluding section discusses the wider implications of the reported results. The consequences for science education are considered, in particular the viability of the approach under scrutiny. Also theoretical points are raised, relating to aspects of the Piagetian and Vygotskian perspectives that have exposed the potential difficulties. Finally and perhaps most importantly given the focus of the book, attention is paid to the implications for how we think about peer collaboration. It is argued that the research strengthens the claims that can be made about collaboration and learning, while simultaneously and somewhat paradoxically showing that collaboration must always be interpreted with reference to the wider context within which it is framed.

## The Potential Relevance of Group Consensus

As it happens, the research that provided the initial clue to the importance of consensus addressed a much simpler scenario than the one of present concern (Tolmie and Howe 1994, Howe and Tolmie 1998a). Far from requiring children to engage with scientific controversies, to treat experimental procedures as means to resolution and to relate outcomes to controversies, this research was concerned with how groups of children test hypotheses chosen from lists generated by researchers and not seriously discussed by the groups themselves. The hypotheses related to the factors relevant to the pressure of water and the size of shadows, and the main concern of the research was the efficacy of a computer-based system that was designed to support these factors' appraisal. Support was provided through the system for such investigative procedures as controlled manipulation of variables and accurate observation of outcomes.

Because the emphasis was on procedures, the system involved expert tutoring, being informed by many of the tutoring principles that Vygotsky and his successors have identified. Wood's (for example, 1986) concept of 'contingent prompting' was especially significant. However, in contrast to the individualised presentation that Vygotskian principles seem to imply (but recognising classroom realities, particularly where computers are involved; for example, McAteer and Demissie 1991), the support was geared towards collaborative group work. The collaborative context turned out to have no adverse effect whatsoever: when the system was tested with children aged 9–14 years, on-task performance was good and progress in a range of investigative skills was carried forward to individual post-tests a few weeks later.

Taking the results as a whole, there were signs that a key element in ensuring success was a task design that required children to achieve consensus over which hypotheses they subscribed to and which they should test. It appeared that because consensus forged a unitary position before exposure to prompting, co-ordination was facilitated with the computer's expert intervention. This set us thinking. Suppose that the consensus was not over listed hypotheses but rather over beliefs that were articulated and debated during peer collaboration, and suppose also that these consensual positions became the subject of experimental investigation with expert support. Perhaps this would be sufficient to eliminate any incompatibilities between collaboration and tutoring. Certainly, the achievement of consensus prior to tutoring would draw a clear line between debate and expert input, possibly reducing the adverse effects of the latter upon the shape the former took. In addition, even if the consensual position was transitory and possibly even grudging, it would still have been defined by the children themselves. As a result, expert tutoring in how to appraise the position might be seen as serving the children's own goals rather than being perceived as imposing alternative views. Thus, when the children came to draw their conclusions at the end of the task, they might treat the issues defined by their debate as having been facilitated rather than undermined by the expert. By these means, then, Piagetian concerns about deference to participating authorities might be addressed.

In view of the above, a method of task organisation was considered which would allow children to debate the conceptual material of science, reach a consensus over the issues at stake, test the consensual position empirically whilst being tutored in appropriate procedures, and draw conclusions from the outcomes of testing. However, many questions remained about the method's viability in practice. The supporting evidence provided by our research was indirect, incomplete, and entirely post hoc. Empirical investigations elsewhere in the literature proved singularly uninformative. Nevertheless, theoretical considerations were not discouraging: co-ordination of ideas is a central process in both Piagetian and Vygotskian accounts of how knowledge grows, and we would argue that consensus is a particular form of such co-ordination.

Indeed, consensus is a form of co-ordination that lies midway between what Piaget and Vygotsky themselves proposed. Piaget (for example, 1985) stressed the *individual* co-ordination of ideas. He saw peer collaboration and debate as providing impetus towards such co-ordination, but nevertheless suggested, in contrast to consensus, that the co-ordination itself need not be socially achieved. By contrast, Vygotsky (for example, 1978) accorded great significance to *social* co-ordinations, with tutoring seen as the route to the joint constructions between experts and learners upon which learning depends. Nevertheless, Vygotsky regarded these constructions as internalised, or appropriated, directly; and not, as proposed for consensus, as tools in more active processes whose outcomes depend in addition on initial positions and the evidence obtained from testing. This midway status is what, more than anything, made the envisaged role of consensus seem promising: since, as noted already, collaboration and tutoring are both now known to be relevant, the indications are of learning processes that lie between what Piaget and Vygotsky proposed and of task organisations which support these. Embedded within activities which also involve debate, tutoring and concluding, consensus would create a method of task organisation of precisely this kind. The question was whether it would prove a more effective tool for promoting active learning and genuine gain than collaboration or tutoring alone. It was this question that we addressed in the studies that are reported next.

## Studies 1 and 2

### Basic Design

It was, in other words, theoretical considerations as much as previous investigations that made the proposed method seem worth pursuing, and that led to the two studies that are central to this chapter. In contrast to their predecessors, these studies involved tasks where children were engaged in controversies regarding science phenomena, introduced to experimental procedures as tools for resolution, and encouraged to draw conclusions from what use of the procedures showed. The studies were also explicitly concerned with both conceptual and procedural learning, as measured by change in knowledge and understanding from pre-tests presented prior to the tasks to post-tests presented several weeks afterwards. To test whether consensus operated as envisaged, there were four types of task organisation with each type presented to collaborating groups. The four types are detailed in Table 6.1 and can be summarised as follows: Type 1, which involved all of debate, consensus, tutoring and concluding; Type 2, which was identical to Type 1 except that the debate was structured so as not to end in consensus; Type 3, which was identical to Type 1 except that investigative activity was group-directed rather than guided by a tutor; and Type 4, where the groups did not hold a debate and therefore did not reach a consensus, but were guided by a tutor.

*Table 6.1* Types of task organisation used in the studies

|         | Debate | Consensus | Tutoring | Concluding |
|---------|--------|-----------|----------|------------|
| Type 1  | Yes    | Yes       | Yes      | Yes        |
| Type 2  | Yes    | No        | Yes      | Yes        |
| Type 3  | Yes    | Yes       | No       | Yes        |
| Type 4  | No     | No        | Yes      | Yes        |

In accordance with the line taken above, we hypothesised that *conceptual* learning with the Type 1 tasks (where the consensus should prevent the benefits of debate from being undermined by tutoring) should be at least as good as with the Type 3 tasks (where there was no tutoring to 'interfere' with the debate), and better than with the Type 2 tasks (where there was no consensus to protect the benefits of debate) and the Type 4 tasks (where there was no debate in the first place). We also hypothesised that *procedural* learning with the Type 1 tasks (where the consensus should prevent the benefits of tutoring from being diluted by explicitly contrasting viewpoints) should be at least as good as with the Type 4 tasks (where there were no contrasting viewpoints to interfere with the tutoring) and better than with the Type 2 tasks (where there was no consensus to protect against dilution) and the Type 3 tasks (where tutoring did not occur). The main issue for the studies is whether these hypotheses were confirmed.

Details of one of the studies (Study 1) can be obtained from Howe et al. (2000), although being recently completed the other study (Study 2) has yet to be reported in full. In summary, though, the first point to note is that there were two major differences between the studies. First, Study 1 compared the effects of expert tutoring by a computer with expert tutoring by a person, while Study 2 focused exclusively on person tutoring. The computer versus person contrast was motivated by the authority issue which, as noted earlier, has been central to Piagetian thinking. Furth (1988) has proposed that computers have a weaker authority relation with children than, say, teachers, meaning that the integration of tutoring with peer collaboration might be easier with computers than with persons. In addition, the subject matter of Study 1 was children's beliefs about the factors relevant to shadow size, while the subject matter of Study 2 was their beliefs about the factors relevant to the transfer of heat. Research by Howe (1998) and Osborne et al. (1990) indicates that children's beliefs in the domain of shadows lack theoretical structure, in the sense that they do not revolve around causal mechanisms (see Harré and Madden 1975 and Wellman 1990 for the importance of causal mechanisms to the concept of a 'theory'). By contrast, children's beliefs in the domain of heat transfer are highly theoretically structured. Since Howe et al. (1995a) and Tolmie et al. (1993) have shown that the presence versus absence of theoretical structure can influence the way collaborative activity proceeds, it seemed imperative in the interests of generalisability to respect this contrast in the way the research was designed.

### Outline of Procedures

*Pre-test*

Apart from the differences over mode of presentation and subject matter, the two studies were equivalent. They were both conducted with primary school children from P5 (9–10 years of age), P6 (10–11 years) and P7 (11–12 years) classes. Their initial pre-tests were both in two parts: Part I tested conceptual understanding and was administered as written assignments to whole classes, while Part II tested procedural understanding and involved individual interviews. For Part I of the Study 1 pre-test, the children were shown apparatus comprising a lamp, a screen, a movable frame located on a track between the lamp and the screen, and triangles which could be slotted into the frame. This apparatus allowed the manipulation of lamp brightness, object size, object reflectivity, object–screen distance and lamp–screen distance, and much of Part I involved the children completing a written exercise in which they were required to predict and explain the consequences for shadow size of manipulating one or more of these five factors. In addition, though, items were included where the children were asked to consider equivalent factors in real-world contexts; for example, Jack (of Beanstalk fame) and the Giant (object size) in a pantomime under bright and dim spotlights (lamp brightness).

Part I of the Study 2 pre-test proceeded in a roughly parallel fashion, comprising mainly apparatus-based and real-world items. Containers varying in width, height, thickness, material and reflectivity were either presented to the children or described to them. They were asked to predict whether cold (hot) water in the containers would warm up (cool down) quickly or slowly, to explain their predictions, and (given the centrality of mechanisms within this domain) to outline how factors used to explain predictions achieved their effects. Real-world items followed; for example, a white rubber hot-water bottle filled with hot water and left overnight.

For Part II of the pre-tests in both studies, the children were presented with ideas relating to two of the five factors introduced in Part I; for example, 'Triangle colour doesn't matter for shadow size', 'The width of the container is important to how quickly or slowly warm water will cool down'. With reference to the apparatus used in Part I, the children were asked: a) how they would establish whether the factor under scrutiny operated as stated; b) why they had made their selection; c) what outcomes they predicted and what this would tell them about the factor of interest; and d) what (after testing) occurred and what conclusions could be drawn.

*Group tasks*

Using the pre-tested children, 72 triads were formed for Study 1, with equal numbers assigned to the computer and person versions of the tasks. For each version, nine triads were each assigned to each of the four types of task organisation. For Study 2, 36 triads were formed, with nine assigned to a person version of the four types of task organisation. Assignment to triads was random, apart from the stipulation that each triad would contain children from the same school class. Assignment of triads to type of task organisation (and for Study 1, computer versus person presentation) was also random, except that age band (P5, P6 or P7) was equalised across each task type/mode of presentation combination. As with the pre-test, the tasks were presented in two parts, Part A and Part B, which were separated by a couple of weeks. The groups came one by one for each part, and their activities were videotaped throughout.

Part A for Types 1 and 3 was intended to create 'debate plus consensus'. It started with the children being given sets of cards and asked to predict privately and without discussion what would happen if the apparatus used in the pre-test was manipulated in certain ways; for example, what would happen to shadow size if there was a small grey triangle at the middle distance from the screen with the lamp at the brightest setting but also at the middle distance from the screen. Subsequently, the children were asked to discuss their predictions, reach an agreed position, and ascertain empirically if they were correct. Having done this, they were asked to discuss why things turned out the way that they did and, based on their discussion, to agree and write down what makes a difference to outcome and what does not matter.

Part A for Type 2 started in the same way, with private predictions, but to achieve 'debate without consensus' the children were asked to justify their predictions without being required to resolve their differences. They were also asked to interpret outcomes but not told to reach and write down an agreed position. Part A for Type 4 also started in the same way but, to avoid either debate or consensus, moved simply to the outcome of apparatus manipulations. The children were always led through the initial private predictions by a researcher, but if they were assigned to computer presentation in Study 1, the computer (a low-end Macintosh) took over thereafter. The computer presented task instructions and (in Types 1 and 3) recorded consensual statements via typed-in messages. In Study 2 and under person-presentation in Study 1, task instructions for Part A were presented via workbooks and consensual statements were noted on cards.

Part B of the group task for Type 1 involved the children testing two ideas that they had written down during Part A and receiving expert tutoring while they did this. Essentially, they were presented with cards showing the full set of ideas generated by their group; for example, 'Container width doesn't matter for how quickly things cool down', and instructed to choose one idea for testing first. They were encouraged to discuss how they should use the apparatus to see if the idea was correct. If their choices amounted to controlled experimentation, they were given positive feedback and allowed to proceed with the test. Inappropriate decisions triggered 'contingent prompting' (as adapted from Wood 1986 by, for example, Howe and Tolmie 1998a) before testing was allowed. After testing, the children were asked to note outcomes, to discuss whether additional tests were required (and if so, to conduct them), and to talk about and draw conclusions about the validity of the idea from the test(s) carried out. Following this the entire cycle was repeated and a second idea tested.

Part B of the group task for Types 2 and 4 was identical to Type 1, except that the ideas presented to the children at the start were described as 'some of the ideas that people have about [domain]', rather than related to Part A decisions. For Type 3, Part B of the group task was identical to Type 1, except for the removal of prompting. When the group task was computer-presented in Study 1, the computer conveyed task instructions, recorded the children's choices (for example, of ideas to test, and of apparatus settings), and provided the Type 1, 2 and 4 prompts. When the group task was person-presented in Study 1 (and throughout Study 2), instructions were provided by workbooks, choices were recorded on cards and prompts were given by a researcher. In both studies, all children who participated in the group tasks (and who were not absent from school) were post-tested about two weeks after completing Part B. Post-test procedures were equivalent to pre-test, but new items were used throughout.

*Scoring*

In Study 1, two scores were derived from Part I of the pre- and post-tests to measure conceptual understanding of the factors affecting shadow size. As detailed in Table 6.2, these were: a) explanation of predictions (EP), which tapped understanding of how factors manipulated via the apparatus affect shadow size; and b) application to real world (AP), which tapped understanding of how the same factors operate in everyday contexts.

*Table 6.2* Pre- and post-test measures

| Conceptual Measures (Part I) | | Procedural Measures (Part II) | |
| --- | --- | --- | --- |
| Measure | Study | Measure | Study |
| Explanation of predictions (EP) | 1 and 2 | Choice of apparatus settings (CS) | 1 and 2 |
| Application to real world (AR) | 1 and 2 | Reasons for choice (RC) | 1 and 2 |
| Understanding of causal mechanisms (CM) | 2 | | |

These scores led to values of 0 to 9 across both the pre-test and the post-test. The same two scores were also used with Study 2 to test conceptual understanding of heat transfer. In addition, though, since the Study 2 subject matter required an understanding of causal mechanisms, as was previously explained, there was a third (CM) score which also produced values between 0 and 9.

With Part II in both studies, the main scores derived from the pre- and post-tests to measure procedural understanding related to apparatus settings, the aspect of investigative activity that, in Types 1, 2 and 4, was subject to prompting. As can be seen in Table 6.2, these scores were: a) choice of settings (CS) which related to the appropriateness of the selected setting; and b) reasons for choice (RC) which related to the acknowledged need for controlled manipulation. In both cases, the scores could range from 0 to 8 across each of the pre- and post-tests. In both studies, 25% of pre- and post-tests were scored by two independent judges, and interjudge agreement was between 90% and 100% for the full set of measures.

Pre-test scores were subtracted from post-test to give measures of pre- to post-test change; and, as noted earlier, change scores were treated as indices of learning. They are therefore the main focus of the 'Results' section to follow. However, as will become clear, they were supplemented by indices of collaborative activity obtained by coding the videotapes and the written/typed-in statements. These indices had the twofold function of a) checking (via measures of debate, consensus and expert tutoring) that the types of task organisation had operated as intended; and b) providing information about how any effects were achieved. They too were checked for interjudge reliability across a 25% sample, with the correlations between judges ranging from $+0.71$ to $+1.00$.

## Summary of Results

Insofar as the differences between pre- and post-test scores can be taken as indices of learning, there can be little doubt that the children learned from the collaborative experience. Across the studies, pre- and post-test comparisons provided five assessments of conceptual learning (2 x EP, 2 x AR and 1 x CM) and four assessments of procedural learning (2 x CS and 2 x RC). On eight of these comparisons (the exception being AR in Study 2), post-test scores were significantly higher than pre-test ($p < 0.01$ to $p < 0.001$). Thus, progress was undoubtedly made, but how did this bear on the central concerns? The key issues are: a) whether pre- to post-test change patterned with type of task organisation in the hypothesised fashion, and how this related to mode of presentation; b) how any type effects were achieved, and whether in particular consensus played a facilitative role. These issues will be considered in turn.

*Pre- to post-test change*

Before looking at pre- to post-test change as a function of task type or mode of presentation, preliminary analyses were carried out to explore the effects of such background variables as participant age, gender and pre-test score. Although several of these variables related to pre- to post-test change, none did so in a fashion which interacted with task type or mode of presentation; hence in what follows background variables are ignored. Focusing then on type and mode, Table 6.3 shows the results which relate to the first hypothesis, that *conceptual* learning with Type 1 should be at least as good as with Type 3 and better than with Types 2 and 4.

*Table 6.3* Mean pre- to post-test change on conceptual measures as a function of task type

|  | | Type | | | |
|---|---|---|---|---|---|
|  | 1 | 2 | 3 | 4 | Significance |
| *Study 1* | (n = 52) | (n = 53) | (n = 49) | (n = 52) | |
| EP (Total) | +2.19$_a$ | +1.43$_{ab}$ | +0.90$_b$ | −0.02$_b$ | F = 4.19, $p < 0.01$ |
| Computer | +2.04 | +1.19 | +0.80 | −0.04 | |
| Person | +2.36 | +1.67 | +1.00 | 0 | |
| AR (Total) | +1.08$_a$ | +0.03$_b$ | +0.39$_b$ | +0.19$_b$ | F = 4.00, $p < 0.01$ |
| Computer | +1.00 | +0.31 | +0.16 | −0.12 | |
| Person | +1.16 | +0.30 | +0.62 | +0.50 | |
| *Study 2* | (n = 25) | (n = 25) | (n = 25) | (n = 27) | |
| EP | +1.04 | +0.64 | +0.96 | +0.78 | ns |
| AR | +0.20 | +0.08 | +0.24 | +0.11 | ns |
| CM | +1.36$_a$ | -0.28$_b$ | +1.60$_a$ | +0.70$_b$ | F = 3.26, $p < 0.05$ |

Note: 54 pre-tested children were assigned to each type in Study 1 and 27 were assigned to each type in Study 2. Reduced numbers here and in Table 6.4 reflect absence from school on the days scheduled for the collaborative tasks and/or post-tests. When subscripts within a row differ the means are significantly different ($p < 0.05$) on a Scheffé test.

As can be seen from Table 6.3, Study 1 provides strong support for the hypothesis: pre- to post-test change was greater with Type 1 than with Types 2 and 4, and the difference was statistically significant. Indeed, pre- to post-test change was also greater with Type 1 than it was with Type 3, even though the prediction here was only that it should be at least as good. The pattern of results was not affected by mode of presentation: as Table 6.3 shows, the means for computer and human presentation were very similar, and neither the main effect of mode nor the type–mode interaction proved to be statistically significant.

Support for the conceptual hypothesis was more qualified with Study 2, with only one statistically significant result in Table 6.3. Nevertheless, the significant difference is in the predicted direction with Type 1 (and now Type 3) outstripping Types 2 and 4. Moreover, the difference relates to CM and therefore to understanding of causal mechanisms. Mechanisms are not only central to theoretically structured domains like heat transfer, but also, in an earlier study by Howe et al. (1995a), were found to make the running as regards equivalents of EP and AR change. In that study, children's beliefs about the factors relevant to heat transfer progressed a few weeks after their beliefs about causal mechanisms, but as a demonstrable consequence of advances in the latter. This relationship may be important in the present context, for while Howe et al. post-tested three to eight weeks after their group tasks, the present research was restricted to around two weeks. With more time, the type effects on CM may have worked through to EP and AR. This seems a plausible explanation given that Types 1 and 3 still showed more EP and AR change in Study 2 than Types 2 and 4 (see Table 6.3), even though these differences were not statistically significant.

The second hypothesis was that *procedural* learning with Type 1 should be at least as good as with Type 4 and better than with Types 2 and 3, and Table 6.4 presents the relevant data.

*Table 6.4* Mean pre- to post-test change on procedural measures as a function of task type

| | 1 | 2 | Type 3 | 4 | Significance |
|---|---|---|---|---|---|
| *Study 1* | (n = 53) | (n = 52) | (n = 51) | (n = 52) | |
| CS (Total) | +1.66 | +1.74 | +1.59 | +1.79 | ns |
| Computer | +1.67 | +1.85 | +1.36 | +2.00 | |
| Person | +1.66 | +1.63 | +1.81 | +1.59 | |
| RC (Total) | +1.91$_a$ | +1.37$_{ab}$ | +0.86$_b$ | +0.73$_b$ | $F = 2.96, p < 0.05$ |
| Computer | +2.63 | +1.41 | +1.04 | +0.92 | |
| Person | +1.15 | +1.33 | +0.69 | +0.06 | |
| *Study 2* | (n = 26) | (n = 26) | (n = 25) | (n = 26) | |
| CS | +1.35$_a$ | +0.42$_b$ | +0.64$_{ab}$ | +1.23$_{ab}$ | $F = 2.40, p < 0.05$ |
| RC | +1.04 | +1.50 | +1.04 | +1.35 | ns |

Note: When subscripts within a row differ the means are significantly different ($p < 0.05$) on a Scheffé test.

Support for the hypothesis can be obtained from the fact that the statistically significant effects in both studies were exactly as expected, although these effects were limited to the RC measure in Study 1 and the CS measure in Study 2. Once more, though, there were no statistically significant differences as a function of mode of presentation, confirming the equivalence of computers and persons that was observed for conceptual change.

*Impact of collaborative activity*

Whether they had the hypothesised consequences or not, there is little doubt that the task types were implemented as intended. The incidence of debate could be ascertained from the frequencies with which explanations were proposed (PE), accepted (AE) and rejected (RE) during the Part A dialogues. The frequencies turned out to be zero with Type 4 in both studies and significantly greater than zero with the other types.

The incidence of consensus could be ascertained from the number of written/typed-in statements (TC) and from the number of group members agreeing (AG) with Part A claims. The incidence of TC was zero (of necessity) with Types 2 and 4 and significantly above zero with Types 1 and 3; the incidence of AG was zero with Type 4 and significantly less than Types 1 and 3 (although above zero) with Type 2. Finally, indices of expert tutoring in Part B such as prompting for control of 'non-focal factors' (PN), prompting for manipulation of 'focal factors' (PF) and 'back-up explanation' (EX), were zero with Type 3, but significantly above zero with the other types.

However, while the task types operated as intended, there was also a tendency for the quest for consensus in Types 1 and 3 to push the level of debate not simply beyond Type 4 but also beyond Type 2, such that Types 1 and 3 > Type 2 > Type 4 for PE, AE and RE. This raises the question of whether the type effects on conceptual learning shown in Table 6.1 could have been consequences of enhanced debate rather than mediated by consensus. Reassuringly, the data show no direct association between PE, AE or RE and the conceptual measures. The two consensus measures TC and AG were, on the other hand, consistently and directly implicated in conceptual learning, and further patterns of correlation suggested that this was because they were providing a framework which rendered Part B of the group task conceptually meaningful. In particular, conceptual change (that is, EP and AR) in Study 1 was also predicted by the total number of valid tests that were conducted in Part B (VT), and by its close associate, the number of unprompted valid tests (UV). These were relatively frequent in absolute terms in Type 1, but even within Type 1 were also predicted by TC and AG. Changes in explanation of causal mechanisms (that is, CM) in Study 2 were predicted by the extent to which explanations were agreed in Part B, and this in turn was a direct consequence of TC and AG.

Since debate was viewed as having potential antipathy to procedural learning, the relatively high levels of debate in Types 1 and 3 were not expected to bear on the observed patterns of procedural change (that is, CS and RC), and this proved to be the case. Once more, however, there was correlational evidence to support the direct and positive involvement of consensus, as indexed by TC and AG. In Study 1, all tutored children, (that is, Types 1, 2 and 4) acknowledged the need for controlled manipulation during the group task. However, it was only the Type 1 children who were able to sustain this through to post-test and therefore demonstrate superior RC change. Sustaining amongst the Type 1 children was associated with TC and AG. Likewise, in Study 1 the absence of type effects over CS change was largely due to post-task gains in the Type 3 children which eclipsed the immediate benefits that the other children obtained from tutoring. TC and AG were strong, and unique, predictors of Type 3 CS change.

In Study 2, the picture was even simpler: TC and AG were predictive of CS and RC change for both the Type 1 and Type 3 children, but VT and UV (the measures of valid testing) were also relevant, and the higher frequency of these in the Type 1 groups was the reason why the children from these groups showed greater CS change than their Type 3 counterparts. What this means, though, is that the constellation of factors that predicted conceptual learning in Study 1 turned out to predict procedural learning in Study 2, and once more the probable explanation is subject matter differences over mechanisms. In Study 1, consensus may have paved the way for an 'empiricist' perspective, such that test results achieved in Part B of the group tasks (that is, VT and UV) could be used as evidence about conceptual knowledge, to the benefit in Type 1 of the latter. An empiricist perspective was less important in Study 2 because, revolving around mechanisms, conceptual advance with heat transfer rests upon theoretical insight rather than evidence from data. As a result, test results achieved in Part B would not have been given conceptual significance. However, by the same token, procedural implications may have been pushed into focus.

## Discussion

In other contexts, the differences between Studies 1 and 2 would warrant detailed discussion. They endorse the evidence alluded to above (Tolmie et al. 1993, Howe et al. 1995a) which suggests that the presence or absence of theoretical structure influences collaborative activity. More generally, they indicate that the presence or absence of theoretical structure is an issue that should be borne in mind by developmental psychologists (for example, Keil 1990) who are attempting to understand the nature of 'domain-specific' learning processes. Thus, the differences between the studies are important, but nevertheless the key issues in the present context rest more with the similarities. As signalled earlier, there are three such issues, relating respectively to current approaches to science education, Piagetian and Vygotskian perspectives upon cognitive growth, and the role of peer collaboration in the promotion of learning. These issues will be discussed below.

## Current Approaches to Science Education

As noted from the outset, the task used in the two studies (and modified as a function of type) was not a laboratory convenience. Rather, it was modelled on exercises that are currently popular in science classrooms, because they are seen as co-ordinating conceptual and procedural teaching and/or as mimicking professional science practice. The studies have nothing to say about professional practice, but they do bear on the co-ordination of teaching and their message is positive. They endorse the view that conceptual understanding and procedural skill can be simultaneously boosted by activities where children engage with controversies, learn experimental procedures as means to resolution and draw conclusions from what use of the procedures shows. However, they also indicate that to make the most of such activities, they should be embedded within an analogue of the Type 1 task. In other words, engagement with controversies should be achieved via peer debates which end with consensus, procedures should be introduced as means to investigating consensual positions and tutored accordingly, and consensual positions should be the focus of conclusions.

On the other hand, given the Type 1 format, the studies suggest that it is irrelevant whether task instruction and tutoring are delivered by computers or by persons-cum-workbooks. The implication is therefore that practitioners wishing to emulate the Type 1 procedures can follow their personal preferences and/or local constraints when thinking about presentation. Computer-presentation can proceed with minimal intervention, but it may not be to everyone's taste. Person-presentation requires less technical know-how, but it probably means small groups receiving undivided attention, especially during tutoring, while their classmates work unsupervised. Practitioners will vary in how they weigh such considerations, but the key point is that as regards outcome this does not matter: the Type 1 task is robust against mode of presentation. The reasons for this robustness can only be speculative, but they may be part and parcel of the steps taken in the Type 1 design to minimise the tutors' authority over the children's ideas. If authority had been rendered more or less irrelevant by virtue of task organisation, then Furth's (1988) point about the weaker authority potential of computers loses force.

## Status of Piagetian and Vygotskian Perspectives

Manipulations of authority relations can, of course, only bear on the results if the Piagetian approach, which treats authority as counterproductive, continues to have relevance. However, this surely has to be accepted: since achieving a meaningful sense of consensus depends on viewpoints being explored, the Piagetian emphasis on debate receives strong support from the studies' results. Nevertheless, as emphasised already, the focus on consensus is itself more than what Piaget would have contemplated. Moreover, one feature of the Study 1 results is also hard to reconcile with a Piagetian stance. As noted above, valid testing (both the total number of tests and the number unprompted) was positively associated with conceptual learning, and valid testing turned out to be more frequent with the Type 1 tasks than with the Type 3. However, the only difference between the Type 1 and Type 3 experience was over expert tutoring, and thus the number of valid tests and (paradoxically) unprompted valid tests must have been a consequence of this. The implication, then, is that tutoring was needed to allow the conceptual benefits of debate and consensus to be fully realised, a conclusion that is a far cry from what Piaget would have proposed.

Yet just as the Piagetian perspective emerges from the studies as relevant but qualified, so does the Vygotskian. Tutoring proved beneficial, as Vygotsky would have predicted; and in Study 1, to both procedural learning and conceptual. Nevertheless, its relevance cannot have been to create social products which the children then internalised. The process of internalisation cannot explain why the Type 1 children in Study 1 carried the messages of tutoring through to post-test, while the Type 2 and 4 children fell away. Equally, it cannot explain why the Type 3 children in Study 1 managed, post-group, to regain lost ground. Such results point to a learning process which accords a more substantial role to individual reflection and sense-making than Vygotsky would have envisaged. This said, the results also show that the reflection and sense making must be strongly influenced by the overall context of activity, since they were after all variable across task types. Importantly, such contextual framing concurs with other aspects of the Vygotskian approach. Nevertheless, this concurrence serves only to emphasise the inconsistencies within the Vygotskian framework, inconsistencies which the present studies suggest should be resolved by downplaying internalisation.

In simultaneously challenging internalisation and supporting contextual framing, the studies concur closely with results that we have presented elsewhere. For instance, as further evidence against internalisation, Howe et al. (1990, 1992b) and Tolmie et al. (1993) have reported children progressing from pre-test to post-test after peer collaboration, yet producing patterns of post-test performance that differed markedly from those observed during the collaborative activity. Indeed, repeated post-testing in two investigations showed understanding growing during the post-group period, building on the collaborative experiences but going beyond these. The processes at stake here are not fully understood, but there is no doubt that in these investigations, too, individual reflection played a central role. Nevertheless, as with the present studies, this earlier work also showed that the value of peer collaboration (and, by inference, the reflection it stimulated) was dependent on the broader task context. In this work too, what might seem like subtle differences in task organisation created major variations in the significance accorded to peer collaboration and the amount that was learned. Yet while the present results concur closely with this picture, they also go beyond it: they show for the first time that contextual framing affects not only the extent of learning but also the integration of potentially disparate elements.

## The Role of Peer Collaboration

In both the present studies and their predecessors, the emphasis has been on framing from the immediate task context. However, the gender differences that emerged in one earlier piece of work have also led us (see Howe and Tolmie 1998b) to make explicit acknowledgement of wider socio-cultural experiences. We therefore concur wholeheartedly with Bruner's (1996) claim that 'learning and thinking are always situated in a cultural setting and always dependent upon the utilisation of cultural resources' (p. 4). Yet no matter whether the emphasis is on the immediate activity or experience in general, the reality of framing has one important consequence: there will always be more to peer collaboration than the collaborative activity itself. Other chapters in the book endorse this point, even though their research perspective may differ from (and, on the face of it, seem opposed to) the one adopted here. Nevertheless, it is easy to make the point without recognising its key implication for methodology – that if there is more to peer collaboration than the collaborative activity, we cannot hope to make progress by focusing on collaboration alone. This highlights what is perhaps the major limitation of research in the field to date, an undue emphasis on factors (for example, social relation or ability differences between collaborators) that are *specific* to the collaborative experience. Such factors are important, but as Crook (1994) also recognises, they are only part of the problem. We also need to attend to the wider context within which collaborative activity occurs.

Yet while the studies we have been reporting emphasise the need to view peer collaboration as part of a much wider whole, via their endorsement of consensus they also encourage a bold perspective upon collaboration itself. Consensus is, by definition, a relation between peers: one can agree with authorities, but consensus requires roughly equal status. Therefore, saying that consensus optimises benefits amounts to claiming that collaborative activity plays a necessary and irreplaceable role in the learning process. This means that by introducing consensus into the equation, we must go considerably beyond the position tacitly endorsed at the start of the chapter. There, peer collaboration was presented as a tried-and-trusted strategy for engaging children with controversies and promoting understanding – a beneficial approach, without doubt, but not necessarily the only one that could be employed. Through consensus a stronger position has emerged, one that treats collaboration not simply as usable but also as essential if learning is to be maximised. It is unclear at present how widely the position can be said to apply; whether it is specific to science or whether its relevance is general. Certainly, the fact that it is underpinned by theory means that generality can be hypothesised, and undoubtedly should be the subject of further research. Nevertheless, the fact that it has been endorsed in one context is itself of significance, for it shifts the agenda away from peer collaboration in comparison with non-collaborative methods and on to strategies for optimising collaboration itself. As we rethink collaborative learning, this seems an important consideration to bear in mind.

## Acknowledgements

The studies to be described in this chapter were supported by ESRC awards R000233481 and R000236714 to Christine Howe and Andy Tolmie. Thanks are due to the ESRC for their support, to the children and teachers from the participating schools, and to Michelle Moore, Catherine Rattray, Stuart Ross, Nick Sofroniou and Claire Stevens for assistance with data collection and coding. Address for correspondence: Professor Christine Howe, Department of Psychology, University of Strathclyde, 40 George Street, Glasgow G1 1QE (e-mail: c.j.howe@strath.ac.uk).

## References

Bruner, J. (1996). *The Culture of Education*. Cambridge, MA: Harvard University Press.
Crook, C. (1994). *Computers and the Collaborative Experience of Learning*. London: Routledge.
Damon, W. and Phelps, E. (1989). 'Critical distinctions among three approaches to peer education'. *International Journal of Educational Research*, 5, 331–43.
Department for Education (1995). *Science in the National Curriculum*. London: HMSO.
Furth, H.G. (1988). 'Piaget's logic of assimilation and logic for the classroom'. In G. Forman and P.B. Pufall (eds) *Constructivism in the Computer Age*. Hillsdale, NJ: Lawrence Erlbaum Associates.
Harré, R. and Madden, E.H. (1975). *Causal Powers: A Theory of Natural Necessity*. Oxford: Blackwell.
Howe, C.J. (1998). *Conceptual Structure in Childhood and Adolescence: The case of everyday physics*. London: Routledge.
Howe, C.J., Rodgers, C. and Tolmie, A. (1990). 'Physics in the primary school: peer interaction and the understanding of floating and sinking'. *European Journal of Psychology of Education*, 5, 459–75.

Howe, C.J and Tolmie, A. (1998a). 'Computer support for learning in collaborative contexts: prompted hypothesis testing in physics'. *Computers in Education*, 30, 223–35.

Howe, C.J and Tolmie, A. (1998b). 'Productive interaction in the context of computer-supported collaborative learning in science'. In K. Littleton and P. Light (eds) *Learning with Computers: Analysing productive interaction*. London: Routledge.

Howe, C.J., Tolmie, A., Anderson, A. and Mackenzie, M. (1992a). 'Conceptual knowledge in physics: the role of group interaction in computer-supported teaching'. *Learning and Instruction*, 2, 161–83.

Howe, C., Tolmie, A., Duchak-Tanner, V. and Rattray, C. (2000). 'Hypothesis testing in science: group consensus and the acquisition of conceptual and procedural knowledge'. *Learning and Instruction*, 10, 361–91.

Howe, C.J., Tolmie, A., Greer, K. and Mackenzie, M. (1995a). 'Peer collaboration and conceptual growth in physics: task influences on children's understanding of heating and cooling'. *Cognition and Instruction*, 13, 483–503.

Howe, C.J., Tolmie, A. and Mackenzie, M. (1995b). 'Computer support for the collaborative learning of physics concepts'. In C. O'Malley (ed.) *Computer-Supported Collaborative Learning*. Berlin: Springer Verlag.

Howe, C.J., Tolmie, A. and Rodgers, C. (1992b). 'The acquisition of conceptual knowledge in science by primary school children: group interaction and the understanding of motion down an inclined plane'. *British Journal of Developmental Psychology*, 10, 113–30.

Keil, F.C. (1990). 'Constraints on constraints: surveying the epigenetic landscape'. *Cognitive Science*, 14, 135–68.

Kruger, A.C. (1992). 'The effects of peer– and adult–child transactive discussion on moral reasoning'. *Merrill-Palmer Quarterly*, 38, 191–211.

McAteer, E. and Demissie, A. (1991). *Writing Competence across the Curriculum*. Report to Scottish Office Education Department.

Nussbaum, J. and Novick, S. (1981). 'Brainstorming in the classroom to invent a model: a case study'. *School Science Review*, 62, 771–8.

Osborne, J., Black, P., Smith, M. and Meadows, J. (1990). *SPACE Project Research Report: Light*. Liverpool: Liverpool University Press.

Osborne, R. and Freyberg, P. (1985). *Learning in Science*. Auckland: Heinemann.

Piaget, J. (1932). *The Moral Judgment of the Child*. London: Routledge.

Piaget, J. (1985). *The Equilibration of Cognitive Structures*. Chicago, IL: University of Chicago Press.

Rogoff, B. (1990). *Apprenticeship in Thinking: Cognitive development in social context*. Oxford: Oxford University Press.

Scottish Office Education Department (1993). *Environmental Studies 5–14*. Edinburgh: HMSO.

Thorley, N.R. and Treagust, D.F. (1987). 'Conflict within dyadic interactions as a stimulant for conceptual change in physics'. *International Journal of Science Education*, 9, 203–16.

Tolmie, A. and Howe, C.J. (1994). 'Computer-directed group activity and the development of children's hypothesis-testing skills'. In H.C. Foot, C.J. Howe, A. Anderson, A. Tolmie and D. Warden (eds) *Group and Interactive Learning* (pp. 139–44). Southampton: Computational Mechanics Publications.

Tolmie, A., Howe, C.J., Mackenzie, M. and Greer, K. (1993). 'Task design as an influence on dialogue and learning: primary school group work with object flotation'. *Social Development*, 2, 183–201.

Vygotsky, L.S. (1978). *Mind in Society*. Cambridge, MA: Harvard University Press.

Wellington, J. (1998). 'Practical work in science: time for reappraisal'. In J. Wellington (ed.) *Practical Work in Science: Which way now?* London: Routledge.

Wellman, H.M. (1990). *The Child's Theory of Mind.* Cambridge, MA: Bradford Books.

Wood, D. (1986). 'Aspects of teaching and learning'. In M. Richards and P. Light (eds) *Children of Social Worlds: Development in a social context* (pp. 191–212) Cambridge: Polity Press.

# 7

# The Role of Adult Guidance and Peer Collaboration in Child Pedestrian Training

*Andrew Tolmie, James Thomson and Hugh Foot*

Given the present widespread concerns about the effectiveness of formal educational systems, and the extensive research being conducted into ways of improving them, it is not surprising that a great proportion of work on collaborative learning is focused on school-oriented activities, such as science, mathematics, literacy and music. However, the growing influence on accounts of interaction and learning of sociocultural theorists such as Cole (1996) and situated learning theorists such as Lave and Wenger (1991) serves as a reminder that we are essentially dealing with processes which originate and have a natural ecology within *informal* learning contexts. It is for this reason, arguably, that it has often proved difficult to establish collaborative learning approaches within the classroom, despite their demonstrated efficacy: they are imported practices that may sit uncomfortably alongside the entrenched methods of formal education. This is not to call into question the value of research on collaboration and learning within formal settings. Indeed, finding ways of marrying formal and informal learning practices might well be the key to the reinvention of educational systems. A fuller understanding of the operation of collaborative learning processes within informal contexts is needed, though, to help steer attempts to effect any such marriage. Thus work in informal settings, particularly where the topics dealt with are outside those of the school curriculum, constitutes a central part of current research efforts.

The acquisition of pedestrian skills can be argued to be the informal learning context par excellence. The vast majority of inhabitants of industrialised societies reach adulthood possessing a complex array of skills and strategies for interacting safely with motorised traffic (van der Molen 1981). They typically acquire these skills and strategies, moreover, in the total absence of any formal instruction outside the occasional road safety lesson of demonstrably limited effectiveness (see, for example, Ryhammer and Bergland 1980, Ampofo-Boateng and Thomson 1990). We know very little in fact about how this learning actually takes place. We know rather more, however, about how it can be deliberately supported, which may provide some clues as to the nature of the processes involved, although of course any inferences must be drawn with caution. So, for instance, there is considerable evidence that practical training which provides children with supervised experience of such environments is amongst the most effective means of promoting learning of the skills and strategies required to solve the problems posed by traffic environments. The teaching of general rules, as in the Green Cross Code, is of little benefit in comparison (Thomson et al. 1996).

Indeed, the efficacy of practical training methods has been demonstrated both at the roadside *and* using simulations. Thomson and Whelan (1997), for example, had adult volunteers working with groups of three 5–6-year-olds at a time, identifying safe places to cross roads. The children were taken to a range of roadside locations, set hypothetical road-crossing goals and asked what routes they would use to achieve these goals. They were then engaged in dialogue aimed at helping them to recognise the features (for example, blind bends or junctions between roads) that would make certain routes unsafe, why these features were hazardous (for example, because they obscured oncoming traffic), and what they should do when confronted with them (for example, walk along the road to a safer location). Four to six half-hour training sessions of this kind led to a 300% improvement in unsupported performance. Ampofo-Boateng et al. (1993) used the same method to train 5-year-olds in safe place identification, but in this case compared the effects of activity at roadside locations and around a table-top model of a road layout containing similar features. They found that both produced the same level of improvement in subsequent unsupported selection of safe crossing places at the roadside, and, importantly, in the rationale offered for selecting these places.

On the face of it, these findings might be taken to suggest that the critical characteristic of practical training is simply that it provides children with *exposure* to the specifics of traffic environments in such a way as to allow the gradual delineation of general principles. This account would be consistent with Piagetian and various information processing models of learning in arguing for the construction of generalised understanding out of a series of concrete experiences. It would also fit in with data showing a reduction in pedestrian accident rates with age despite increased exposure to traffic environments (see, for example, Christie 1995), suggesting that experience may be a vital component in the undirected acquisition of pedestrian skills. However, on closer inspection it is unclear from previous research how far improvements in children's performance following practical training are in fact attributable to actual contact with traffic features, and how far to interaction with and input from trainers or other children being trained alongside them, since these two elements have typically been confounded. It is possible to partially disentangle these variables across different studies, though, and the signs are that, whilst experience is important, social input also has a crucial role. Certainly, Rivara et al. (1991) apparently had less success with a practical training method which involved modelling and positive reinforcement of behaviour, in contrast to the more discursive approach used by Thomson and colleagues. The importance of social input would, moreover, help explain the otherwise counterintuitive finding that training via simulations can be as successful as training at the roadside. If traffic features provide important 'hooks' for certain kinds of dialogue, then to the limited extent that roadside and simulated environments are equated with respect to the availability of these, the same type of interaction would be possible in both contexts, allowing learning to proceed in the same fashion and to the same level.

This leaves open, however, the question of what kind of discursive social input might be most important. On the one hand, Damon and Phelps (1989) and Rogoff (1990), amongst others, argue that *adult scaffolding* or structured guidance of the performance of an activity (for example, taking a novice through the steps involved in baking a cake) is a central means by which children acquire skilled *behaviour*. If this were the critical element in the practical training methods used by Thomson and Whelan (1997) and Ampofo-Boateng et al. (1993), it would explain the improvement they found in children's ability to construct safe road-crossing routes for particular kinds of road layout. It is also possible to envisage something of the same kind of guidance being spontaneously provided by parents during pedestrian journeys with their children, albeit in a less intensive and less organised fashion. It is unclear, though, how support of this type for children's route planning in a limited number of specific instances would lead to the growth of any more generalised strategies for locating safe places for crossing roads (or, in terms of the earlier analogy, how being guided through the steps involved in cake baking would lead to an appreciation of the need to select an appropriate oven temperature for the cake materials being used). Such broader insights seem to entail the acquisition of *conceptual* models of traffic environments, and the building up of understanding of *why* particular routes are preferable, not just what route to use under which circumstances. That practical training does in fact result in learning of this kind is indicated by the improvements found in children's ability to explain why certain routes were safer in terms of, for example, the visibility of cars, and their own visibility to drivers. Given the well-established effects of *peer discussion* on conceptual growth, via disagreement and explication of reasoning (see, for example, Damon and Phelps 1989, Tolmie et al. 1993), this must be considered to be a potential source of such learning where training takes place in groups, even if the parallels to children's everyday roadside activity are less obvious.

To summarise, then, it is plausible that practical training in pedestrian skills may to an extent provide more intensive versions of spontaneously occurring processes of learning about traffic environments, and there are indications in past research that social input is central to the effectiveness of such training. It is not immediately apparent, however, which elements of social input might be most important, beyond the fact that these appear to be of the kind usually associated with collaborative learning. The remainder of this chapter reports on two studies which were designed to explore in detail the role of both adult guidance and peer discussion in practical pedestrian training, in an attempt to provide clarification on this point. The chapter concludes by addressing some implications of this work for both the acquisition of pedestrian skills and broader models of interaction and learning in informal contexts.

## The Effect of Peer Collaboration and Adult Guidance

Study 1 attempted to distinguish straightforwardly between the effects of the two broad types of social input outlined above. It did this by examining the impact of practical training in which children were asked to make road-crossing judgements using computer animations of traffic environments, working either *on their own under adult guidance* or *collaboratively in peer groups*. Simulations were used because of their convenience relative to the roadside, especially for the purposes of recording the interactions that took place during the training sessions. Training in this case focused on 'visual search'; that is, identification of the features, both static (for example, road layout, parked vehicles) and dynamic (for example, type of traffic and pattern of flow), that need to be attended to in making road-crossing decisions. Individual pre- and post-tests were used to establish learning outcomes, and analyses of dialogue and activity during training were conducted to examine how this learning related to the processes in train under the two conditions.

Prior to training, all participants (49 children aged 6–8 years) were pretested on their ability to identify relevant and ignore irrelevant features for road crossing, both within computer simulations and at the roadside. The computer description task involved the presentation of twelve ten-second simulations, varying in terms of road layout (straight roads to complex junctions), amount of traffic, and presence of distractions (for example, a mother calling her child). Children watched each sequence in turn, and after each were asked to report on what they had seen and heard that a child shown at the roadside would need to know about in order to cross the road safely. For the roadside description task children were taken to a location near their school, where there was a busy straight road, a cross-roads, traffic lights and a blind bend. Standing at this location, they were again asked to say what they could see and hear that it would be important to know about to cross the road safely. Finally, children also undertook a road-crossing decision task, which was designed to examine the relation between ability to pick up relevant features and the quality of actual crossing judgements. Standing at the same roadside location, children were asked to watch the traffic, and shout when they thought it would be safe to walk right across the road (without actually doing so). They did this for five trials or ten minutes, whichever was less. Responses for the computer and roadside description tasks were simply audiotaped. For the road-crossing decision task, the timing of traffic movements and children's decisions were recorded via key presses on a portable computer for subsequent analysis. No feedback was provided on any of the three tasks.

After pre-testing, a sub-sample of the children took part in four training sessions, working in either adult–child dyads (the *adult guidance* condition, n = 18), or groups of three (the *peer collaboration* condition, n = 18). Under the first condition, children worked with the same adult volunteer (one of six postgraduate psychology students, none of whom specialised in developmental work, and who had had no instruction on how to interact other than to help the children). Under the second they worked with a fixed group of other children (all classmates). The remaining children received no training (the *control* condition, n = 13).

The training sessions required children to view a series of animated traffic scenarios, and decide if and when it would be safe for a child depicted by the road to cross. Each scenario (there were twelve in total) showed a flow of traffic, with a single gap allowing time for the child to cross. However, the difficulty of the task was gradually increased by bringing in more complex road layouts, variable vehicle speeds and various distractions. The size of the gap also became smaller, making it harder to spot. In a third of the items, the child in the animation was located in a position where the view of approaching traffic would be impaired (that is, there was no *safe* gap). Overall, the training task was intended to sensitise children to the range of features they should attend to, and why; and also to the need to ignore irrelevant features. Without doing both, they were unlikely to arrive at the correct solutions. The dyads or groups watched each scenario in turn (as often as they wanted), and then made a decision on screen by pressing a 'not safe' or a 'go' button at the right moment.

Once they had made a decision, the computer gave feedback on this (via a prerecorded voice-over), and either directed them on to the next scenario, or asked for a further attempt at the problem. The first three training sessions started at successively harder items; the fourth returned to the beginning to provide an opportunity for recapitulation and consolidation. Each session was stopped after 25 minutes, and all were videotaped.

One to two weeks after training, all the children (bar three, one from each condition, who were unavailable) were post-tested using the same procedures as the pre-test. Once post-testing was complete, children's pre- and post-test responses on the *computer description task* were scored on two dimensions. The first was a standardised index of performance: the ratio of relevant features reported relative to irrelevant, calculated as the difference between the number of relevant (R) and irrelevant (I) features over the total number of features (that is, $(R - I)/(R + I)$). A positive value or shift on this index indicated a favouring of relevant features over irrelevant, and a negative value or shift the opposite. The second dimension was a conceptual measure, the number of elaborations, or spontaneous explanations of why relevant features were important. The *roadside description task* was scored in the same way to give two corresponding indices, ratio (road) and elaborations (road). The *road-crossing decision task* was scored on two performance indices, the mean accepted gap size (that is, the size of traffic gap, in seconds, the child chose as safe), and the mean starting delay (the length of time, in seconds, between the leading car of the chosen gap passing and the child shouting; that is, a measure of their ability to anticipate the presence of the gap). Since children are typically overcautious, and show much longer accepted gap sizes and starting delays than adults, progress on these indices would be indicated by a *reduction* in value.

Pre- to post-test change on each of these six measures was calculated by subtraction and analysed for differences between conditions. The adult guidance children were found to have made significantly greater improvements in both their computer ratio and elaboration scores (see Figures 7.1 and 7.2), with a marked shift in favour of reporting relevant features (equivalent to a 'swing' of 22%), and an increase in elaborations, which were rare at pre-test, to just under three per child on average. There was little difference between the peer collaboration and control children, whose ratio scores actually regressed slightly, and who showed only small increases in elaborations. Reductions in accepted gap size and starting delay (see Figures 7.3 and 7.4) were also largest for the adult guidance children (nearly 3 seconds and 1.5 seconds, respectively), although these differences were not quite significant. Moreover, the adult guidance children showed systematic associations between change on the computer and the roadside tasks. First, increases in the reporting of relevant features and in elaborations on the computer were related to increased reporting of relevant features at the roadside. Second, increased reporting of relevant features on the computer was also related to reductions in starting delay, which were in turn related to smaller accepted gap sizes. Thus the adult guidance condition produced improved attention to relevant features on the computer, and an understanding of why these mattered. This led to better awareness of relevant features at the roadside, more rapid assessment of traffic gaps, and improvement in accepted gap size. None of these changes were evident in either the peer collaboration or control conditions.

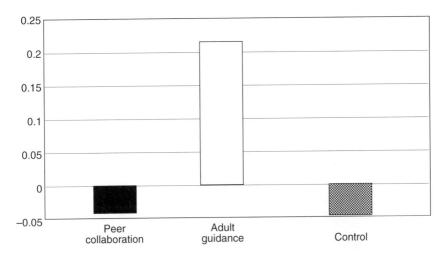

*Figure 7.1*  Change in ratio by condition in Study 1

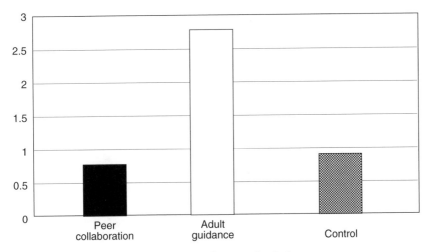

*Figure 7.2*  Change in elaborations by condition in Study 1

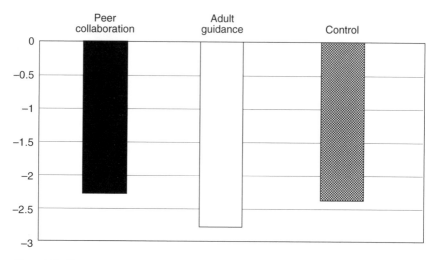

*Figure 7.3* Change in accepted gap size by condition in Study 1

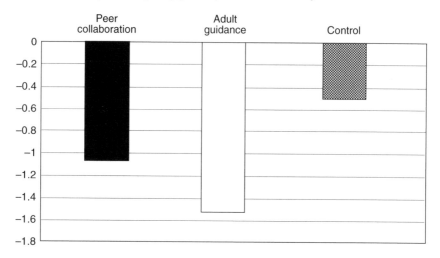

*Figure 7.4* Change in starting delay by condition in Study 1

Having established these differences in learning between their relationship to dialogue and activity during the training sessions was then examined. In order to get a systematic picture of the interaction that had taken place, the videotapes of each session were coded for the incidence of a number of predefined categories of dialogue and on-task activity:

- *suggestions* re crossing decisions; for example: 'it's safe to go now'
- *agreements*; for example: 'yes, I think so too'

- *disagreements*; for example: 'no, not then'
- *explanations*; for example: 'it's safe to go now 'cos no cars are coming'
- *chairing*; that is, utterances concerned with the progress of the task, such as: 'it's my turn'; 'we press this button now'
- *instructions*; for example: 'press the button now'
- *questions*; for example: 'when should I go?'; 'why then?'
- *prompts*; that is, statements, possibly in the form of questions, directing attention to something not yet considered, such as: 'would having the hill there make a difference to crossing?'; 'don't forget about the bend'
- *correct solutions*; that is, the total number of problems answered correctly during the session.

These data yielded good evidence for the differences between the conditions being the result of differences in the pattern of interaction during training (see Table 7.1). At first, children in the peer collaboration condition showed conflict (that is, disagreement and explanation of suggestions) at levels indicative of productive exchange (see Howe et al. 1995). However, this declined over the sessions, and as it did, so did the number of correct decisions. Much of the dialogue (around 30%) was simply chairing, which was negatively associated with on-task performance. In contrast, interaction in the adult guidance sessions led to an *increasing* number of right answers. The initial pattern here was a classic form of scaffolding (see, for example, Wood 1986), with a high incidence of prompts, coupled with occasional instructions, suggesting that adults were steering the child's attention towards critical features and thus to solutions, but without being too directive. These prompts and instructions fell off as children's performance improved; but *explanations* became more frequent. There was also a marked shift towards these explanations being provided by children themselves (18% of all explanations in Session 1 versus 44% in Session 4). It was clear where children's explanations had come from as well. Adult explanations initially followed their own prompts and questions, and the child's suggestions, but over the sessions they increasingly came after child suggestions and explanations. Children's explanations always occurred in reply to adult prompts and adult questions, but steadily increased in incidence. In other words, then, initially the adults provided prompts and asked questions to direct children to what they should be attending to, but also provided an explanatory commentary on these prompts. Over time, the commentary on adult questions and prompts was taken up by children, but adults maintained a commentary on children's input.

*Table 7.1* Study 1: Summary of dialogue frequencies and performance scores in the peer collaboration and adult guidance training sessions*

| Measure | Peer collaboration | Adult guidance |
|---|---|---|
| suggestions[‡§] | high, decrease | high, stable |
| agreements[§] | moderate, sharp decrease | moderate, stable |
| disagreements[†] | moderate, decrease | low, stable |
| explanations[†] | moderate, decrease | moderate, increase |
| chairing[†] | high, stable | high, decrease |
| instructions[‡] | very low | low, decrease |
| questions[†] | low, decrease | high, stable |
| prompts[†] | low, decrease | high, decrease |
| correct solutions[† ‡ §] | decline (3.2 to 2.2) | improve (4.7 to 6.2) |

* High = 10+ per session; moderate = 2–10 per session; low = < 2 per session; very low = < 0.01 per session.
[†] Significant effect of condition.
[‡] Significant effect of session.
[§] Condition x session interaction.

Thus as well as scaffolding action, dialogue in the adult guidance condition showed adult to child transfer of language supporting that action at a conceptual level (cf. Vygotsky 1978). This appeared to aid performance during training, but it also seems likely to have been the source of growth in children's understanding. The implication is that children's progress was underpinned by the *appropriation* of conceptual input from adults, a frequently overlooked aspect of guidance models.

To summarise the key points to emerge from Study 1, children in the adult guidance condition improved significantly more in pick up of relevant road crossing features, and ability to explain the importance of these. This had significant knock-on effects on roadside performance. These improvements were directly attributable to adult–child interaction, especially the issuing of prompts to guide action, *and* the offering of explanations to help understanding of these. Overall, given the differences between the adult guidance and peer collaboration conditions, the results indicate that social input is a crucial aspect of practical training in pedestrian skills, and that the training task itself is not enough to guarantee progress.

## The Effect of Adult–Child Interaction and Adult–Group Interaction

Study 2 was designed to explore in more depth one issue left outstanding by Study 1, namely the apparent failure of peer collaboration to generate any effect on learning. It is tempting to attribute the lack of progress in this condition to the age of the children participating in the study, and a consequent inability to organise productive joint activity. Certainly these children were younger than those typically involved in peer collaboration research in the primary school age range. Moreover, Tomasello et al. (1993) explicitly argue that difficulties with intersubjectivity leave children unable to collaborate effectively until after the age of 7, older than many participants in Study 1.

In fact, though, the peer collaboration condition in Study 1 was not a total failure. The initial training session worked quite well, and it was only after this that performance declined, suggesting that children were successful until the problems got harder. Once this point was reached, it is possible that none of the group members had enough knowledge to propose solutions, so discussion was of no help and they fell back on going through the motions. With better knowledge, the known benefits of peer discussion for improving conceptual grasp might have been more evident.

The obvious way of examining this possibility would be to employ peer collaboration methods of training with more knowledgeable children. However, to do so would be likely to mean confounding traffic knowledge and age, and leading the research away from its start point, the issue of how social input contributes to the success of practical training with *younger* children. The alternative would be to attempt to overcome young children's personal lack of knowledge by using adult guidance *in conjunction* with peer collaboration. This would allow a return, following the simpler distinctions used in Study 1, to the adult–group training format employed by Thomson and Whelan (1997), permitting a check on whether this produces any benefits for learning over and above those of adult guidance on its own.

It would also enable exploration of a further issue to be carried out. Past work (for example, Tolmie and Howe 1994; see also Howe et al., Chapter 6 of this volume) indicates that there are problems integrating productive expert–child and child–child dialogue within the same event, due to these being based on very different processes; that is, co-ordination within the zone of proximal development (cf. Vygotsky 1978) and cognitive conflict and reequilibration (cf. Piaget 1932). The central difficulty is that peer discussion requires a group whose members are of equal status, whereas scaffolding requires interaction between individuals of unequal status. In other words, each contains a condition that undermines the other. This suggests that for adult–group pedestrian training to be effective, there is a need at the very least to ensure that adult input is not so dominant it interferes with children's discussion, and indeed to encourage a degree of separation between the two. However, it should be noted that Thomson and Whelan found adult–group work presented no particular problems, holding out the possibility that the difficulties of integration are sharper in formal contexts. It seems plausible, for instance, that the expert in the classroom is accorded a more exalted and remote status than the expert engaged with novices in a familiar everyday activity, and is therefore more intrusive or dominant. This would square with Hughes and Greenhough (1994), who found that adult guidance improved the on-task performance of 5- and 7-year-olds undertaking training with a peer in the use of Logo (that is, a classroom-oriented context), but that such guidance only had benefits for learning amongst 11-year-olds. The implication is that for younger children the on-task benefits may simply have reflected deference to adult control.

To examine these issues, Study 2 repeated Study 1, using the same method and materials, except that an adult was assigned to work with each peer collaboration group. One further difference was that adults were on this occasion briefed in advance on the interactional style they should adopt, especially the need, when working with groups, to begin by guiding children towards solutions, but to promote a shift to peer discussion wherever possible in order to help children explicate the conceptual basis of judgements for themselves, and to retreat into the background as such discussion became self-sustaining. The adults in this case were eight parent volunteers, recruited via the participating school, who went through a two-hour induction on the software and how to work with groups (including hands-on experience). Each adult trained six children aged 6–7 years; half on a one-to-one basis (the *adult–child* condition, n = 24), and half in a group of three (the *adult–group* condition, n = 24). A further 15 children took part in the *control* condition, giving a total sample of 63 children. Pre- and post-testing was restricted to the *computer description task*, since transfer to the roadside had already been established by Study 1. Otherwise, the tasks and the indices of learning, on-task activity and dialogue were all as before.

Analysis of pre- to post-test change found that the greatest improvement occurred in the adult–group condition, in terms of both the pick-up of relevant traffic features (the ratio score) and explanation of the significance of these (elaborations), as can be seen in Figures 7.5 and 7.6. As in Study 1, children in the adult–child condition showed a marked shift towards reporting relevant features as a result of training (a 22% swing, exactly as before). However, the shift was even greater in the adult–group condition (a 30% swing), although the post-test differences between the training conditions were not significant. The control children showed no shift whatsoever. Similarly, whilst the two training conditions and the control children all showed an increase on average in elaborations, this was only significant in the adult–group condition, because the post-test performance in the adult–child and control conditions was too variable to constitute a clear effect. Overall, then, whilst adult guidance still had an obvious impact, there are signs of *extra* benefits being produced when this guidance was supported by peer discussion. Moreover, these benefits were of the *conceptual* kind anticipated. The adult–group children not only showed more reliable improvement in understanding of why relevant features mattered, for them alone this gain was directly associated with improvements in actual pick up of such features.

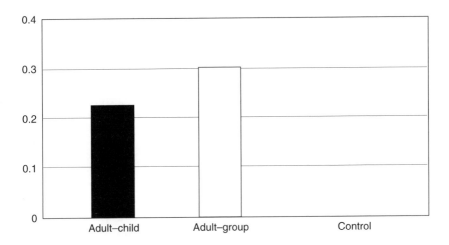

*Figure 7.5* Ratio change by condition in Study 2

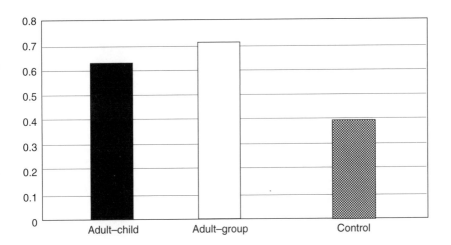

*Figure 7.6* Elaboration change by condition in Study 2

In line with the above, interaction in the adult–group condition contained elements of both scaffolding and conflict, and it was particularly the latter which seemed to have driven change. Adult input was restricted from the outset, save for chairing, questions and prompts (see Table 7.2), and, as in Study 1, these scaffolding behaviours declined as children's performance improved. Adult explanations started at a moderate level, and declined from there, suggesting that guidance typically focused more on support for children's task performance than on conceptual input. In contrast, the level of explanations generated by children was high at the start, and its later decline was probably due to the increased accuracy of their judgements reducing the need for discussion. In line with the conflict model of peer discussion and conceptual learning, there were also more disagreements amongst children in the adult–group condition, and these were positively correlated with both explanations on-task *and* with elaboration change. However, contrary to the caveats about conflict between those of unequal status usually associated with this model, when adults contributed disagreements, these were also positively correlated with elaboration change. The picture that emerges, then, is of adults asking children to suggest solutions, prompting them where these failed to take important features into account. Where there was disagreement between children's suggested solutions, however, this resulted in discussion between them as to why one idea was preferable to another, with the adult taking more of a back seat (although in fact the effect was positive when they did chip in). The first element helped on-task performance, and provided the basis for discussion, but it was the latter that cemented learning.

On-task scores for the adult–child sessions showed comparable levels of performance to the adult–group condition during training, and the interaction measures indicate that adult scaffolding of children's performance took place much as it did there. Thus adult questions and prompts both started at a reasonable level but fell off as children's own performance improved. As in Study 1, however, there were signs of important *conceptual* input coming from adults, in terms of explanations being put forward. Not only was proportionately more input of this kind made by adults here than in the adult–group condition, the level was stable throughout. These explanations were not provoked by disagreements, but followed on from other adult input, as in Study 1. It was also found that adult explanations had a direct impact on children's improved pick up of relevant features at post-test, but not on elaborations. This suggests that in the absence of peer discussion, adult input of this type was capable of providing the conceptual underpinning for children's performance, but in a less explicit, half-glimpsed manner, hence the lower level of elaboration change, and the lack of any mediating effect of this on ratio change for children in this condition. The pattern here was slightly different in fact from Study 1, since there was not the same explicit appropriation of adult explanations by children, although the reason why is not immediately clear.

*Table 7.2* Study 2: Summary of dialogue frequencies and performance scores in the adult–child and adult–group training sessions*

|  | Adult–child condition | Adult–group condition |
|---|---|---|
| a) *Adult input* | | |
| suggestions | moderate, stable | low, decrease |
| agreements[§] | moderate, stable | moderate, decrease |
| disagreements | low, stable | low, stable |
| explanations | moderate, stable | moderate, decrease |
| chairing[‡§] | high, decrease | high, decrease |
| questions[†‡] | high, decrease | high, decrease |
| prompts[‡] | high, decrease | high, decrease |
| | | |
| a) *Child input* | | |
| suggestions[†‡§] | high, stable | high, stable |
| agreements[†] | low, stable | moderate, stable |
| disagreements[†‡§] | very low, stable | low, decrease |
| explanations[†‡] | moderate, decrease | high, decrease |
| chairing[†‡] | low, decrease | moderate, increase |
| questions | low, unstable | low, unstable |
| prompts | non-existent | non-existent |
| correct solutions[‡] | improve (4.5 to 6.2) | improve (4.6 to 5.7) |

* High = 10+ per session; moderate = 2–10 per session; low = < 2 per session; very low = < 0.01 per session).
† Significant effect of condition.
‡ Significant effect of session.
§ Condition x session interaction.

## Conclusions

A number of key points emerge from this research. First and foremost, the two studies confirm that training young children in pedestrian skills via computer simulations (with the advantage this confers of being able to work under practicable and safe conditions) has the potential to produce real benefits at the roadside. However, it is also clear that this is only the case if such materials are used within supportive interactions. In other words, there is good evidence that, as hypothesised, social input is critical to practical training using simulations, though the materials themselves may have an important part to play in facilitating the right input. Moreover, since considerable care was taken to ensure that the computer simulations presented reasonable approximations of real roadside environments (albeit in schematised form), there are grounds for arguing that the role of social input would be likely to extend to roadside practical training, in line with some of the other evidence presented earlier.

The second point is that both adult–child and adult–group approaches were found to be effective, but not in the same way, suggesting that both adult guidance and peer discussion may form a useful part of this social input. So, for instance, Studies 1 and 2 taken together indicate that peer discussion depends on the structure (and implicit knowledge) provided by adult guidance in order to be productive. However, the evidence from Study 2 is that the explicit disputes and explanations generated by peer discussion under these conditions lead to a fuller development of conceptual understanding, and that this improved understanding directly drives performance. In terms of deliberate programmes of practical training, the adult–group combination would appear to be the most effective, as well as the most *cost*-effective, option.

From a theoretical perspective, though, it is the evidence the two studies provide on the functioning of adult guidance, both on its own and in conjunction with peer discussion, that is perhaps most interesting, and this leads on to the third point. The success of the adult–group condition in Study 2 shows it is possible for adult guidance and peer collaboration to be integrated without problem in pedestrian training, and at first sight this might be attributed to the degree of separation the adult volunteers were encouraged to make between their own input and that of the children. There are signs, however, that this was not the crux of the matter and that, as conjectured above, adult input may have a different impact in formal and informal learning contexts. One such sign is that when the adults disagreed directly with the children, this actually had a positive effect, in stark contrast to the established negative effects of expert intervention of this kind in primary school science (for example, Tolmie et al. 1993; see also Hughes and Greenhough 1994). A further sign is the scale of the conceptual input made by adults when working with children on their own, and the willingness of children, in Study 1 at least, to appropriate this input and actively employ it (as opposed to simply echoing it). Both suggest that adult input of this kind is a more natural part of informal learning contexts, and that adults and children alike expect it to be present. Another pointer to the same conclusion is that in Study 1 such input occurred in the absence of any instruction to adults on how to interact.

It is tempting to infer from this that one reason adult conceptual input seems more natural a part of pedestrian training is because this combination of prompting and explanation comes close to mirroring the way in which pedestrian skills are acquired more spontaneously. This is of course speculation, although as noted previously it is reasonably easy to envisage parents assisting their children's learning by shepherding them through the sequence and structure of various pedestrian behaviours (for example, stopping at kerbs, or going to pedestrian lights) and providing an occasional explicit commentary on these behaviours (cf. Lave and Wenger 1991 on the character of apprenticeship learning). At the same time, it is possible that the pattern of effects surrounding adult explanations is simply a function of the age of the children involved in the studies, who as already noted were younger than is typical in research on collaborative learning. Hughes and Greenhough's (1994) evidence on the lack of benefits of adult guidance for younger children would not sit well with this account, but the differences in the pattern of learning in the adult–child conditions in Studies 1 and 2 are explicable specifically in terms of an age effect, the children in the latter being slightly younger than in the former. This suggests there might be a cusp at around 7 years at which children are especially sensitive to the appropriation of adult explanations. If this sensitivity were subsequently undermined by a growth in conceptual autonomy on the part of children, this would lead to an overall pattern of effects consistent with much of the existing literature. There is insufficient evidence here to judge between these two accounts, however. For the present, then, both possibilities merit further research.

## Acknowledgements

Study 1 was funded by the UK Department of the Environment, Transport and the Regions (Project No. S214H). Study 2 was funded by the Economic and Social Research Council (Award No. R000222468). The invaluable contribution made by the researchers on these projects, Kirstie Whelan, Brian McLaren and Sheila Morrison, is gratefully acknowledged.

## References

Ampofo-Boateng, K. and Thomson, J.A. (1990). 'Child pedestrian accidents: a case for preventative medicine'. *Health Education Research: Theory and Practice*, 5, 265–74.
Ampofo-Boateng, K., Thomson, J.A., Grieve, R., Pitcairn, T., Lee, D.N. and Demetre, J.D. (1993). 'A developmental and training study of children's ability to find safe routes to cross the road'. *British Journal of Developmental Psychology*, 11, 31–45.
Christie, N. (1995). *Social, Economic and Environmental Factors in Child Pedestrian Accidents: A research review*. Crowthorne, Berks: Transport Research Laboratory.
Cole, M. (1996). *Cultural Psychology*. Cambridge, MA: Harvard University Press.
Damon, W. and Phelps, E. (1989). 'Critical distinctions among three approaches to peer education'. *International Journal of Educational Research*, 13, 9–19.
Howe, C.J., Tolmie, A., Greer, K. and Mackenzie, M. (1995). 'Peer collaboration and conceptual growth in physics: task influences on children's understanding of heating and cooling'. *Cognition and Instruction*, 13, 483–503.
Hughes, M. and Greenhough, P. (1994). 'Is it better to work with a peer, an adult or both? A systematic comparison with children aged 5, 7 and 11 years'. In H.C. Foot,

C.J. Howe, A. Anderson, A. Tolmie and D. Warden (eds) *Group and Interactive Learning* (pp. 53–9). Southampton: Computational Mechanics Publications.

Lave, J. and Wenger, E. (1991). *Situated Learning*. Cambridge: Cambridge University Press.

Molen, H.H. van der (1981). 'Blueprint of an analysis of the pedestrian task – 1: method of analysis'. *Accident Analysis and Prevention*, 13, 175–91.

Piaget , J. (1932). *The Moral Judgement of the Child*. London: Routledge and Kegan Paul.

Rivara, F.P., Booth, C.L., Bergman, A.B., Rogers, L.W. and Weiss, J. (1991). 'Prevention of pedestrian injuries to children: effectiveness of a school training program'. *Pediatrics*, 88, 770–5.

Rogoff, B. (1990). *Apprenticeship in Thinking: Cognitive development in social context*. Oxford: Oxford University Press.

Ryhammer, L. and Bergland, G.W. (1980). *Children and Instruction in Road Safety*. (Uppsala Reports on Education, No. 8). Sweden: University of Uppsala.

Thomson, J.A., Tolmie, A., Foot, H.C. and McLaren, B. (1996). *Child Development and the Aims of Road Safety Education: A review and analysis*. (Department of Transport Road Safety Research Report No. 1). London: HMSO.

Thomson, J.A. and Whelan, K.M. (1997). *A Community Approach to Road Safety Education Using Practical Training Methods: The Drumchapel Report*. (Department of Transport Road Safety Research Report No. 2). London: HMSO.

Tolmie, A. and Howe, C.J. (1994). 'Computer-directed group activity and the development of children's hypothesis-testing skills'. In H.C. Foot, C.J. Howe, A. Anderson, A. Tolmie and D. Warden (eds) *Group and Interactive Learning* (pp. 139–44). Southampton: Computational Mechanics Publications.

Tolmie, A., Howe, C.J., Mackenzie, M. and Greer, K. (1993). 'Task design as an influence on dialogue and learning: primary school group work with object flotation'. *Social Development*, 2, 183–201.

Tomasello, M., Kruger, A. and Ratner, H. (1993). 'Cultural learning'. *Behavioral and Brain Sciences*, 16, 495–552.

Vygotsky, L.S. (1978). *Mind in Society: The development of higher psychological processes*. Cambridge, MA: Harvard University Press.

Wood, D. (1986). 'Aspects of teaching and learning'. In M. Richards and P. Light (eds) *Children of Social Worlds: Development in a social context* (pp. 191–212). Cambridge: Polity Press.

# 8
# Applying a Dialogical Model of Reason in the Classroom

*Rupert Wegerif*

Recently there has been an increasing number of studies in psychology informed by dialogical rather than monological theoretical assumptions. In the area of cognition and learning this 'dialogical turn' implies a move away from explanation in terms of underlying cognitive structure toward descriptions of the dynamic construction of meaning in conversations (for example, Edwards and Potter 1992). In this chapter I argue that accepting dialogical assumptions does not mean abandoning useful models of cognition but that, on the contrary, models of cognition that follow from dialogical assumptions can be used very effectively to guide educational practice. I will make this argument through a discussion of the findings of several research studies in which a dialogical model of reason was applied to teaching in classrooms. This chapter has five main sections: the first outlines what I mean by the dialogical paradigm, the second discusses the nature of dialogical models, the third offers an explicitly dialogical model of reason for education, the fourth describes research applying this model in classrooms and the fifth and final section discusses the significance of the findings of this research for rethinking collaborative learning.

## The Dialogical Paradigm

Those who use the term 'dialogical' often refer to the Russian writers Bakhtin and Volosinov. Volosinov puts the dialogical position very clearly when he writes:

> [M]eaning is like an electric spark that occurs only when two different terminals are hooked together.

And further, that:

> In essence meaning belongs to a word in its position between speakers; that is, meaning is realised only in the process of active, responsive, understanding. (Volosinov 1929, pp. 102–3)

The claim being made is that meaning is never simply given but is always created out of the interaction between different voices and different perspectives. This implies the further claim that when people understand or know something they do so dynamically in a communicative act and not statically in a structure (Wells 1999, p. 77).

To understand the significance of the dialogical turn it is necessary to consider the contrasting monological paradigm that can still probably be said to represent the mainstream in psychology. The monological paradigm in science generally seeks to find the universal laws and structures underlying surface phenomena. The ideal motivating this endeavour is to produce a single logically coherent model of everything independent of perspective. The monological paradigm is often accused of overlooking the fact that knowledge is never independent of social, historical and biological contexts that give it meaning. One aspect of the contextual background required to interpret knowledge claims is their position within conversations including what could be described as the long-term conversations of a culture. The dialogical claim from Bakhtin and Volosinov is that any utterance needs to be seen as a link in a chain of communication (Bakhtin 1986, p. 69). Dialogicality means not merely that participants in interactions respond to what other participants do, they respond in a way that takes into account how they think other people are going to respond to them. Rommetveit calls this circularity 'atunement to the atunement of the other' and points out, first, that it influences most human behaviour, and, second, that it is impossible to understand the effects of this circularity using monological representations (Rommetveit 1992). Monological models assume closed systems with regular and therefore discoverable relationships between inputs and outputs. If human behaviour has to be understood in much the same way as we interpret meaning in a continuing dialogue then, as Rommetveit claims, monological models are inappropriate.

In the monological paradigm it is normal to see models as a way of getting a handle on reality which we can use to inform interventions that change things. For those who adopt the assumptions of the dialogical paradigm, on the other hand, the role of models is not so straightforward. 'Post-structuralist' writers such as Foucault and Derrida apply some of the assumptions of the dialogical paradigm to question both the feasibility and the desirability of producing useful models of human behaviour. This theoretical position is an influence on those discursive psychologists who side-step the issue of the 'reality' or 'usefulness' of their accounts in favour of a focus on examining the rhetorical conventions applied by others (for example, Edwards 1996). In the following sections I will take 'reason' as a paradigmatic case to show that dialogical models of cognition are possible and can be applied as a useful tool for changing reality.

## The Concept of a 'Dialogical Model' of Reason

Models of reason in psychology that refer to logical structures in the mind reflect a strong tradition in the philosophy of rationality linking human reason to formal logic and mathematics. The social philosopher Habermas challenges this monological tradition in accounts of reason and proposes an alternative dialogical account of reason that he calls 'communicative rationality'. I do not intend to outline his argument here but merely to draw from it features that can be used to characterise dialogical models of cognition in general. Habermas begins his account of communicative rationality by drawing a distinction between 'a success-oriented attitude' and 'an attitude oriented to reaching understanding' (Habermas 1991, p. 286). While he does not dismiss the strategic or profit-maximising rationality that issues from a success-oriented attitude he argues that this kind of rationality is a parasitic derivative of the more fundamental communicative rationality issuing from an attitude oriented to reaching understanding. Use of the word 'attitude' carries with it the danger of being interpreted as only referring to individual states, whereas Habermas makes it clear that he is referring to ways in which participants in a dialogue can orient themselves to each other or what he refers to as the 'structural properties' of intersubjectivity. For this reason I will use the term 'intersubjective orientation' in place of attitude. I propose that, in some form or other, an account of intersubjective orientation is a necessary feature of dialogical models of cognition.

To understand what an account of reason as an intersubjective orientation might mean in practice we have only to turn away from the specialist discourse of philosophy and psychology to ordinary language use. When we describe someone as a 'reasonable' person we do not normally mean that he or she is good at abstract logic or at mathematics, but that he or she listens to what others say to him or her and responds appropriately. This everyday idea of what it means to be 'reasonable' describes the 'intersubjective orientation' of seeking mutual understanding.

An account of intersubjective orientation may be necessary to a dialogical model of reason but in itself it is not sufficient for a useful model that could be applied to education. In Habermas' account of communicative rationality a second level of description of reason is often referred to as the social rules governing what he calls an 'ideal speech situation' but he never actually gives details of what these rules are. At one point he quotes approvingly an account by Alexy of the procedural rules that might be used to structure a speech situation in which unforced agreement could be achieved, these are participation rules of the kind that every participant has an equal right to participate and to question claims (Habermas 1990, p. 92). Procedural rules of this kind are not in themselves reasoning, but it may be possible that reasoning can result from the interaction of agents each following a few simple procedural rules. One metaphor for understanding how following social groundrules can lead to reasoning is provided by computer simulations of complex adaptive systems.

Whilst computer models of cognition based on the analogy of information processing implement monological assumptions, computer simulations of complex adaptive systems are based on an implementation of the complex feedback loops used by Rommetveit to characterise dialogicality. Casti argues that such simulations represent a new scientific method distinct from methods of experiment and linear mathematical modelling that were developed in the study of closed and relatively noncomplex systems (Casti 1997). A complex adaptive system is any system in which several agents reciprocally adapt to each other. Once agents reciprocally adapt to each other, the circular feedback loops involved produce a level of complexity that makes reduction to a monological model impossible. One solution adopted to studying complex adaptive systems is to simulate them with programs in which multiple agents are each given a set of rules of behaviour and possibly also rules on how to adapt those rules and then set loose to interact. Such studies have found that the interaction of many agents each following simple rules can result in the 'emergence' of new self-organising systems that can not be predicted or explained by the rules that the agents are following. One striking example is the simulation of flocking behaviour which was achieved by giving virtual birds three simple rules to guide their flight, keep a minimum distance from neighbours, fly at about the same speed as neighbours and always fly towards the perceived centre of the mass of birds. Understanding flocking had been seen as a hard problem until this simulation clarified how it might work (Waldrop 1992, pp. 241–3). An illustration of 'emergence' in complex adaptive system closer to dialogues is provided by Robert Axelrod's various demonstrations of the emergence of apparently co-operative behaviour in simulations of social interaction (Axelrod 1997).

The conclusion of this brief discussion of approaches to dialogical modelling is that a dialogical model of reason has to take some account of the possibility of different intersubjective orientations, and could consist of a description of the social groundrules followed by agents in an interaction. In the next section I will describe the development of a specific and useful dialogical model of reason.

## A Dialogical Model of Reason for the Classroom

The dialogical model of reason implemented in research which I describe below began with a characterisation of 'types of talk' found empirically in collaborative learning in classrooms. The three 'types of talk' described by Mercer (1995) can also, as a later article made clear (Wegerif and Mercer 1997a), be seen as reflecting fundamental intersubjective orientations:

- cumulative talk reflecting an orientation to share and understand each other but without any critical grounding of shared knowledge
- disputational talk where individuals treat dialogue as a competition which they seek to win, and
- exploratory talk which is oriented to sharing knowledge like cumulative talk but with the addition of critical challenges and explicit reasoning.

Of these three intersubjective orientations, the one found most educationally desirable by teachers was exploratory talk. This combines features of cumulative talk, being a kind of co-operation, with features of disputational talk, because it includes challenges and competition. To turn this idea of orientation into a useful model that could be applied in a classroom we needed to specify it more closely in terms of social groundrules. Teacher-researcher Lyn Dawes, Neil Mercer and I developed the following list of social groundrules, partly influenced by a survey of the literature on effective collaborative learning (see review in Mercer 1995, pp. 90–5), partly influenced by the philosophy of rationality (see discussion above, and Wegerif 1999), but mainly based on our experience in classrooms. From these different sources seven groundrules were put forward:

1. All relevant information is shared
2. The group seeks to reach agreement
3. The group takes responsibility for decisions
4. Reasons are expected
5. Challenges are acceptable
6. Alternatives are discussed before a decision is taken
7. All in the group are encouraged to speak by other group members

It is noticeable that the first three of these groundrules are shared with cumulative talk. These are rules that help to unite the group and to create a positive atmosphere for group work.

Wegerif and Mercer (1997a) characterise dialogical reason through a hierarchy of levels of analysis. Intersubjective orientations are realised within any given social and historical context through the use of specifiable groundrules. Each groundrule is in turn realised by a specifiable range of 'communicative actions' by which I mean utterances or gestures classified by their function such as to put forward a claim or to support group solidarity. Similarly each such communicative action is realised in a given context by a limited set of phrases, words, grammatical features, gestures, intonations, and so on.

## Applying this Dialogical Model of Reason

We explored the impact of explicitly teaching dialogical reason in three separate studies.

*Study 1* looked at the effects of explicitly teaching dialogical reasoning on children's understanding of citizenship issues and on group reasoning tests over a ten-week period in one class of approximately 30 8–9-year-old children with a matching control class.

*Study 2* was a similar but larger study in which we worked with three target classes of approximately 30 children each in three schools with three similarly sized matching control classes. As in the first study, all children were aged 8 or 9. In this study different tests were used to focus on the effect of explicitly teaching dialogical reasoning on individual reasoning. We also looked at the effect of teaching dialogical reasoning on conceptual understanding in science. In addition, the study was partly designed to explore the transfer of this method of teaching from the original school to other schools.

*Study 3* is continuing and is called the Raising Achievement through Thinking and Language Skills. This study was initiated by teachers and is mainly run by teachers with part funding from the Local Education Authority. Our involvement is continuing and focuses on the further development and dissemination of practical teaching methods.

We asked different questions in each study. One of the major themes of the first two studies was the improved use of information and communication technology (ICT) in the classroom. Another major theme of study 2 and of study 3 was the effect on the whole classroom as a discursive community. In this chapter I will focus on the effect that the explicit teaching of groundrules of dialogical reason described above had on the talk and the reasoning of children. I will limit myself to the published results of the first two studies, as study 3, which is still continuing, has not yet produced analysed data.

## An Educational Programme to Teach Dialogical Reason

All three studies included the explicit teaching of dialogical reason. In the first two studies Lyn Dawes took the lead in devising a series of ten 'talk lessons' around the groundrules outlined above. Each of the talk lessons had three phases: teacher-led discussion, small-group work and whole-class plenary. The groundrule or rules being taught in each lesson was made explicit at the beginning and revisited in the plenary. Each lesson began with explicit modelling by the teacher of the use of the groundrule that the lesson was focusing on and possibly some of the language strategies associated with it. (Examples of language strategies might be using 'Why?' to challenge, 'because' to give reasons or asking all in the group to agree before taking a decision.) Each lesson included small-group work in mixed-ability and mixed-gender groups of three. The teacher visited each of the groups in turn to support their use of the groundrules and language strategies. At the end of the lesson the groups reported back to the class and the teacher once again emphasised the aims of the lesson.

The early lessons in the series were designed to raise awareness of different ways of talking together and to teach the communicative preconditions of exploratory talk, such as effective listening, giving information explicitly and co-operating as a group. Later lessons encouraged the use of all the groundrules in critical discussions of issues in different areas of the curriculum.

Full details can be found in a practical book for teachers (Dawes et al. forthcoming). To illustrate the 'talk lessons' approach I will describe one of the key early lessons in the series. The class teacher begins by telling a story, she then asks the class to discuss it in groups of three, giving each group just one worksheet containing questions to talk about and answer boxes to fill in. After this activity the children are brought together again into a whole-class group and asked to give feedback first on what they had thought about the story, but then also on the ways in which they had talked about it together. How did they reach a group decision? What sort of thing worked and what didn't? The teacher then leads the children to suggest rules for working together. These rules are written down by one of the children on the board as they are produced. The teacher then goes through each rule to discuss it further. Some of the rules are usually inappropriate, like 'Don't talk unless you have your hand up', but others will fit the groundrules of dialogical reasoning that we have proposed. The teacher leads this discussion to produce a final set of 'class groundrules for talk'. This list of groundrules is then to be displayed prominently on the wall of the classroom. In all succeeding talk lessons these rules can be referred to as 'our rules for talk'.

Encouraging children to take an exploratory orientation and to use these groundrules meant working with teachers not simply to 'teach' these groundrules, but to turn the classroom into a social and physical environment that supported and rewarded their use. The groundrules displayed on the wall were important for this, as were the seating arrangements and the frequent reminders from the teacher that the way groups talked together was as important and valued as the answers that they came to. Equally important was the way that the teacher talked with the class. Using our talk lessons led the talk of the teachers to change almost as much as the talk of the children.

In the first two studies these lessons were taught every week for approximately ten weeks, with each lesson lasting about one hour. The teachers we worked with were also encouraged to apply the same teaching approach to other lessons.

## Impact on Curriculum Learning

In both study 1 and study 2 we looked at the effect of teaching exploratory talk on the quality of interaction in collaborations around computers. In study 1, using qualitative analysis and quantitative measures we showed that the intervention programme led to longer and deeper discussion of citizenship issues presented through educational computer software and so could be shown to serve the stated aims of the citizenship curriculum in England. In study 2 we also demonstrated that the groundrules we taught helped conceptual change and learning in science. Pre- and post-test questions given to 20 children using a simulation designed to prompt reasoning about friction showed a statistically significant learning gain. The more important method for us was the analysis of the talk of groups of children working around this science simulation. This analysis showed apparent learning in the talk of the children. We related this learning to the outcome measures by linking episodes in their talk to changes in the answers they gave to our questions about the nature of friction. These two studies of talk around curriculum-related activities used computer-based tasks specially designed to support learning through reasoning together. They are reported in more detail in Wegerif et al. (1998).

## Reasoning Test Results

To help explore the questions about improvements in group and individual reasoning we used pre-intervention and post-intervention testing with Raven's matrices in both study 1 and study 2. The Raven's test consists of a series of shapes where the children have to discover the pattern in order to continue the series. Results on this test correlate well with other academic achievement measures, and it is said to be the best measure of 'g' or the concept of general intelligence (for example, Carpenter et al. 1990, p. 428). The literature on the concept of 'g' and the design and normal use of this test is based on a monological model of the nature of reasoning. We used this test specifically to explore the relationship between our dialogical model of reasoning and the more traditional monological idea of reason that these tests had been developed to measure. In this we were not so much concerned to deny the concept of general intelligence as to show how this concept can be usefully re-described as a specific way of using language.

In both of the first two studies we used a similar design giving different versions of the Raven's matrices test to individuals and to groups in target and control classes before and after a ten- to twelve-week intervention. The groups were mixed-ability and mixed-gender groups of three selected by the teacher. In the first study we divided the 60 questions of the Raven's progressive matrices into two equally difficult tests of 30 questions each. We gave one of these tests to the children working in groups of three and the other to the same children working as individuals three days later. The same procedure was repeated at the end of the intervention programme. In the second study we had a similar design but used the full 60 questions of the Standard Progressive Matrices (SPM) for the groups and the 36-question Coloured Progressive Matrices (CPM) for the individuals. In the first smaller study with one target class and a matching control class we found a statistically significant improvement in both groups' results and individual results (reported in Wegerif 1996). In the second study using three target classes and three control classes we found a significant difference between conditions only for the individual test score improvements (reported in Wegerif et al. 1999). While the target group scores improved overall by 10% and the control scores remained the same, this difference between the conditions was not found to be significant. Some of the difference between the results of study 1 and study 2 may also be accounted for by the different tests used, since the full SPM of 60 questions proved to take a very long time when each question was discussed in groups. There was also a difference in the results obtained for each of the three classes, with the biggest improvement in test scores in the class of the teacher-researcher (Lyn Dawes) who originated the programme and the test scores staying much the same in the class of the teacher who we had found it hardest to keep in touch with.

In all our studies we have found that the role of the teacher is crucial. To effectively teach the groundrules of dialogical reason each teacher has to change their own way of talking with pupils so as to model and encourage questioning and reasoning. This is not a simple or automatic procedure that can be communicated with a few lesson plans – it requires commitment from teachers and no programme will produce uniform results.

The children in study 2 showed an improvement in their individual test scores after a programme teaching essentially social groundrules. These findings support the claim that children learn to reason better as individuals through personally appropriating strategies used first in dialogue with others. This finding fits well with Vygotsky's claim that, as he put it, 'all that is internal in the higher mental functions was at one time external' (Vygotsky 1991, p. 36), meaning that the ability to perform cognitive tasks when acting alone stems from a prior socialisation process when the same or similar tasks are performed with the help of others.

However, these test results do not tell us very much about the effects of the groundrules of dialogical reasoning on group processes. It was clear from our observations that these groundrules were not taught equally effectively in all classrooms, were not appropriated equally by all groups and were not used all of the time even by those groups who did use them effectively some of the time. In addition to test results it is obviously important to look at the actual talk of children together.

### Exploring Changes in the Talk of Children

In both study 1 and study 2 we selected focal groups, three per class, said by the teacher to be representative of the ability of the class, and we videotaped their talk around Raven's test problem before and after the intervention. When we transcribed these sessions and analysed the differences between the talk after the intervention programme and that before, we found marked differences for most target groups. These changes included an increased overall amount of talk as well as an increased use of terms associated with explicit reasoning, such as 'because', 'agree' and modals, and an increase in the number of long turns at talk. We were able to link these general features of language change to specific instances of successful problem solving. In other words, groups successfully solving problems in the post-test that they had failed to solve in the pre-test tended to use the key words we had noted and longer turns at talk. The aim of our analysis was to explore the effect of changes in the groundrules that groups were using on the way that they used language as a tool for thinking. We did this using quantitative methods such as counting key words and long turns, and also by using a computer-based concordancer which enabled us to quickly produce lists of key words in their immediate contexts in order to explore changes in the way that key words were used. These methods were used to demonstrate that the findings of more detailed qualitative studies could be generalised (see Wegerif and Mercer 1997b for an account of this approach). Detailed qualitative analysis is crucial to our claim to provide evidence for the effectiveness of our dialogical model of reason. The next sub-section gives a small illustration of this kind of analysis.

## An Example of Children Thinking with Language

The group we illustrate below, Susan, George and Trisha, scored 39 SPM questions right in the pre-test, and after our lessons they scored 47. There were eight questions that they had failed to solve in the pre-test which they managed to solve in the post-test. Focusing on the talk around these questions enabled us to compare successful talk with unsuccessful talk with the same problems and the same children.

What follows is a shortened version of the full analysis that can be found in Wegerif and Mercer (2000). Line numbers refer to the original full transcripts. Other than the use of line numbers the transcripts are presented without special conventions and punctuated to be readable.

*A. Extract from Susan, George and Trisha talking about the problem (problem B12 – see figure 8.1) before our talking lessons*

| 1 | Trisha: | Square and diamond, it's 2 |
|---|---|---|
| 2 | George: | No it's not |
| 3 | Trisha: | It is 2 |
| 4 | George: | No it's not |
| 5 | Trisha: | It is |
| 6 | George: | No it's not |
| 7 | Susan: | It's that one, 6 |
| 8 | Trisha: | It is |
| 9 | George: | No it's not it's got to be a square and a circle |
| 10 | Trisha: | It's that, it has to be that, it has to be that, it has to be 6 because look they've only got that [*pointing to the pictures*] |
| 11 | Susan: | Look first they are starting with one of them things over [*pointing*[ and then it has to be black |
| 12 | George: | Right, 6 |
| 13 | Susan: | No it isn't George |
| | | [*talk continues around problem B12 for a further 11 turns with dispute over the correct answer turning into a physical struggle over control of the pencil*] |

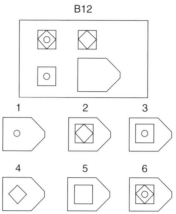

*Figure 8.1.* Raven's SPM. Problem B12

*B. The same group doing the same problem after the lessons: extracts from the beginning and the end of the session.*

| | | |
|---|---|---|
| 1 | Trisha: | That has got to be a diamond, a square with a diamond with a circle in that one, number 6, do you agree? |
| 2 | George: | No, what do you mean? |
| 3 | Trisha: | OK, no it's got to be square |
| 4 | Susan: | I think it's number 6 – that's the one |
| 5 | George: | No it ain't |
| 6 | Susan: | I think it's number 6 |
| 7 | Trisha: | No 'cause it's got to swing round every time, so there is a circle in it |
| 8 | Susan: | Yes but it hasn't got a circle in there has it and that one has [*indicating*] |
| 9–20 | | [*They continue for 12 turns looking at different options but getting no nearer a solution, then Trisha comes up with something new*] |
| 21 | Trisha: | Look that's got a triangle, that's got a square, look that's got a square with a diamond with a circle in, that's got a square with a diamond in and that's got a square with a circle in so that's got to be a square |
| 22 | George: | I don't understand this at all |
| 23 | Trisha: | Because look on that they've taken the circle out yes? So on that you are going to take the circle out because they have taken the circle out of that one |
| 24 | George: | On this they have taken the circle out and on this they have taken the diamond out and on this they have put |

them both in, so it should be a blank square because look it goes circle square

25   Susan:      It's got to be a blank square. Yeah it is.

26   George:     Do you agree on number 5, do you agree on 5?

27                [*George writes '5', which is the correct answer*]

In the pre-intervention talk George challenges Trisha's first suggestion ('It is 2', line A3) without giving a reason. Trisha offers no further justification for her suggestion. This leads into a series of exchanges typical of the type of talk we call 'disputational', in which participants simply assert their opposing views without reasoning.

After the intervention Trisha is the first to propose an answer (line B1), but this time she does this not as a statement ('it is 2') but as an elaborated hypothesis with a question encouraging debate ('That has got to be a diamond, a square with a diamond with a circle in that one, number 6, do you agree?', line B1). George asks for more explanation (line B2). This time his challenge prompts Trisha to attempt to be more explicit. Through this effort Trisha appears to see that she is wrong and changes her claim.

Many features of the talk are different in the second transcript section. Explicit reasons for claims are given (for example, lines B8, B22, B25), challenges are offered with reasons (for example, line B7), several alternatives are considered before a decision is reached (in the full transcript, answers 6, 3 and 4 are explicitly suggested in turn and decided against before 5 is agreed upon), and the children can be seen seeking to reach agreement together (for example, lines B23–27). Explicit reasoning may be represented in talk by the incidence of some specific ways of using language, and we can see here some 'key features': the hypothetical nature of claims is indicated by a preceding 'I think' (line B4 and B6), reasons are linked to claims by the use of 'because' or ''cause' (lines A10, B7 and B24) and agreement is sought through the question 'do you agree?' (lines B1 and B26). Explicit reasoning requires the linking of clauses and leads here to the incidence of a greater number of longer utterances in the post-intervention talk than in the pre-intervention talk. As I wrote earlier, this same group solved a total of eight new problems in the post-test which they had failed to solve in the pre-test. When we compared talk that led to the group solving these problems correctly with talk that led to wrong answers, we found that there was a clear association with the number of these key linguistic features. We used a concordancer not only to count terms but also to explore the contexts in which they were being used (see Wegerif and Mercer 1997b). We found that terms such as 'because', terms introducing a reason clause, were used to point to verbal context in the more successful talk, whereas in less successful talk 'because look' frequently occurred on its own with children pointing physically at the picture. This different way of using 'because' is illustrated in the transcript extracts above:

A10   *Trisha:*   It's that, it has to be that, it has to be that, it has to be 6 because look they've only got that [*pointing to the pictures*]. (*Unsuccessful talk. Pre-intervention*)

B23   *Trisha:*   Because look on that they've taken the circle out yes? So on that you are going to take the circle out because they have taken the circle out of that one. (*Successful talk. Post-intervention*)

In comparing these two ways of using 'because', we see a shift in the talk from pointing to the physical context (line A10) to pointing to a verbal context which the children construct together (line B23). This is a general finding of the impact of explicitly teaching the groundrules found also in the first study. This shift is also apparent in the far greater number of long turns at talk found in the more successful talk.

In pointing to the process of 'taking the circle out' (line B23), Trisha is pointing to something that cannot be pointed to directly in the picture. It exists only in words. In the next line (line B24) George repeats what Trisha says and applies the same process of 'taking out' to the diamond as well, saying: 'they have taken the diamond out'. Turning back to Figure 8.1 we can see that this combination of taking the circle out and taking the diamond out described the solution to the problem. Once Trisha has made this relationship verbally explicit George is able to see it and he echoes Trisha's construction, repeating her 'taken the circle out' construction and applying it to the diamond as well the circle (perhaps the element of repetition in language here helps George appropriate this 'concept' or way of using words for himself).

Further exploration showed that this use of language to make relationships and processes visible was generally found to be the case in the more successful talk of all the groups. Expressions such as 'the same', 'getting fatter', 'that and that make that' or 'add that to that and you get that' were all used for this purpose.

## The Significance of These Findings for a Dialogical Understanding of Collaborative Learning

It is interesting that in the example just quoted we can see the group learning to use language to think about virtual operations such as subtraction ('taking the circle out'). In the transition from the language of the pre-test to the language of the post-test, there is a shift from performing quasi-physical operations on the picture without naming them to using language to describe, reflect on and generalise those operations. This shift is accompanied by the use of more complex utterances with increased use of embedded clauses – in other words, a new kind of structure is visible in the language used. The results of the individual reasoning tests that we used suggest a connection between the way that the children used language to think together and the way that they then solved problems working on their own. All this suggests the possibility that applying the groundrules of exploratory talk is leading here to the genesis of structures of thought within dialogues which are then appropriated by individuals. This does not necessarily imply a model of cognition incompatible with the idea that cognition is also located in the brain. As Harre and Gillet propose, it is possible that the neural pathways of the brain are organised to reflect rules originating in the social use of language rather than the other way round (Harre and Gillet 1994, p. 77).

The new science of complexity theory can provide useful metaphors to think about collaborative learning. The idea that agents each individually following simple rules can produce an emergent self-organising system that is not reducible to those rules has already been applied by many writers to suggest a possible account for such higher mental faculties as reason and self-consciousness (Edmonds 1997, Juarrero 1999). It is also useful for thinking about how our dialogical model of reason worked in the classroom. We succeeded in increasing the quality of reasoning and learning in group work by influencing the social groundrules that the children followed when working together. We did this by working with teachers to change the kind of behaviour that the social and physical environment of the classroom supported and rewarded.

The use of computer simulations to explore complex adaptive systems has led to claims about some general features of such systems which can offer a further analogy for thinking about the nature and role of the 'intersubjective orientations' or 'types of talk' that our model of reason started with. Some initial sets of rules given to interacting agents, will tend to produce dissipation into uninteresting randomness, whilst other rules will lead the system to move towards a rigid structure where no creative change can occur. The transition point between these two extremes, sometimes evocatively referred to as 'the edge of chaos', is where the most interesting creative evolutionary 'emergence' is found (Coveney and Highfield 1995, p. 273). In the classroom, exploratory talk – talk supporting reasoning – was defined in relation to two other fundamental types of talk found in classroom groups: cumulative talk, in which children tend to agree uncritically, and disputational talk, in which they compete with each other.

Taken to their extremes, both cumulative talk and disputational talk do not lead to the construction of new understandings. With cumulative talk the group always tend to lock in too quickly to solutions without critically considering alternative possibilities, and disputational talk tends to fragmentation reflected in short disjointed turns at talk. The groundrules of exploratory talk do not directly teach children how to think. They serve to open up and maintain an intersubjective space of creative diversity in which alternative solutions to problems are generated and allowed to develop and compete as ideas without threatening either group solidarity or individual ego-identity. However, if our pedagogy served to open up and maintain a creative space between collaborators, it was also successful in making that creative freedom work to support the needs of the education system. In other words, effective collaborative learning opens a space free from the constraints of identity in which difference is allowed free play within a framework in which the products of that creative diversity are put to work to serve social ends.

## Conclusion

Thinking about collaborative learning from a dialogical perspective shifts the focus of attention away from abstract cognitive structures and toward the ways that people respond to each other in dialogues. Our research explored this perspective by developing and applying a dialogical model of reason consisting of an intersubjective orientation that we called 'exploratory' and a set of groundrules specifically designed to support collaboration in the classroom. This dialogical model proved an effective support for teachers. Its implementation resulted in a significant improvement in the quality of collaborative learning and reasoning. A fine-grained analysis revealed that the groundrules of exploratory talk worked to create a situation in which the evolution of ideas was supported. This situation promoted the generation of a variety of responses and then encouraged these alternatives to compete within a collaborative social framework that allowed the best ideas to be shared between all participants and jointly developed. This analysis suggests that one potentially valuable direction to pursue in the project of rethinking collaborative learning might be the application of models and concepts drawn from the use of simulations to study emergent properties in complex adaptive systems.

# References

Axelrod, R. (1997). *The Complexity of Cooperation: Agent-based models of competition and collaboration*. Princeton, NJ: Princeton University Press.
Bakhtin, M. (1986). *Speech Genres and Other Late Essays*. Austin: University of Texas Press.
Burbules, N. (1993). *Dialogue in Teaching*. New York: Teachers College Press.
Carpenter, P., Just, M. and Shell, P. (1990). 'What one intelligence test measures: a theoretical account of the processing of the Raven Progressive Matrices test'. *Psychological Review*, 9(7), 404–31.
Casti, J. (1997). *Would be Worlds*. New York: Wiley.
Coveney, P. and Highfield, R. (1995). *Frontiers of Complexity*. New York: Faber and Faber.
Dawes, L., Mercer, N. and Wegerif, R. (forthcoming). *Thinking Together*. Birmingham: Questions Publishing.
Edmonds, B. (1997). 'Modelling socially intelligent agents'. AAAI Fall Symposium on Socially Intelligent Agents, Cambridge, MA, USA.
Edwards, D. (1996). *Discourse and Cognition*. London: Sage.
Edwards, D. and Potter, J. (1992). *Discursive Psychology*. London: Sage.
Habermas, J. (1990). *Moral Consciousness and Communicative Action*. Cambridge: Polity Press.
Habermas, J. (1991). *The Theory of Communicative Action. Vol. 1*. Cambridge: Polity Press.
Harre, R. and Gillet, G. (1994). *The Discursive Mind*. London: Sage.
Juarrero, A. (1999). *Dynamics in Action*. Cambridge, MA: MIT Press.
Leibniz, G. (1973). *Leibniz: Philosophical writings* (ed. G. Parkinson; trans. M. Morris and G. Parkinson). London: Dent and Sons.
Mercer, N. (1995). *The Guided Construction of Knowledge: Talk amongst teachers and learners*. Clevedon: Multilingual Matters.
Rommetveit, R. (1992). 'Outlines of a dialogically based social-cognitive approach to human cognition and communication'. In A. Wold (ed.) *The Dialogical Alternative: Towards a theory of language and mind*, (pp. 19–45). Oslo: Scandanavian Press.
Volosinov, V.N. (1929). *Marxism and the Philosophy of Language*. Cambridge, MA: Harvard University Press, 1986.
Vygotsky, L. (1991). 'The genesis of higher mental functions'. In P. Light, S. Sheldon and B. Woodhead (eds) *Learning to Think*. London: Routledge.
Waldrop, M. (1992). *Complexity: The emerging science at the edge of order and chaos*. London: Penguin.
Wegerif, R. (1996). 'Using computers to help coach exploratory talk across the curriculum'. *Computers and Education*, 26(1–3), 51–60.
Wegerif, R. (1999) 'Two images of reason in educational theory'. *The School Field*. 9(3–4), 77–107.
Wegerif, R. and Mercer, N. (1997a). 'A dialogical framework for researching peer talk'. In R. Wegerif and P. Scrimshaw (eds) *Computers and Talk in the Primary Classroom* (pp. 49–65). Clevedon: Multilingual Matters.
Wegerif, R., and Mercer, N. (1997b). 'Using computer-based text analysis to integrate quantitative and qualitative methods in the investigation of collaborative learning'. *Language and Education*, 11(4), 260–71.
Wegerif, R. and Mercer, N. (2000). 'Language for thinking'. In H. Cowie, D. Aalsvoort and N. Mercer (eds) *New Perspectives in Collaborative Learning*. Oxford: Elsevier.
Wegerif, R., Mercer, N. and Dawes, L. (1998). 'Software design to support discussion in the primary classroom'. *Journal of Computer Assisted Learning*, 14(3), 199–211.

Wegerif, R., Mercer, N. and Dawes, L. (1999). 'From social interaction to individual reasoning: an empirical investigation of a possible socio-cultural model of cognitive development'. *Learning and Instruction*, 9(5), 493–516.

Wells, G. (1999). *Dialogic Inquiry: Toward a sociocultural practice and theory of education.* Cambridge, UK: Cambridge University Press.

# Part IV
# Identity, Motivation and Affect

# 9
## Gender Identities and the Process of Negotiation in Social Interaction

*Patricia Murphy*

## Introduction

Central to a Sociocultural approach to understanding learning is the concern for the mediated nature of cognition. As Bruner observes, 'Although meanings are "in the mind" they have their origins and their significance in the culture in which they are created' (Bruner 1996, p. 3). As part of the process of meaning making, children have to situate their experiences in their appropriate cultural contexts in order to make sense of them. It is through interaction with others that children come to understand culture and the ways in which it constructs reality. Learning therefore relies on the ability of humans to understand the minds of others; that is, intersubjectivity – 'shared understanding based on a common focus of attention and some shared presuppositions that form the ground for communication' (Rogoff 1990, p. 71). The ability to be inter-subjective allows children to negotiate meanings. This is one reason that classrooms have been reconceived as communities wherein learners participate in settings that are orchestrated by teachers and simultaneously created, enacted and experienced by learners (Lave 1988). Collaboration between learners is an essential feature of such a setting. The term 'collaboration' is used here to describe children actively communicating and working together, talking and sharing their cognitive resources to establish joint goals and referents, to make joint decisions, to solve emerging problems, to generate and modify solutions and to evaluate outcomes through dialogue and action (Hennessy and Murphy 1999).

To understand negotiation within interaction in classrooms, individual's actions have to be considered in their social context; that is, 'the immediate practical goals being sought and the enveloping socio-cultural goals in to which they fit' (Rogoff 1990, p. 139). In classrooms teachers' representations of schooling and of subjects are manifest in complex and wide-ranging ways, subject discourse being just one aspect of this manifestation. These instantiations of social orders, or as they will be termed here social representations, in teachers' practices provide children with resources to interpret and make sense of learning activities. How children take these up and create meaning from them, however, is mediated by the social and cultural bases of their experiences. It is expected therefore that children's understandings of the values, rules and common representations of school and of science classrooms will influence their interactions with each other and their ability to negotiate and develop shared reference.

Collaboration is a 'social structure' (Dillenbourg et al. 1995). Social identity emerges through collective activity 'where social identities reflect the individuals' efforts to situate themselves in their societies in relation to social representations of their societies' (Duveen and Lloyd 1986, p. 220). Penuel and Wertsch (1995) argue that

> identity formation must be viewed as shaped by and shaping forms of action, involving a complex interplay among cultural tools employed in the action, the sociocultural and institutional context of the action, and the purposes embedded in the action. Taking human action as the focus of analysis, we are able to provide a more coherent account of identity, not as a static, inflexible structure of self, but as a dynamic dimension or moment in action. (pp. 84–5)

It is this conceptualisation of identity as a moment in action as children situate themselves in relational activities with others that is seen as significant in the interpretation of children's behaviours in social interactions. Children's actions are understood to be shaped and realised as they resolve the tensions between the influences of various and divergent social representations (Ivinson and Murphy 1999). The evidence examined in this chapter of children's interactions in science classrooms is interpreted in relation to social representations of the subject, schooling and gender. The influence of each being understood to penetrate classrooms in complex ways.

For example, gender-codified social and cultural stereotypes interact with children's own developing cognitive understanding of what it is to be a boy or a girl. Both the extant social structures and children's own preferences influence their views of what constitutes appropriate activity. Duveen emphasises the transition from 'external identities as children are incorporated into the social world through the actions of others to internalised identities as children become independent actors in the field of gender' (Duveen 1999). An outcome of different socialisation patterns is that children develop different ways of responding to the world and making sense of it, ways that influence how they learn and what they learn. In this way children learn to value those activities, traits and behaviours associated with their gender. Consequently gender becomes a self-regulating system which needs to be understood as an evolving set of values and activities. The more children engage in gendered activities, the more they develop the skills and understandings associated with them, understandings which emerge as gender-related ways of being in the world.

Murphy (1997, 2000a) has documented general features of these gender-related ways of being that reveal the different views of *salience* that girls and boys may bring to the same activity; views that influence the tasks they perceive and the solutions they judge to be appropriate given the *same* circumstances. Furthermore, these differences in worldviews can lead to differences between children in the values, and rules that they consider apply in a learning situation. This can limit their ability to negotiate shared reference or, if negotiation occurs, can influence how social representations are taken up and are realised in the shared reference developed.

Classrooms taken as mini-cultures differentially privilege ways of acting, ways of being and ways of knowing. Teachers mediate between the learner's personal meanings and the culturally established meanings of the wider society. This chapter looks in particular at the differences that emerge between children and children and teachers in their perceptions of tasks and solutions and the consequences of these for negotiation within a collaborative learning situation. Neither the sources of these differences nor their consequences are visible to teachers or children. Evidence from case study research of classroom practice provides examples of how children invested in science activities, the circumstances of gender mediation and its consequences for individuals' participation and hence learning.

## The Research Study

The research has carried out detailed observations in three primary schools over extended periods of time. Teachers' interest in and commitment to collaborative learning determined the choice of schools in the study. For the purpose of this chapter the evidence from one case study school[1] where observations extended over a year is drawn on. In the school discussed, children aged 9–10 years old were observed as they undertook their normal science classes. The extent of the observation means that the evidence allows consideration of (i) the same group of children carrying out different activities; (ii) the same child in different group situations; and (iii) different groups carrying out the same activity.

To understand teachers' approaches and their consequences for children's learning, teachers' intentions were established, both in their approach to science and to learning generally. How these intentions were put into practice in the activities selected and in the interactions with and support given to children was observed and recorded using video and audio. Target groups of children identified by teachers were observed in depth. To complement the observations, interviews were carried out with the teachers and target children.

Children's perceptions of activities and of teacher's intentions, their level of engagement with tasks, their interactions with others and their views of working within groups were also explored to understand how teachers' and children's approaches influenced learning. There is a distinction made here between activities introduced by the teacher and tasks which are children's reconstructions of an activity.

The majority of children thought working with others was good because of the sharing of ideas. The children were able to articulate their understanding of the teacher's agenda for group work.

## Findings

Four examples have been selected. The first is of successful negotiation and the second of unsuccessful negotiation for the same 'mixed-gender' group of children carrying out different activities. The third case shows one of the children from the group in a 'same-gender' group situation and how this mediated his negotiation of alternative reconstructions. The fourth case is of unsuccessful negotiation in a 'mixed-gender' group where children's recognition of cues about the subject and its goals in relation to the values and rules for schooling differed.

### The Topic

The teacher introduced the topic of 'Water' by explicitly linking children's science learning and their everyday lives. This was seen as an essential aspect of a constructive approach to learning that the teacher valued. He also wanted children to understand the significance of science acting in the world. The first activity for children was therefore to conduct a survey at home of water consumption. This was to provide them with insights into the scale of need for 'clean water' which set the scene for the activity that followed.

### Case 1: Group 1, Activity 1

Case 1 shows an example of a successful negotiation. In the example two boys and a girl were engaged in a science activity to find out the best medium for filtering water. The teacher expected the children to collaborate to decide what they were trying to find out, what procedures to undertake to find this out, what variables to control and what to measure. A planning sheet was provided to support their initial thinking by asking a series of key questions. This provided further cues to what was considered to be an appropriate solution; that is, the goal of the task. The children had to predict an outcome and explain it. The final decisions they had to agree on were what equipment to use and how to record and communicate their findings. The children were expected to listen to each other and exchange views.

*Ruth:*    He [*the teacher*] wants you to listen to other people's ideas and I have started doing that now. Discuss which is the best idea.

*Lee:*    He [*the teacher*] puts two people together he thinks will work, who have the same ideas. Trouble is, we get new ideas once we start. He wants us to discuss what we should do and then come up with a final result of what to do.

Children were provided with four materials to test; gravel, sand, peat and soil, to see which one would clean the best or, as one of the children said, 'We were trying to clean dirty water and seeing what would be the most effective way.' Children were given plastic cups to put the filtering medium in and were expected to make holes in the base of it (this had already been demonstrated).

The children in their initial planning decided to use five holes per pot, the same amount of each filtering media and the same amount of pond water. With this much agreed including their common goal, the children went off to collect equipment. They did not allocate tasks, they assumed them and let each other know by talking out loud about what they would do. For example, Ruth commented as she left the group to collect cups, 'We need cups don't we?'

The teacher returned to the group to monitor progress.

*Teacher:*    Have you formulated a hypothesis or a prediction of which one will be best?

*Sam:*    Yes, we thought gravel.

The teacher confirmed that this was the view of the other two group members and then left. The children started to carry out their investigation and to monitor each other's decisions.

*Ruth:*    So you are going to start making the holes then?

*Lee:*      Five holes.
*Sam:*      OK, we want five holes.

Ruth went to get the water. In her absence the boys, who found making the holes difficult, altered the decision.

*Sam:*      [*who is making the holes*] After a couple of years we should have five holes!
*Lee:*      Why don't we just make it three holes?
*Ruth:*     [*Returns to the group*].
*Sam:*      Ruth, we're only having three holes. OK? Because they're big holes.
*Ruth:*     OK.

The children were negotiating changes in procedural decisions and offered explicit explanations for them. Each contributed to the activity and continually monitored procedures and shared observations. The teacher monitored the activity by observing from afar and asking questions periodically. This meant he could provide appropriate support when necessary. The teacher's questioning technique placed the decision making in the children's control. Furthermore, by repeating children's comments he gave them value.

*Teacher:*   What's happened?
*Sam:*       The sand's all come through with the water.
*Teacher:*   What's actually in the jar?
*Sam:*       Sand and water.
*Ruth:*      Sand.
*Teacher:*   Is that telling you that the sand is filtering out the dirt or not?
*Sam:*       No – the water's got dirtier – it's dirtier than when it started.
*Lee:*       The peat's gone down with it – but the gravel.
*Ruth:*      The gravel hasn't.
*Teacher:*   Is that telling you that the gravel is better than the ... ?
*Lee:*       Yeah, yeah.
*Teacher:*   Is it?
*Lee:*       No – no, it doesn't really.
*Teacher:*   Why has the sand and peat gone down through it and the gravel hasn't?
*Sam:*       Because [*the holes*] are too big.
*Ruth:*      The gravel's hard and it won't fit through the holes.
*Teacher:*   Listen to what she's saying.
*Ruth:*      Because the holes are too big and we've made the holes like that.

*Teacher:*   So what do you think you could do?
*Ruth:*       Make the holes smaller.

The teacher's questioning enabled the children to make explicit their thinking to inform their planning.

On the basis of their findings the children rejected each of the filtering media. They agreed to test two additional ones, grass and paper, and the teacher supported this decision. After this investigation the group concluded that paper was the most effective of the filtering media and could hypothesise why this was the case.

*Teacher:*   How does the paper work?
*Sam:*       Has it got tiny holes in it?
*Lee:*       Has it got such minute holes you'd have to use a microscope to see them?
*Ruth:*      Yeah.

Two underlying features of this example need to be noted to understand the interpretation of the next. First, the children understood the practices and requirements of scientific investigations and could mobilise these in developing shared reference about the task and the interpretation of its outcomes. Second, the teacher established ways of working with children where he explicitly required them to explain and justify their actions and interpretations. The children determined them but it was the teacher who validated them.

*Case 2: Group 1, Activity 2*

Case 2 is an example of unsuccessful negotiation by the same 'mixed-gender' group of children carrying out a different activity.

In the activity that immediately followed, the class had to consider rates of dissolving. The progression in scientific ideas from learning about ways of dealing with solid impurities to dealing with soluble ones (evaporation was a phenomenon investigated later in the same topic) was in the teacher's mind, but not made explicit to the children. The activity focused on observing the phenomenon of dissolving and investigating variables that influence it, in this case temperature. The teacher provided a worksheet for this and the same planning sheet as in the last activity. In the worksheet the activity is set in the context of a domestic setting. The context frames the problem as one affecting a person, Megan's father, who cannot get his sugar to dissolve in his tea. Megan suggests that this is because he waits too long before adding the sugar. The worksheet continues and frames the scientific investigation in isolation from the human dilemma; that is, 'to find out how the time taken for sugar to dissolve depends on the temperature of the liquid'.

In the initial planning stage for this activity, it appeared that the children could not agree on a procedural strategy.

| | |
|---|---|
| *Ruth:* | We're going to have two tests. One putting the sugar in straight away, and then five minutes later. |
| *Lee:* | Rubbish, not just straight, five minutes. Not just two tests. I think we should have at least three, and one where you put it in after ten minutes. |
| *Ruth:* | No, we're not asked to do that. |
| *Lee:* | Two tests won't give us the proper answer. |

The teacher intervened as the exchange between the children became heated. His expectation was that a shared task could be developed if the children discussed what they were trying to find out; that is, what the independent variable was. The following is an extract of the teacher–child interactions where the teacher is guiding the children's attention to what he judged to be the relevant aspects of the activity. This is described by Wood (1998) as contingent teaching 'which helps children to construct local expertise ... by focusing their attention on relevant and timely aspects of the task, and by highlighting things they need to take account of' (pp. 80–1).

| | |
|---|---|
| *Teacher:* | Why did he [*Lee*] suggest another reading after ten minutes? |
| *Ruth:* | But nobody puts their sugar in ten minutes later, do they? |
| *Teacher:* | I know, but what are you trying to find out? |
| *Ruth:* | How much the sugar will dissolve. |
| *Lee:* | How much the sugar will dissolve in water at different temperatures. |
| *Teacher:* | So what's the thing you are changing each time? |
| *Ruth & Lee:* | The temperature of the water. |
| *Teacher:* | Right, that's the thing you're interested in. |
| *Ruth:* | I know but ... nobody likes cold tea. |

Lee's task was the same as that identified in the worksheet. The cues that had salience for him corresponded to the teacher's representation of the subject. He understood the goals and the rules for evidence collection in the same way as the teacher intended. The girl was aware of these rules too and indeed they informed her approach to the first activity of cleaning water. However, she gave salience to other cues provided by the teacher about the subject in terms of its role in the world reinforced by the cues in the worksheet. Her commitment was to the human dilemma posed as she experienced it. As Lave observes, 'a problem is a dilemma with which the problem solver is emotionally engaged' (Lave 1988, p. 175).

For Ruth the context of the activity was salient; this view of salience being linked to gendered ways of relating to the world where girls seek social purpose in their solutions to justify the subject, whereas for boys the subject criteria have value in their own right (Murphy 2000b). Finding out how much sugar would dissolve in cold water was not relevant to Megan's father's dilemma. As she observed on several occasions, 'nobody drinks cold tea'. For Ruth the problem was to use her science to solve the father's dilemma and to provide evidence to support Megan's assertion. The teacher in his practices made the everyday and the scientific visible and related in the setting. Ruth's perception of the activity and her task were congruent with the teacher's and her own representations of the subject and her understanding of appropriate ways of interacting with the world. The introduction of the everyday was used by the teacher as a 'hook' to create bridges for children into the discourse practices of the subject. It was these practices that had priority in the teacher's representation of the subject. His objectives were to develop the procedural knowledge necessary to establish relationships that had general application.

In collaborative interactions children are expected to examine the strengths and weaknesses of alternative perspectives. Learning occurs as each group member's perspective is analysed and inferior ideas are rejected and superior views proposed and accepted (Kruger 1993). This assumes, however, that the 'common focus of attention' and 'shared presuppositions' that Rogoff (1990) refers to are available. The teacher's interactions assume that the common focus; that is, the shared problem, is available because for him there is no discontinuity between his perception of the problem and the representations of the subject. The source of the discontinuity for Ruth is not available to him precisely because of his social and cultural history. Consequently, how he is able to mediate between the learners' personal meanings and culturally established meanings is constrained. What followed exemplifies this.

| | |
|---|---|
| *Teacher:* | I'm not sure why you don't want to do it. You haven't given him [*Lee*] a good reason why not. |
| *Boy:* | You're just thick. |
| *Girl:* | Tea – quicker in five minutes instead of five minutes later. |
| *Teacher:* | Yes that's the situation. |
| *Girl:* | Why should I have to do what the boy wants? |
| *Teacher:* | But he's come up with a suggestion. |
| *Girl:* | Yeah, a suggestion and you want me to do it. You think it's a good idea? |

| | |
|---|---|
| *Teacher:* | I do think it's a good idea. |
| *Girl:* | But if I don't, do I still have to do it? |
| *Teacher:* | Is it going to tell you something? You give him a good reason why you shouldn't do it. |
| *Boys:* | Yeah. |
| *Teacher:* | No, no, that's not the right way to do it. [*This is said to the boys*] I can understand his reason for doing it ... but I can't understand your reason for not doing it. |
| *Girl:* | Right, the situation is that someone wants their sugar to dissolve quicker in their tea, right? So we, so nobody, but they still want warm tea or hot tea but they don't want it cold. |
| *Teacher:* | You're too hung up on this rather than what it is you're trying to find out. |
| *Girl:* | Maybe. |
| *Teacher:* | Would it be a big hardship if you did it? |
| *Girl:* | Be more to write up [*laughing*] but you'd find out more yeah. |

Ruth, along with other girls, tended to act as the scribe a group as she commented: 'I get lumbered with the writing.' She was now put in the position of recording a task which had no meaning for her, an activity that was deeply disempowering.

| | |
|---|---|
| *Boy:* | You need to put down three tests and how we're going to do the third test. |
| *Girl:* | You love watching me do this don't you, when it's your way. |
| *Teacher:* | Perhaps it'll be fair if someone else writes it. |

The teacher, whilst being unaware of the reason for the lack of meaning for Ruth in the activity, was alert to the disempowering nature of her participation.

*Case 3: Group 2 with a student from Group 1 (Lee) and a different activity*

Case 3 shows one of the children from the group discussed in a 'same-gender' group situation and how this mediated his negotiation of alternative reconstructions.

Lee was observed in a group of four boys engaged in an activity where the supports offered by the teacher were the same, as were the expectations to develop a shared task and a procedural strategy. The activity took place prior to the topic on water when the children were studying forces. At the planning stage the children had to formulate a hypothesis about what will effect how far a toy car travels down a ramp. Lee's hypothesis was that it was the length of the ramp that was significant, for another boy, James, it was the height of the ramp. For many minutes each boy offered their alternative views whilst the others watched. Both boys' frustration was clearly visible. Finally Lee tried to draw the others in to support him. The excerpt below shows Lee negotiating.

*Lee:*      The longer the piece of wood [*that is, the ramp*] the more time the car has to build up [*speed*].
[*Turns to Daniel*]
Can I say that we [*the group*] think the longer the piece of wood the more time the car has to build up?

Daniel agreed with Lee, but the other two boys disagreed.

*Mark:*      Why?
*Lee:*      More time to build up speed.
*James:*      I don't think so. I think if it's the longer kind of wood it won't go so far.
*Lee:*      Why yes it would, because the car will have more time to build up it's speed so it will go further.
*James:*      That's only if it's steep. If it's about that high [*demonstrates 10 cm*] it's not going to go very far is it? If it's about that high [*demonstrates 30 cm*] it's going to go further.

James then got down on the floor and demonstrated using the ramp and car. 'It goes much further if you have it like that.' Daniel and Mark both observed the demonstration and agreed with James. Lee made no attempt to model his thinking. When the three boys returned to the table Lee summarised the investigation for the group.

*Lee:*      We will have two different lengths of wood, a long bit of wood and a short bit of wood. We will make the slope longer and higher.

Everyone agreed on this compromise straight away as it gave value to both boys' ideas. Mark and Daniel were anxious to keep the others calm.

     Lee was not prepared to give up his reconstruction of the task. He was one of the children who had talked about the problem of losing ideas in collaborative activities.

*Lee:*      I like working on my own because then I have got my ideas and not other people's. It is all my ideas.

He was prepared to compromise, in contrast with his interaction with Ruth, and combine the two hypotheses, as were the other boys. This compromise can be understood in a number of ways. First, all the children in the interviews and questionnaire strongly expressed the belief that boys think alike, as do girls, but that boys' and girls' thinking is different. They therefore assume compatibility of mind in single-gender groupings and actively seek it. Second, Lee had to consider his position as a member of a community of boys. Science mattered to Lee, and doing well also mattered, which the other boys were aware of. He therefore had to deal with the possibility of being labelled as a 'nerd', a 'keener', a 'boffin'; titles that diminish a boy in the peer culture in schools. The boys, when talking about the activity, referred to Lee's 'Mega stress telling us all what to do'; 'Lee organised it all'. Organising activity is typically associated with girls' behaviour, hence this was another threat to Lee's identity in this situation. Compromise helped him to maintain a safe identity. A third factor was the boys' and Lee's understanding of science practices. Their knowledge of validity in relation to evidence was at an early stage of development. The consequences of the compromise for the validity of their data were unknown to them, as the interaction with the teacher that followed revealed.

| | |
|---|---|
| *Teacher:* | Can you go through what it is you are going to do now? |
| *James:* | I am going to find out whether the car goes further different heights on different slopes – on shorter slopes and on longer slopes. |
| *Teacher:* | Are you thinking that you'll have a longer and a shorter slope as well? Can I suggest that you use one type of slope? |
| *Lee:* | But we want to try and find out … which length of slope and which height of slope will work best. |
| *Teacher:* | That's two different tests then isn't it? Maybe you could do that afterwards. Compare the heights first, then compare the slopes afterwards. |

The teacher recognised the tension between having an agenda for the children and letting them pursue their own concerns. 'Knowing what you want them [the children] to start looking at … but not wanting to push them along that avenue particularly … I let them try to work through their own method.' This was a significant feature of his practice in that he tried to move the locus of control towards the children in their investigations in science and to maintain this.

As the children moved off it became clear that Lee was resisting the teacher's suggestion. He collected two pieces of wood.

| James: | We don't need that. We're using this. |
|---|---|
| Lee: | We're doing two slopes. |
| James: | You only need one slope. |
| Lee: | No, two. You see we're going to do two tests – one after the other. |

In spite of this last comment the boys confounded the two variables in their tests and consequently had difficulty interpreting their findings. In Case 2 the teacher intervened and imposed a particular construction of the activity because there was conflict in the group. The construction imposed accorded with the majority view so did not undermine his practice, as he described it, of allowing children autonomy. In this situation the children had developed shared reference. He did offer guidance about the need to test one variable whilst holding others constant, but he did not model the consequences if this was not done.

### Case 4: Group 3, Activity 1

Case 4 exemplifies differences in boys' and girls' recognition of cues about the subject and its goals in relation to the values and rules for schooling generally and the possibilities for learning and for individual's participation that this allowed. In the final example, James and Daniel are in a mixed-gender group on the same activity as in the first example – cleaning dirty water using four filtering media. Negotiation was problematic in the mixed group in contrast to the first example. The group consisted of two girls, Cathy and Diane, and two boys, James and Daniel. The children had the same supports as the group in the first example.

They did not reformulate the task together and what purpose their evidence had to serve. They therefore had no agreed strategy, but a series of procedures to enact. Cathy stayed at the table and 'organised' whilst the others searched for equipment and materials.

| Cathy: | Right have we got a cup? So we got a ruler, get a cup, put holes in it, and put the cup on top of the jar. |
|---|---|

Cathy also oversaw procedures.

| Cathy: | [*To Daniel*] No wait, wait. Measure for the different materials. |
|---|---|
| Diane: | He is, look. |

Cathy reading from the planning sheet:

| Cathy: | Right. To make our test fair we'll keep the things the same, same material, keep the water the same level. We will look for |
|---|---|

the cleanest water and count the stones and no, no, yeah, we'll look for the cleanest water and measure the height, using the graph we'll record.

Diane, Daniel and James, continued to assemble materials. Cathy monitored what they were doing.

*Cathy:*      No, we need the same amount remember – the same amount.

Daniel and James told her they had the same amount.

*James:*      It's just the jug's bigger.

When Cathy looked at the jars, it appeared as if there were differences between them in the amount of water. James and Daniel had used a ruler to measure the water and knew that the amounts were the same. When corrected, Cathy made no further comment before going on to tell them what they needed next.

*Cathy:*      Right now we need the sand after.

Unlike in the other group, the children found it hard to allocate tasks and resolve disagreements through negotiation. Cathy was significant in this in that she monitored and organised action but continued to be marginalised in the actual activity itself. Sometimes this marginalisation was by choice; at other times group members, both the boys and the other girl, excluded her.

The group had three jars with a cup in each jar. In the cups were the different filtering media. James poured dirty water into the cup with the gravel.

*Cathy:*      Is this the gravel? This is the gravel.
*James:*      I think this is going to be the cleanest.

However, the water came through with some dirt retained. Both boys were concerned that their procedures were wrong, and tried to explain what they saw as a wrong result.

*Daniel:*     Wait a minute. Wait a minute. I think I know what's gone
              wrong.
*Cathy:*      Is there something wrong?
*James:*      The jars are not clean at the bottom that's why.
*Daniel:*     No they're not clean.

The girls started pouring water into the next sample without talking this over with the boys. The boys objected and suggested repeating the investigation.

*Cathy:*      Which one's the cleanest so far? Looks like the cleanest so far is the sand.

*Daniel:*     Yes, but there's not so much [*water*] coming out.

*James:*     What we really need to do is tip them into separate jugs and see which one's the cleanest, I think.

The boys were beginning to consider how to judge cleanliness both in terms of the state and the amount of water. The group had not discussed this before. James questioned the results of the experiment.

*James:*     I think the gravel's wrong. I don't think the gravel is the cleanest.

The children argued about the results. Cathy was concerned that they were not doing what the teacher wanted.

*Cathy:*      We're meant to be doing work not arguing.

*Daniel:*     We're not arguing. We're just –

*Cathy:*      We're meant to be working as a group.

*Daniel:*     I think we should start again and we should do it properly.

*Diane:*      We can see [*the cleanest*], can't we?

*Daniel:*     I think we should start again.

*Diane:*      That's the cleanest.

*Daniel:*     No, you call that clean. Look at this.

*James:*     I think we should start again.

*Diane:*      I don't.

*James:*     Because then we can measure how much water got through, got through the first time. And another thing and if we never measured it [*the dirty water added*], it wasn't a fair test either.

*Diane:*      It was.

*James:*     Yeah and it wasn't a fair test. So I think we should start again.

*Diane:*      Well I don't think so.

*James:*     That's because you don't want to … then we can measure. If we start again, we can measure how much water. Because we ruined it anyway.

*Cathy:*      That one's the cleanest.

*Daniel:*     Let's try it out again and see.

*Diane:*      We've already done it. It's a waste of time.

It appeared that the children did not have a common focus. The boys were concerned with the validity of evidence. They prioritised this in their reconstruction of the activity. The girls prioritised the routines and expectations of school rather than the subject. For them this entailed getting on, engaging in activity, and coming up with an answer. It was also important to be seen to co-operate and share.

> *Cathy:*  We have to learn to work with other people. We have to help each other to do things. We have to get the same idea. If we have different ideas, we'll all have to decide on another one 'till we all agree on the same idea.

Their own learning in relation to science appeared to be neither clear to them nor apparently significant. Rather, they took up procedures as rituals; for example, planning to use a graph which was inappropriate for representing the data. This difference in priorities has been related to the form of feedback that girls and boys typically receive in primary schools (Dweck et al. 1978). Davies and Brember (1995) found that by the end of primary school girls were more anxious to do as they were told and to please their teachers. Boys expressed less concern to observe rules or about being reprimanded. This gendered view of the institutional order does not necessarily lead to one or other gender dominating in group situations. Cathy has been referred to as a 'girl organiser' following her interpretation of the teacher's cues. In this comment Cathy indicates her view of what routines dominate and her role in them.

> *Cathy:*  We do one thing each so it is fair. No one else could think so I thought of something and I tell Diane. I get the teacher so they wouldn't start arguing.

Here fairness is to do with the social aspects of co-operation, not the scientific procedure of controlling variables. James, Diane and Daniel each recognised Cathy's role as organiser. For Diane this was unproblematic. James accepted her in that role because she facilitated his participation in the group. Daniel appeared to tolerate it.

> *Diane:*  Cathy tells us what to do – I don't mind. I follow Cathy's advice. I just ignore James, we take turns.
>
> *James:*  Cathy says something and that was it. She decides. Diane gets in the way, she just gets on my nerves. Cathy listens to me, Diane doesn't listen. I was left out. Cathy helps me.
>
> *Daniel:*  James and I did all the work. Cathy can be stubborn.

The lack of joint discussion meant that the children's presuppositions were not made available for joint reflection. Hence when the boys began to question the procedures and results they were unable to explain their concerns, assuming that 'fairness' was understood in the same way by the others. Similarly, the girls were unable to understand the boys' concerns because of their view of what was salient and their different views of 'fairness'. The teacher intervened only when disagreements arose, assuming that the co-operative action he observed represented shared understanding. This assumption is common in classrooms. At the point where he intervened he could not determine the source of the problem as the goals that the girls identified he had not anticipated. Hence the lack of a common task was not evident, only a disagreement about whether procedures had been 'fair'. Again he assumed that fair was being used in the scientific way as for him this perception of fair dominated any social interpretation because of the scientific cues he had made available.

## Summary

Little attention is paid in classrooms to the tasks that children perceive and their interpretations of what is an appropriate response to them; that is, the cues they consider salient. This is because in practice it is assumed that tasks are given, rather than constructed. As Clancey (1993) puts it: 'Information is created by the observed, not given because comprehending is conceiving, not retrieving and matching' (p. 91). In this research a distinction was made between activity that teachers orchestrate in which cues to the intended task are embedded in a variety of ways, and the tasks that children conceive; intended tasks being what Newman, Griffin and Cole (1989) refer to as 'strategic fictions'. Bredo (1999) adds to this view of tasks and extends it to consider the implications if such a perspective is disallowed in classrooms.

> Any sequence of interactions can have multiple interpretations and be aligned to different goals … Behaving as if there were only one interpretation, one descriptive framework, is a possible way of interacting. It is a form of interaction, however, that is likely to make it painful or difficult for others who may have a different interpretation to join the 'dance'. (p. 39)

The 'dance' that is of concern in this chapter is learning about scientific ways of knowing and acting. Case 2 provided evidence of the painful experience that Bredo refers to when children are cast in the role of the 'wallflowers' at the dance.

The findings indicate the difficulties that arise for children and teachers if a common focus of attention and shared presuppositions about situations are assumed rather than established. Negotiation of alternative views essential to collaboration can only occur if the source of the differences between children is understood by the children, if they have the ability to articulate their perspectives to group members, and if others in the group have the experience and understanding to make sense of them. Ruth (Case 2) concluded about her own participation:

*Ruth:*  We had an argument. I wanted two tests but I didn't have a good reason and Lee did so we went with Lee's idea.

This means that not only was her participation marginalised, but she was also made to feel responsible for it.

The constructivist approach to learning that dominates science education in the UK does not perceive the child as involved in *relational* activities with others. Nor, of course, is the wider plane of community (Rogoff 1990) taken into account when analysing individual behaviour. Consequently eliciting children's interpretations of interactions that take into account alternative views of salience related to diverse social representations does not feature in curriculum schemes, teacher training or professional development in science education.

The teacher in the case study was aware of the role that prior scientific knowledge played in the children's learning about science. He was unaware of the impact of other influences on learning. Hence he elicited children's *scientific* understanding about learning situations without attention to the tensions that arose from competing views of salience that individuals had to resolve. To act differently teachers need access to models of children's tasks and the interpretations that they are based on. These are essential to inform them of the bridges that individuals need to understand the goals and intentions of the subject and the intended subject learning. Currently the bridges or 'hooks' used in science are relatively crude. The use of everyday settings and applications are problematic because they assume a ubiquitous view of relevance and trivialise the complex process involved in meaning making.

They fall far short of the authenticity that a Sociocultural approach considers essential to engage children and support subject learning. Activity is considered to be authentic if it is coherent and personally meaningful; and purposeful within a social framework – the ordinary practices of the culture. The interpretation of these two dimensions is not, however, straightforward (Moschkovich 1995), as Case 2 revealed. The teacher's cues represented science investigations as directly applicable to the solution of everyday problems without attention to whether the problem legitimately required the type of evidence argued for. Evidence of the relationship between temperature and rate of dissolving can explain the phenomenon of the troublesome sugar *and* many others. It is the application that determines the type of evidence required.

The investigation that Ruth proposed provided satisfactory evidence to explain the *specific situation*. The issue was therefore of different goals being available for the intended task. These alternative goals are, however, only available if the specific situation is accorded salience. The teacher and Lee did not give salience to the specific situation as it was not part of their '*interpretative horizon*' (Roth 1997). To enable intersubjectivity the interpretative horizons of participants in social interaction need to be understood. The task for teachers to develop this understanding is considerable; they have also to make this understanding available to children. The evidence from the research suggests that children can develop this understanding if given access to others' thinking. In the activity, Lee's responses to Ruth's suggestion were quite aggressive and dismissive: 'That's a rubbish idea'; 'You're just thick.' Later, after observing the video excerpt, he commented: 'I thought Ruth was barmy, just getting it wrong. I didn't understand what she meant. I do now, I hadn't realised it till now, I hadn't thought about it.'

The research provides insights into the mediating effects of gender on children's views of salience. Another effect noted was the way in which peer-group culture mediates children's actions. The cultures that girls and boys describe vary considerably (Kruse 1996, Ivinson and Murphy 1999). For example, the male peer culture is characterised as competitive and tough, involving mickey-taking or teasing. Girls speak of collaborative, caring, safe cultures. Lee's actions in the same-gender group were shaped by his perceptions of the peer culture and his concern to be seen to be successful in science and to achieve credit for his ideas. When teachers intervene to support children's negotiations these influences are rarely considered. Yet the 'imaginary gaze' of critical peers is a major threat to children's social identities and significantly affects how they learn to position themselves in subjects, positions that can constrain their future learning. A further constraint arises from children's learned assumptions of gender-appropriate roles. For example, organisation and scribing are low-status roles associated with female participation. These roles prescribe girls' participation in social interactions in that they shape the interpretative horizon available to them and influence how others regard them. Thus roles in groups need to be considered in terms of the possibilities they allow for participation.

A Sociocultural view of learning sees thinking and action as inseparable. As Clancey puts it: 'To be perceiving the world is to be acting in it' (Clancey

1993, p. 95). Planning is 'a dynamic process, not merely of reaching goals through carrying out planned actions but of forming goals which may emerge or be modified during the course of an activity' (Leont'ev 1981). Planning in science is typically carried out at the beginning of an activity. Rarely is there an expectation that explicit review and reformulation of plans may be needed to maintain intersubjectivity. To support this process children need to be encouraged to make explicit their emergent goals and need tools to support them in this.

The children in Case 4 would have benefited if planning sheets provided strategic guidance about learning goals that was reinforced in the wider subject discourse of the classroom. Typically goals are assumed to be shared and unproblematic, and planning support focuses on the subject practices to achieve assumed subject goals. These are not distinguished from other school-related goals. The different goals of schooling and subject learning can have antagonistic effects, as emerged in Case 4. These effects need to be considered in teachers' monitoring of children's interactions and provision for them made in the guidance for planning. If opportunity for reflection on meanings that emerge are built in to the practices of classrooms then plans can be refocused, goals reconsidered and intersubjectivity maintained.

The messages of the research for teaching and learning in science are considerable. They suggest that currently the models of practice available to teachers and learners are narrowly conceived. Hence the practices have not been developed to support negotiation in social interaction in subject cultures. The research does, however, show how these practices might be developed. The issue is whether there is potential to reconceptualise approaches to science education in ways that recognise the cultural process of meaning making. In the English education system this appears unlikely. Currently there is a retreat to simplistic models of mind that is reflected in formal assessment procedures based on the 'bell curve' conception of human ability, and the introduction of nationally prescribed pedagogic approaches that limit the time and the organisational possibilities for science learning. Research is needed to establish how a cultural approach allows children to develop different, more useful and robust understanding in contrast with other approaches if this retreat is to be halted.

## Note

1 This case study was part of an earlier project Collaborative Learning in Primary Science (CLAPS) which involved a team of people: the author, Eileen Scanlon, Kim Issroff, Barbara Hodgson and Liz Whitelegg, based at the Open University.

# References

Bredo, E. (1999). 'Reconstructing educational psychology'. In P. Murphy (ed.) *Learners, Learning and Assessment*. London: Paul Chapman.

Bruner, J. (1996). *The Culture of Education*. Cambridge, MA: Harvard University Press.

Clancey, J. (1993). 'Situated action: a neuropsychological interpretation, response to Vera and Simon'. *Cognitive Science*, 17(1), 87–116.

Davies, J. and Brember, I. (1995). 'Attitudes to school and the curriculum in Year 2, Year 4 and Year 6: changes over four years'. Paper presented at the European conference on Educational Research, Bath, UK.

Dillenbourg, P., Baker, M., Blaye, A. and O'Malley, C. (1995). 'The evolution of research on collaborative learning'. In P. Relman and N. Spade (eds) *Learning in Humans and Machines*. Oxford: Pergamon.

Duveen, G. (1999). 'Representations, identities, resistance'. In K. Deaux and G. Philogene (eds) *Social Representations: Introductions and explorations*. Oxford: Blackwell.

Duveen, G. and Lloyd, B. (1986). 'The significance of social identities'. *British Journal of Social Psychology*, 25, 219–30.

Dweck, C.S., Davidson, W., Nelson, S. and Enna, B. (1978). 'Sex differences in learned helplessness 11. The contingencies of evaluative feedback in the classroom'. *Developmental Psychology*, 14, 268–76.

Hennessy, S. and Murphy, P. (1999). 'The potential for collaborative problem solving in design and technology'. *International Journal of Technology and Design Education*, 9, 1–36.

Ivinson, G. and Murphy, P. (1999). 'Researching the construction of school knowledge, identities and pedagogic practice in single sex classrooms'. Paper presented at the American Education Research Association Annual Meeting, Montreal, Canada.

Kruger, A.C. (1993). 'Peer collaboration: conflict, co-operation or both?' *Social Development*, 2(3), 165–82.

Kruse, A.M. (1996). 'Single sex settings: pedagogies for girls and boys in Danish schools'. In P. Murphy and C. Gipps (eds) *Equity in the Classroom: Towards effective pedagogy for girls and boys*. London: Falmer Press.

Lave, J. (1988). *Cognition in Practice: Mind, mathematics and culture in everyday life*. Cambridge: Cambridge University Press.

Leont'ev, A.N. (1981). 'The problem of activity in psychology'. In J.V. Wertsch (ed.) *The Concept of Activity in Soviet Psychology* (pp. 37–71). Armonk, NY: Sharpe.

Moschkovich, J. (1995). *Assessing Students' Mathematical Activity in Context of Design Projects: What are authentic assessment practices?* Palo Alto, CA: Institute for Research on Learning.

Murphy, P. (1997). 'Gender differences – messages for science learning'. In K. Härnqvist and A. Burgen (eds) *Growing up with Science*. Cambridge: Jennifer Kingsley.

Murphy, P. (2000a). 'Equity, assessment and gender'. In J. Salisbury and S. Riddell (eds) *Gender Policy and Educational Change. Shifting agendas in the UK and Europe*. London: Routledge.

Murphy, P. (2000b). 'Science education – a gender perspective'. In J. Seers (ed.) *Issues in Science Teaching*. London: Routledge.

Newman, D., Griffin, P. and Cole, M. (1989). *The Construction Zone: Working for cognitive change in school*. Cambridge: Cambridge University Press.

Penuel, W. and Wertsch, J. (1995). 'Vygotsky and identity formation: a sociocultural approach'. *Educational Psychologist*, 30, 83–92.

Rogoff, B. (1990). *Apprenticeship in Thinking: Cognitive development in social context*. Oxford: Oxford University Press.

Roth, W.M. (1997). 'Situated cognition and assessment of competence in science'. Paper presented at the 7th Conference of the European Association for Research in Learning and Instruction, Athens, August.

Wood, D. (1998). *How Children Think and Learn* (2nd edn). Oxford: Blackwell.

# 10
## Motivation and the Ecology of Collaborative Learning

*Charles Crook*

The editors of this volume invite us to 'rethink' collaborative learning. My own motives for doing so arise from an uneasy awareness that many who write about collaboration are at odds over whether and why it is a good thing. Thus, within the pages of one recent book we find quite opposing judgements on the benefits of learning collaboratively: one chapter notes that 'there is a substantial body of empirical evidence demonstrating the positive effects of social interaction for learning' (Littleton and Hakkinen 1999, p. 20); whilst another claims 'research suggests that there is nothing particularly special about working in small groups, at least with regards to cognitive outcomes like learning' (Schwartz 1999, p. 197).

Indeed, Schwartz argues that, despite its long history as a topic in psychology, collaboration has been rather poorly theorised. In particular, he suggests that the ingredient of human 'agency' has been excluded from its definition: collaborations are not viewed as motivated. I agree with this diagnosis. Although I am less comfortable with Schwartz's suggestion that such a neglect indicates researchers' over-concern with the contextual arrangements for collaboration; or that, therefore, 'there are times when it is worthwhile to minimise the emphasis on the cultural environment in which we swim' (Schwartz 1999, p. 203). In fact, I wish to argue that the settings in which collaborations get organised – the tide in which we swim – should be a natural starting point for any analysis. Moreover, that includes any analysis that takes 'agency' seriously. To do this, I believe it helps to mobilise the notion of 'ecologies' and thereby to analyse the actual spaces within which collaborations are either constrained or resourced.

In order to summarise the arguments to be developed here, it is necessary to simplify some key concepts, not worrying for now about how their definition ought to be more hedged about with qualifications. In this spirit, it can be said that 'collaboration' refers to certain forms of productive joint engagement. 'Ecology' is about the immediate environments within which such activity is supported – the artefacts, the technologies, and the spaces for acting. Then, a significant organising idea is that arrangements for collaborating evoke in us a more or less agreeable emotional reaction. This is an idea that is not well-explored. However, I suggest it helps us understand certain conflicts (such as that illustrated above) over whether collaborating is good for learning outcomes, or not. For the experiences evoked in collaborations are highly variable and such variability is most likely implicated in learning outcomes. Schwartz's agency and motivation could be mobilised at this point. Yet, I shall argue, we cannot properly systematise this variation of experience unless we foreground the idea that any collaboration is, in the end, a form of co-ordination with a supporting environment. In short, taking on the felt *experience* of collaborating requires us to take more seriously the *ecologies* of collaboration. Doing so helps us understand the variety of engagement enjoyed by collaborators and, thus, the variety of learning outcomes that arise. A consideration of ecology also helps us act more effectively as educational designers: for we may better design circumstances in which the productivity of joint engagement can be optimised.

In what follows I shall first try to be more precise about 'collaboration' as a social psychological concept. I shall then consider the status of 'ecology' as a metaphor for organising analyses of how collaborations occur. Finally, I shall illustrate the ecological approach with some empirical examples.

## The Collaborative Experience

On entering this arena, we surely want to know 'what counts as collaboration?' and 'what collaborations count?' Unfortunately, in practice, such questions prove slippery. I suggest below some problems with the way collaboration has been conceptualised in discussions of learning. In particular, I shall suggest that collaboration might be usefully characterised as an experience with a distinctive and important emotional dimension.

There certainly have been attempts to characterise how collaborative interactions can vary in quality. Yet the terms in which that variation has been sought suggest a preoccupation with notions of cognitive skill. On this view, collaborators – as individuals – possess resources of, say, predicting, hypothesising, reasoning, reviewing, and so forth. When they are learning as individuals, those resources are suitably deployed for getting problems solved. When individuals learn as collaborators, those resources are suitably *co-ordinated*. Indeed, in the case of collaboration, the public nature of the problem-solving discourse allows researchers to classify and count constituent cognitive acts. On the whole, this is what has been done by those researchers who have tried to characterise the form and variety of collaborative encounters (for example, Webb 1986). Those who are oriented towards a cognitive skills emphasis tend to focus on two general themes for characterising variability in the collaborative communication. The first concerns discrepancies between the collaborators in terms of their cognitive resources at the outset of interaction. This would encourage research on mixed-ability groupings (Bennett 1991), or research on the consequences of (otherwise matched) collaborators starting with different cognitions about the problem in hand (Howe 1996). The second research line concerns how smoothly collaborators manage cognitive co-ordination: how individually preferred cognitive moves become comfortably integrated with a partner's preferences. This has encouraged studies on the implication and control of cognitive *conflict* within such contexts of interaction (Doise 1985).

## Collaborating as Motivated

There is no question that research in these traditions has been valuable. Yet the underlying theoretical perspective does lack scope. In particular, conceptions of collaborative learning that foreground cognitive skill fail to represent collaboration as something that is *motivated*. The quality of a collaborative encounter may depend just as much on the participants' enthusiasm for engagement as it does on their harmony of knowledge, or their experience at resolving cognitive conflict. In practice, researchers often tend to neutralise this issue of motivation by arranging that the situations they observe recruit good-natured volunteers who agree to be interested by the problems they are invited to solve. Moreover, perhaps researchers suppose that motivation is never more than a benign issue in collaboration. For it may be argued that whether a learner is motivated by a learning task is no more of a problem in a collaboration than it would be when the task is conducted alone. Such reasoning might dispose of any idea that motivation has a special relevance to collaborating.

However, the issue of motivation becomes less benign if it is supposed that there are emergent properties associated with learning through collaborative interaction. For being within a collaboration may provoke reactions of an affective nature: responses that are distinctive to that form of encounter. Such responses could then be relevant to the motivation of greater (or lesser) task engagement. Finally, 'task engagement' determines how far cognitive skills become mobilised and deployed. Such an analysis is implicit in the paper by Schwartz (1999) mentioned earlier: 'people need to choose whether and when to collaborate and whether to go beyond the minimum necessary to meet the rules of collaboration' (p. 198). To develop this claim, Schwartz invokes the notion of 'agency'. He suggests that this is a neglected form of experience arising within occasions of joint problem solving. For Schwartz, the core of agency as a motivational notion is what he terms 'effort after *shared* meaning'. Note that this is an individualistic, rather than a social, concept. It thereby encourages inquiry 'into the properties of individuals that make collaborative behaviours emerge' (p. 198). Finally, Schwartz characterises such interpersonal agency as an aspect of our human nature: when collaborating, we are naturally inclined to work towards attaining this state of mutual understanding.

Here I shall attempt to tune more finely this notion of 'effort after shared meaning': reflecting, in turn, upon the 'natural', the 'effortful' and the 'shared' features of what is proposed.

### Motivation as Seeking Shared Meaning

If human beings are 'naturally' disposed to act collaboratively, we might expect participation in such arrangements to evoke agreeable emotions in us. Elsewhere (Crook 1994, p. 225), I have argued that observations of human development strongly suggest that joint cognitive engagement can have affective and motivational potency in and of itself (perhaps 'effortlessly'). From the earliest months of infancy it seems that we are attracted by the forms of synchrony that joint human action can furnish. A close observer of such events has remarked that 'only humans have the kind of appetite a one-year-old begins to show for sharing the arbitrary use of tools, places, manners and experiences' (Trevarthan 1988, p. 55). Argyle (1991) complements this claim with observations about the attraction of joint activity for adults. Thus, the experience of mutual knowledge – a cognitive synchrony, as it were – appears to be something that people readily strive to achieve. Given that human history is significantly about the evolution of social problem solving (Humphrey 1976), then it is reasonable that positive emotional states should be associated with the behavioural synchronies involved.

A more problematic feature of 'effort after shared meaning' is the understanding of 'effort'. It implies a strong *intent* to achieve shared meaning. Yet moments of powerfully felt shared meaning clearly can arise following rather little effort on our part. The point is that effort is not a necessary condition for realising the motivating experiences of a collaboration. Krauss and Fussell (1991) provide an accessible illustration. They discuss the potency of mutual knowledge that is experienced when, for example, one New Yorker meets another – perhaps as strangers both away from their common home. This gives rise to pleasure that needs very little 'effort' of construction. If the case of roving New Yorkers is not sufficiently like collaborating, consider an illustration closer to formal learning. Consider two individuals who, separately, have been working on some problem and, separately, have achieved familiarity with it (say, some computer puzzle that we have authored). My expectation is that if their activity is now arranged to intersect, if they are convened by us for a collaborating session at the computer, then at that time they will most likely experience a pleasantly animated feeling from the intersection. Such an experience reflects awareness that their understanding of the problem domain overlaps: an awareness that it is understanding shared. They will experience this even though the basis for it is in what they have done (previously) as individuals. They still register that this has created an agreeable mutuality, albeit not something created through *joint* activity – for there was none. Yet that shared understanding is now available as a resource: it can be recruited into the (now joint) activity, and it may come to motivate that convened collaboration further and faster.

Of course, whether joint activity has the informality of New Yorkers meeting abroad or the formality of collaborative learning, if the pleasure of co-ordination is to be savoured then the participants must launch into more active investment of effort – more organised work directed at controlling and extending the shared meaning. That is, if collaborators' effort was not necessary to precipitate the shared meaning, such effort may become important to sustain and elaborate it. Nevertheless, the basic emotion we are discussing here seems often to be available without any great orchestration on the collaborators' part. The collaborators' shared culture (say, that of common institutional context) may serve to furnish the currency through which shared meaning may be experienced within joint activity. This should encourage psychologists to understand how such optimal scenarios are provided – particularly for would-be or reluctant collaborative learners.

The final ingredient of 'natural effort after shared meaning' to consider is the 'sharing'. Here the challenge is to discover more of how the positive affect arising from collaborating relates to different conditions of things being shared. It is natural to think first of depth or extent of common knowledge as the basis on which the quality of sharing might vary. Doubtless this is significant. But also important may be the degree of 'intimacy' associated with the common knowledge. If when collaborators convene their shared meanings are very widely shared by others, then the joint experience may not be very engaging. However, if the shared meaning is more idiosyncratic or if it does arise from unique effort that learning partners have made as collaborators, then such intimacy of understanding may be especially motivating. This is a perspective recently applied to understanding the appeal of joke-telling (Cohen 1999). Yet, regrettably, the general argument still remains speculative. The research agenda on the processes of collaborating has been rather narrow in its focus. It has dwelt upon situations that tend to have no history. It also admits rather little concern for the motivational quality of participation.

This exploration of the experience of collaborating (inspired by Schwartz's 'effort after shared meaning') need not imply that joint activity is always and everywhere vigorously sought, for we readily discover that joint activity can arouse both positive *and* negative emotions. I have documented some of the variety of such experience by observing young children collaborating in pairs around classroom computers (Crook 1994, chapter 7). In some pairs, discourse was mobilised to discover and negotiate an expanding resource of shared experiences (as, perhaps, their teachers had hoped). Moreover, often this entailed conversational contributions that seemed to cultivate an intimacy from the situation: marking events in such a way as to appropriate them into a particularly personalised narrative of shared experience. On the other hand, some collaborative pairings exercised conversational moves that were more about wrestling to contain competing individual ambitions (such as one partner wishing to solve the problem and another wishing to escape and do some other, more preferred activity). Still others would involve one member of a pair manoeuvring to ensure that the version of shared meaning to evolve was the one that he or she had predetermined as desirable. An important point about this variety is that it exists despite the collaborative talk being rather similar in terms of its more cognitive profile. These pairings are all similarly animated, often quite symmetrical in terms of contributions, and those contributions can be equally sophisticated in cognitive terms. Yet, the affective tone within these encounters can be very different; the intimacy of shared meaning also can be very different. Probably we would also find that the learning outcomes associated with such variability were different.

In sum, the position I wish to defend regarding the concept of collaboration is as follows. To be a collaborator is to enter into an interpersonal exchange in which it is understood that there should be a sustained investment in constructing shared meaning. Talk and action is recruited towards negotiating, updating and reviewing that achievement. Progress in this enterprise will involve both a cognitive and a motivational dimension. Cognitively, the participants become resourced by an evolving 'platform' of meanings from which new explorations can take off. Motivationally, we find that participants can become more closely engaged through a certain potency associated with the experience of shared understandings. The affect arising from this cognitive synchrony is something human beings seem inclined to enjoy. In this setting, it can serve to animate and sustain a cognitive exploration – to an extent that might be beyond what could be achieved in solitary conditions of learning. Yet that quality of affect is not an easy or an inevitable consequence of the contract for joint activity.

This sketch of what it is to be within a collaborative relationship refers to somewhat delicate forms of social alignment. The sense of having realised something that is genuinely 'shared' may often be quite fragile. It may be a hard-to-win prize. It may become unevenly felt by the collaborators. In particular, how these occasions are experienced may not be simply determined by the sheer will or 'effort' brought into them by participants. Certainly, human agency and the effort after shared meaning are significant ingredients that can be usefully imported. But they are ingredients that are not immutable properties of individual collaborators. They are psychological reactions that *situations* evoke. They occur because people act within a cultural context: because they share certain experiences within that local culture. The possibility of powerful joint activity must depend a great deal on the context of the collaborative occasion itself. Because circumstances of joint activity are precarious in this sense, there can be no assumption that learners will energetically seek out collaborative opportunities. It cannot be assumed that they will naturally seek out opportunities to exercise some generic *effort* towards making shared meaning with another person. Faced with a given possibility, they may judge that this will not be the inevitable payoff. Or they may judge that the logistics of co-ordinating defeat the anticipated gains. At least within formal educational settings, it may be more realistic for researchers to think in terms of how the circumstances for a potential collaboration are made more optimal: how they are designed and engineered, with expectations that putative collaborators can more readily fall into them to productive effect.

I wish to marry up this line of thinking about the *experience* of collaborating with a line of thinking that is, broadly speaking, 'ecological'. The point is to maintain that for collaborators, the quality of the experience felt – in practice – is variable. Moreover, such variability is best approached by orienting towards the social, cultural and material conditions surrounding the collaborative occasion. So, if learning outcomes following collaborative study are mixed, then this may reflect varying qualities of affect aroused by the circumstances of the collaboration. And this, in turn, may be understood by reference to the ecology of the joint activity that was entered into.

## The Ecological Metaphor

The term 'ecology' recently has been recruited by Nardi and O'Day (1999) into a discussion about people's relationships to information technologies. These authors are frank in admitting that their use of the concept is strictly metaphorical. So, also, is my own use here. Ecology is a helpful term to invoke because it invites a principled attention to certain neglected aspects of collaborating.

First, the term reminds us that an organism's activity is always a form of co-ordination with an environment. In the study of collaboration, there has been a tendency to decouple the collaborators' talk from the material circumstances in which it is embedded. Analysts need to recover this 'mediated' character of social interaction. Second, an ecological perspective is one that addresses the potentially systemic character of social exchanges. What collaborators do is not bounded by the circumstances of a researcher's convened 'session'. On this view, we are invited to consider how the fate of a collaboration is to be understood in terms of its position within some larger picture of organised human activity. In particular, to consider interdependencies: to consider how, for example, tinkering with parameters in one region of this 'system' has knock-on effects elsewhere. Finally, ecology offers us the notion of 'niche'. Importing that idea into the study of collaboration would require us to notice the organisational coherence of various settings – say, institutional settings – in which the practice of collaborative learning is pursued.

Ecological perspectives have enjoyed some influence in psychology. In the study of perception, Gibson (1968) stimulated a significant research tradition concerned with how structure in the visual array furnishes 'affordances' for the management of activity within space. Ecological studies of child development have revealed how parameters of the built environment constrain or facilitate patterns of social and playful development (Barker and Wright 1954, Smith and Connolly 1980). Similarly, Bronfenbrenner's work (for example, 1979) develops this into a larger systemic analysis of how child development is governed within a culture's institutions and spaces. Finally, studies of how we interact with technologies stress how patterns of use arise from the affordances of material design (Norman 1988). This may include the larger-scale (social) design issues of space management within workplace settings (Bannon 1986).

Arguably, the ecological perspective has been most vigorously pursued in relation to features of the environment that seem to have fairly direct relationships with human action – or where the sophistication of the actors is less advanced (as, say, with children). This may be because the problem confronting any ecological analysis of human activity is that human beings are so active in imposing *meanings* upon the paraphernalia of their material world. The spaces, artefacts and technologies of our worlds are *interpreted*. Their 'properties' as items to be co-ordinated with are complicated by the meanings we impose upon them. Moreover, different people may build very different meaning relationships into the environment. All of this makes things difficult for researchers and theorists. In practice, these complexities may have distracted researchers from taking a strongly ecological approach: from making the material environment the starting point for their analyses of human action. Perhaps it encourages theorising to be developed on a more cognitive plane. The conceptual vocabulary for analysis becomes pitched more at the level of mental structures rather than at the level of embodied and situated activity.

Yet it should be possible to grapple with the complexities introduced by the fact that human actors impose meanings on the cultural context in which they act. I suggest it is necessary to do this. Because, otherwise, we cannot make adequate sense of how collaborations can be successful (and how success may be designed for). Making this sense requires us to become ecological. Thus, it requires us to register the systemic nature of the activity, to understand how collaborating implicates artefacts or technologies and to characterise the cultural niches within which it is orchestrated. These possibilities perhaps are best captured through considering concrete examples in which the ecologies for collaborative learning are illustrated and research needs identified. I turn to this task in the next section of this chapter.

## On Resourcing Collaborators

If we wish to optimise the collaborative experience of learners, I suggest there are two broad research challenges for the design of educational interventions. The first involves a concern for the character of the resources that collaborators interact around: that is, what they refer to at the time that they are actually engaged in a session of joint learning. This becomes an 'ecological' interest because it insists that the quality and prospects for interaction depend upon the co-ordinations that are made possible by locally available resources. This line of enquiry is more familiar, as it resonates with the typical format for research investigation in this area. Namely, it tends to take discrete occasions of orchestrated collaboration as the 'empirical unit' of concern.

There is a second line of enquiry that is less familiar. It is based on recognising that formalised occasions of joint learning are only one way in which collaboration can occur. Collaborative learning may also simply crystallise out of learning communities: occurring as rather informal and improvised occasions. Such collaboration is not something that is prompted through the official demands of some curriculum (or the stage directions of some researcher). The challenge presented by this more informal case is different. It is one of understanding how the corporate experiences of some learning community are best designed to optimise such opportunities, by making them seem attractive. This becomes an 'ecological' interest because it locates individual collaborators within a larger *system* of (learning) activity. It also seeks a greater degree of *interdependence* between social experiences in a learning community – rather than parcelling them into circumscribed occasions of joint learning activity (the most popular empirical unit).

I will discuss what is involved in this more corporate and improvised situation first, and then turn to the ecological dimension of the more planned and self-contained circumstances of a collaborative learning 'session'. For each case, I will endeavour to illustrate some empirical possibilities by reference to some examples from work of my own.

### Ecology and Informal Collaboration

With the advent of accessible and powerful computer-mediated communications, there is some question as to whether the communal nature of traditional educational practice is necessary at all. Perhaps this technology will be the final lever for a 'deschooling' (Illich 1973) of society. Yet if there is something to defend here it is surely something to do with the potential for peer interaction that a community context for learning affords. Whether members of this community actively plan collaborative encounters or whether they crop up casually, the depth of participants' established common knowledge will make a difference to what happens within them. At least, this would be the argument that follows from the conceptualisation of collaborative experience formulated above. Where collaborating partners understand that they have interesting commonalities of knowledge (arising from their participation in the larger learning community), then it is likely that the quality of affect generated by their various encounters will be enhanced. I will expand these observations a little, first in relation to undergraduates.

It is not unusual for undergraduates to remark that the sense of corporate activity (attending the same lectures, doing the same assignments, and so on) is an agreeable aspect of institutional learning. In that case, the sense of shared understanding probably serves a serious motivational function. On the other hand, this does not necessarily ensure that informal and productive collaborations will thereby flourish. Unfortunately, the learning niche students occupy may have other features that obstruct an effort to develop further shared meanings. In particular, if there is a sense of being in *competition* with fellow students, then that structural feature of the learning ecology may impede informal collaborating (cf. Becker et al. 1961). Probably this is happening within many university classes. I suggest this because I can report observations about social affiliation taken from two second-year classes of residential, full-time students taking degrees in chemistry and in psychology.

These students had attended various courses together for two years. They were each shown a composite photograph of the 40 or so fellow students in their respective classes and asked a number of questions about each peer. About two-thirds of the class was sampled as respondents whilst all class members were visible in the photograph.

Figure 10.1 shows a psychologists' affiliation network based on which other students were acknowledged to be at least acquaintances ('known such as to talk with socially').

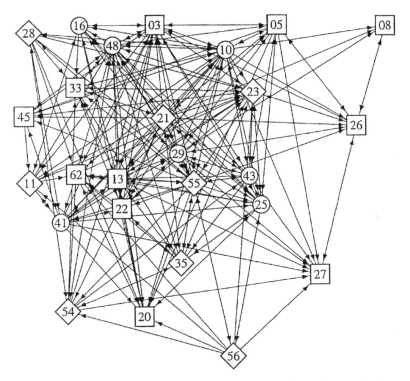

*Figure 10.1* Acquaintance network for a second-year class of chemistry students

Figure 10. 2 shows how the density of this net thins out when the question concerns whether or not a respondent has triggered an arrangement 'to meet up explicitly to talk about course work'. This is clearly an infrequent scenario despite the apparent goal-directed coherence of the underlying community.

The same point is made comparatively (for psychologists versus chemists) in Figure 10.3. Here we see median percentages of the class nominated in response to a number of questions to individuals about their social affiliation. For example, Question 0 merely asks whether a fellow student is recognised. Question 1 is that mentioned above concerning simple acquaintance. Question 2 asks each individual whether he or she has ever 'discussed problems/ideas relating to work/study outside of actual class time', and Question 3 is the one cited above concerning explicit study meetings. The remaining questions concern further possibilities for closeness of social contact.

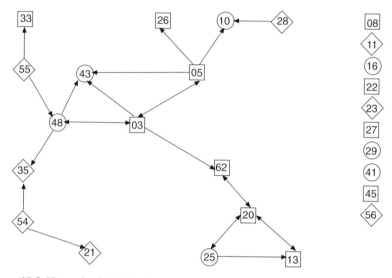

*Figure 10.2* Network of individuals who had organised an out-of-class meeting to discuss work issues at some time during the year.

Observations of this kind are useful for clarifying the extent to which an existing learning community takes advantage of its shared experiences to resource informal collaborative interaction. One would have to say they do not do this very much in the present example. However, this is descriptive research. It is hardly useful for clarifying what circumstances or social processes obstruct the taking of these opportunities. We get a little further with that interest by referring to another study carried out by David Webster and myself at the same university. We carefully sampled a cross-section of students during a period of several weeks when they were revising for final examinations. They reported a number of things about their study strategy, including confirming that it was largely solitary.

Figure 10.4 shows how such study was distributed across the possible spaces provided by the campus infrastructure. Clearly most of it is conducted in areas where social interaction is either prohibited (libraries) or in spaces that traditionally are private (personal study bedrooms) and where neighbours are from a whole variety of degree courses (rather than just one's own).

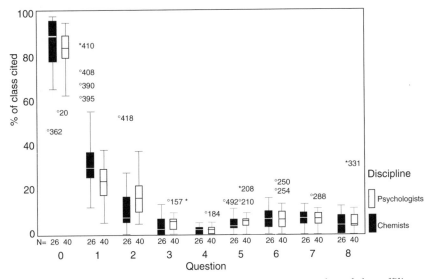

*Figure 10.3* Median percentage of peers cited in answer to a number of class affilia-tion questions for second-year students of chemistry and psychology.

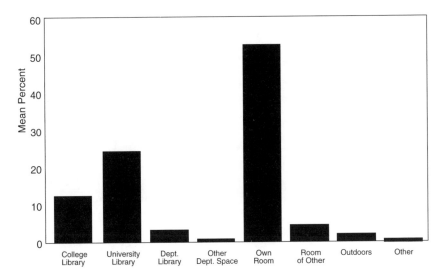

*Figure 10.4* Percentage of study time spent in various locations

This is an issue of ecology. For it encourages us to think about how the activities we wish to cultivate (informal collaborations) might best be supported by the design and provision of a certain kind of space. In the diaries of revision study, there is a notable lack of reference to space conceived for informal encounters; space designed to encourage members of a class who might seek opportunities for collaborative discussion. Our impression was that this university (like most others) lacked significant space of this sort. Not that simply making it available is all that is needed. For example, my own department has reserved an area at its centre for casual use by the community – suitably furnished with round tables, comfortable chairs and refreshment facilities. I believe the space enjoys some success as a support for casual collaborations. Yet I suspect there is still a shortfall in what it achieves. Its limitations arise less through its furniture and situation than through the habits of occupancy that it has attracted. In particular, it enjoys relatively little use by postgraduates or staff. This is 'merely' an issue of office geography and pressures of time, but this reduced constituency of users undermines the sense of the space as a representation or focus of shared concerns. Moreover, the one-sided nature of its occupancy (mainly by undergraduates) may serve to reinforce some of what is unhelpful in the tutor/student divide. Such division may obstruct any grand ambition that what is originally 'tutoring' might move towards becoming 'collaborating'. Yet this example about study space – once opened up for scrutiny – exposes the systemic nature of the activity (informal collaboration) that researcher-designers need to contemplate.

In the end it will be necessary to go beyond simply documenting the state of development of educational ecologies. Researchers must also probe how local space can be designed to 'work': that is, to be richer in its collaborative opportunities. I will refer to just one example of what acting at this level might involve. I have reported elsewhere (Crook 1999) an intervention that considers how new technology might be recruited towards extending the shared knowledge of a primary classroom. The environments of early education and university may appear very different but there is a common underlying need: namely, to create a setting which cultivates, records and exploits common knowledge. In our case, this strategy involved designing an interface to the file system of the classroom's (un-networked) computer. Pupils were given 'home page' style space and a facility for passing text messages. Various areas of the disk were created to display records of work currently being carried out – as well as that from previous years. While the facility has received no formal evaluation, it was clear on the basis of informal contact that it made possible a greater degree of mutual awareness in relation to ongoing class work and products achieved. The example simply illustrates the relevance of new technologies to working on such challenges. While a primary school classroom may be quite hard to influence by this route, a university class should be much easier. For example, the use of websites for undergraduate classes is one point of comparison. Perhaps their future use could echo my example above: moving away from 'delivery' models (repositories for handouts, lecture overheads, or assignment details) towards a more 'community-oriented' model (celebrating the corporate discussions and products of the learning group).

## Ecology and Collaborative Resources

Earlier, I noted that an ecological approach might be mobilised to consider two species of issue. First, the community-level issues (facilitating informal collaborations) and, second, interaction with the more 'local' resources that mediate within particular occasions for collaborating. There is much that could be said about the design of such resources. For example, it seems that the interactivity of mediational means is important to enhance the potency of shared knowledge. Also important is the capacity of a collaborative resource to act as a useful representational support – perhaps externalising for the collaborators difficult abstractions characteristic of the problem domain being studied (Crook 1994). Here, I will mention just one study concerning mediational means: in this case, resources being used by pairs of (undergraduate) collaborators. It is a useful example to conclude on as it touches on a number of points I have tried to develop in this chapter.

Students revising for a final examination on a particular lecture course were invited to convene into (self-selecting) revision pairs. They would take part in a couple of informal sessions and would be assigned to a condition in which the collaborative resource was either their personal notes from lectures, or a set of hypertext web pages built from the lecturer's own notes for these sessions. Evidently, there is much in common between these circumstances. The students have the same purpose (revision for exam), they are oriented to the same target (the syllabus of a lecture course), and they have a similar focal object for collaboration (species of textual notes). Yet the interactions generated seemed to have rather different qualities. Talking around their own notes, students' discussion was more exploratory, more creative and more pitched towards understanding underlying disciplinary ideas. Talk around the web notes was more prone to distraction, more preoccupied with what was 'expected' and more likely to provoke (worried) social comparisons within the pair regarding what they each seemed to 'know about'.

The example again warns against crude forms of assessing collaborations in terms of the amount of task talk sustained. In both conditions there was a lot of task talk. But detailed consideration of how the core material was being explored revealed very different levels of engagement and different sorts of shared experience being developed. Clearly, as mediational means, these artefacts (the two forms of notes) had attracted very different meanings for their users. These differences can only be speculated upon in relation to the larger ecology of which they are products. Thus, it is tempting to suppose that the lecturer's web notes conjure up the metaphor of 'delivery'. They are a version of something that took place (lectures) and the attitudes they invite from collaborative users is perhaps to learn them, and to consider the lecturer/author him- or herself – his or her motives, expectations and agenda. Whereas students' personal notes (albeit composed from the same teaching events) conjure up the metaphor of 'platform' and thereby they invite from the collaborators a more exploratory and open-ended form of use.

The example illustrates the significance of collaborative artefacts as mediational in this sense. Further, it illustrates the challenge to 'human ecology' identified above: namely, that artefacts acquire cultural meaning prior to serving as a focal point for co-ordinated activity. Finally, the example also illustrates something of the systemic nature of what we are considering here, for a development such as educational information technology cannot be viewed as a self-contained form of resource simply added to the educational 'pot'. It is an intervention that has potential knock-on effects throughout the system. In particular, the innocent new resource of web-based lecture notes may well disturb the cultural context of learning in ways that are not easily anticipated.

## Concluding Comments

I began by noting that commentators seem uncertain as to the effectiveness (the learning outcomes) of studying in collaborative arrangements. I then considered the emotional dimension of collaborating: suggesting that the quality of the experience in this sense would have much to do with the prospects for any given collaboration. Broadly defined, the emotions generated seem to centre on the participants' discovery, pursuit and celebration of shared understandings. Expressing this as 'effort after shared meaning' is helpful – unless it invites us only to dwell on 'the properties of individuals that make collaborative behaviors emerge' (Schwartz 1999, p. 198). In the end, much of the variance associated with these experiences of joint activity may not be derived from individual cognitive or personality differences. The significant variance will be found in the configuration of that sociocultural (learning) context within which individuals act. This, therefore, encourages a more ecological approach to theorising collaboration.

Research has tended to neglect the sociocultural conditions that precipitate collaborating. Possibly the neglect of this issue reflects the fact that most occasions of interest for researchers are required, designed (and perhaps rewarded) by the researchers themselves. Yet there is a bigger picture; one that can not easily be derived from looking at only short, self-contained occasions of orchestrated problem solving. Many collaborations for learning will be circumstances that are serendipitous or improvised: they simply arise from living within a learning community. As such, the emotions they create – the engagement that is sustained – will not be fully understood without serious scrutiny of the rich cultural context in which collaborators are positioned.

If we stand back from what goes on in formal education, it is possible to conclude that the biggest question about collaboration is why it does not happen more often. Few students study together informally. Many under-graduates actively resent the direction to 'work in groups'. I do not believe that this undermines claims made above about the synchronies of joint activity being intrinsically attractive to us. From preverbal play to adult conversation, human co-ordination is a powerful motive. Yet any given occasion for co-ordination must be located in a wider system of personal motives and cultural constraints, obligations and responsibilities. Intending collaborators may see much that is complex in the circum-stances of each proposed liaison and in the configuration of each set of material resources. I have suggested that we may enjoy greater purchase on the quality of these experiences (and their value for participants) if we adopt a more ecological perspective. In the end, collaborations are social events that are 'situated': that is, they involve interpersonal co-ordinations around the artefacts and technologies of culture, and they must be precip-itated out of the larger social systems – the larger communities – to which collaborators belong.

## References

Argyle, M. (1991). *Cooperation*. London: Routledge.

Bannon, L.J. (1986). 'Helping users help each other'. In D.A. Norman and S. Draper (eds) *User Centred System Design* (pp. 399–410). Hillsdale, NJ: Lawrence Erlbaum Associates.

Barker, R.G. and Wright, H.F. (1954). *Midwest and its Children: The psychological ecology of an American town*. Illinois: Row, Person.

Becker, H.S., Geer, B., Hughes, E.C. and Strauss, A.L. (1961). *Boys in White*. New Brunswick, NJ: Transaction Publishers.

Bennett, S.N. (1991). 'Cooperative learning in classrooms: processes and outcomes'. *Journal of Child Psychology and Psychiatry*, 32, 581–94.

Bronfenbrenner, U. (1979). *The Ecology of Development*. Cambridge, MA: Harvard University Press.

Cohen, T. (1999). *Jokes: Philosophical thoughts on joking matters*. Chicago, IL: University of Chicago Press.

Crook, C.K. (1994). *Computers and the Collaborative Experience of Learning*. London: Routledge.

Crook, C.K. (1999). 'Computers in the community of classrooms'. In K. Littleton and P. Light (eds) *Learning with Computers: Analysing productive interaction* (pp. 102–17). London: Routledge.

Doise, W. (1985). 'Social regulations in cognitive development'. In R. Hinde, A.-N. Perret-Clermont and J. Stevenson-Hinde (eds), *Social Relationships and Cognitive Development*. Oxford: Oxford University Press.

Gibson, J.J. (1968). *The Senses Considered as Perceptual Systems*. London: Allen and Unwin.

Howe, C.J. (1996). 'Piagetian theory and primary school physics'. In P. Woods (ed.) *Contemporary Issues in Teaching and Learning* (pp. 105–19). London: Routledge.

Humphrey, N. (1976). 'The social function of the intellect'. In P. Bateson and R. Hinde (eds) *Growing Points in Ethology*. Cambridge: Cambridge University Press.

Illich, I. (1973). *Deschooling Society*. Harmondsworth: Penguin Books.

Krauss, R.M. and Fussell, S.R. (1991). 'Constructing shared communicative environments'. In L. Resnick, J. Levine and S. Teasley (eds) *Perspectives on Socially-Shared Cognition* (pp. 173–200). Washington, DC: American Psychological Association.

Littleton, K. and Hakkinen, P. (1999). 'Learning together: understanding the processes of computer-based collaborative learning'. In P. Dillenbourg (ed.) *Collaborative Learning: Cognitive and computational approaches* (pp. 20–30). Oxford: Pergamon.

Nardi, B.A. and O'Day, V.L. (1999). *Information Ecologies*. Cambridge, MA: MIT Press.

Norman, D.A. (1988). *The Psychology of Everyday Things*. New York: Basic Books.

Schwartz, D.L. (1999). 'Agency that drives collaborative learning'. In P. Dillenbourg (ed.) *Collaborative Learning: Cognitive and computational approaches* (pp. 197–218). Oxford: Pergamon.

Smith, P.K. and Connolly, K.J. (1980). *The Ecology of Preschool Behaviour*. Cambridge: Cambridge University Press.

Trevarthan, C. (1988). 'Universal cooperative motives: how infants begin to know the language and culture of their parents'. In G. Jahoda and M. Lewis (eds) *Acquiring Culture: Cross cultural studies in child development*. Beckingham, Kent: Croom Helm.

Webb, N.M. (1986). 'Microcomputer learning in small groups: cognitive requirements and group processes'. *Journal of Educational Psychology*, 76(6), 1076–88.

# 11
## Taking Time Out from Collaboration: Opportunities for Synthesis and Emotion Regulation

*Margarita Azmitia*

Cognitive development is inherently social. Two or three decades ago, when a small group of developmental psychologists working in the neo-Piagetian (for example, Doise and Mugny 1979, 1984, Perret-Clermont 1980, Ames and Murray 1982, Bearison 1982), social learning (for example, Bandura 1977), or Sociocultural (for example, Wood 1980, Greenfield and Lave 1982, Laboratory of Comparative Human Cognition 1983, Rogoff and Wertsch 1984) traditions advanced this position, they caused much excitement among those who had come to doubt the image of the child as the lone scientist or information processor. This view that cognitive development is inherently social actually originated in the early part of the century. In the same way that developmental psychologists from a variety of theoretical perspectives converged on this belief in the 1970s and 1980s, four decades earlier three giants in the field, working relatively independently in Europe and the United States, had advanced similar proposals. Piaget (1932) wrote about the social construction of morality through peer interaction, George Herbert Mead (1934) outlined the foundations of communication and cognition in the early conversations of gestures between care-givers and their infants, and Vygotsky (1929, 1978) discussed the roles of language and social interaction in the emergence and develop-ment of thought.[1] Although Vygotsky paid more attention to historical and cultural contexts than Piaget or Mead, there is still much convergence among their three theories. Since the 1970s, Piaget's and Vygotsky's models, in particular, have been tested, expanded and revised as investiga-tors' efforts have shifted from merely demonstrating the social nature of knowledge construction to explaining it and developing applications for the classroom or workplace.

In this chapter, I will focus on three continuing themes in work on the social contexts of cognitive development. Two of these themes, the process of knowledge construction during collaboration and the broader analysis of the sociocultural context in which this process takes place, have received considerable attention. The third, the role of affect in collaborative cognitive development, has not received much attention in developmental research.

Because the central goal of the chapter is to highlight how a consideration of affective processes can broaden our understanding of collaborative cognitive development, I will adopt the strategy of interweaving the discussion of affect into the presentation of the first two themes. Also, because my expertise lies more in the area of the processes of collaborative cognition, I will devote more attention to this theme than to the discussion of the broader sociocultural context of collaborative cognitive development.

## A Brief Introduction

As evident in the contributions to this volume, many researchers have studied how group members co-construct knowledge during social interaction and how individuals selectively incorporate this collaborative product in their minds. Researchers pursuing this goal have abandoned the overly romantic view that collaboration always leads to development for the more realistic view that the cognitive outcomes of collaboration depend on the nature of the interaction (for reviews, see Azmitia 1996, Rogoff 1998).

Studies on the sociocultural context of collaboration and cognitive development have examined collaborations within and across cultures and linked the patterns of social interaction to societal values and beliefs (for example, Tharp and Gallimore 1988, Goodnow 1990, Hatano and Inagaki 1991, Cole 1996, Rogoff and Toma 1997, Wertsch 1997). Rogoff and Toma, and Hatano and Inagaki, for example, described how Japanese teachers helped their students learn to work together, question each other's beliefs and evaluate and integrate different perspectives.

Another research direction in the sociocultural tradition involves studying communication and collaborative cognitive development in the context of many kinds of relationships,[2] such as teachers and students (for example, Tharp and Gallimore 1988, Murphy, Chapter 9 this volume, Tolmie et al., Chapter 7 this volume), parents and their children (for example, Ninio 1973, Bruner 1977, Callanan and Jipson forthcoming), friends (for example, Azmitia and Montgomery 1993, Hartup 1996, Macdonald and Miell, Chapter 5 this volume), and scientists (Watson 1968, Dunbar 1995, 1997) and other professionals (Hutchins and Paley

1993, Suchman 1993, Csikszentmihalyi and Sawyer 1995, Bennis and Biederman 1997). Except for the work on friendship, however, these studies have seldom considered how the unique properties of particular relationships influence collaboration and cognitive development. In this chapter, I illustrate the sociocultural context of collaborative cognitive development by reviewing research on creative insight and scientific discovery and presenting some of my own work on collaborations between friends.

The third strand of my chapter concerns the role of affect in collaboration and cognitive development. In an earlier paper, Marion Perlmutter and I (Azmitia and Perlmutter 1989) proposed that the availability of a partner may help collaborators reduce frustration when faced with a very difficult problem. At the time that we made this proposal, which drew on the proverb 'misery loves company', we had no data to support it. Over the years, as I have conversed with children, adolescents, and adults following their participation in my studies, many have espoused this view, making such statements as: 'We couldn't figure it out and I felt bad and told Andy we should just stop and ask you to tell us how to do it, but he convinced me to keep trying and we finally figured out what we were doing wrong.'

Having a partner can also make a task more enjoyable and increase motivation, a point that has been made by a variety of developmental and non-developmental scholars (for example, Wood, 1968, Azmitia 1996, Graf et al. 1996, Bennis and Biederman 1997). Participants in our research agree: 'It was fun to work with Sarah 'cause the teacher never lets us be partners', and: 'When I work in a group, I work harder so they don't think I'm lazy.' Singleton participants (the control condition for some of these experiments) often get upset when they discover that other participants are working with a partner. As a 6-year-old boy told me: 'It's not fair that you let some kids come together and I have to come by myself. It'll be funner if I can come with someone.'

While the comments of these participants supported the proposal that working with others generates positive emotions and motivation and can reduce negative affect, it is also the case that at times, partners' frustrations with the task or each other can lead to breakdowns in the communication and interaction. In what follows, I will show that sometimes these breakdowns can be productive because partners use them to work out an idea, to reassess their position, or to reduce negative affect so they can reconnect in a more positive manner. However, frustration can also escalate and cause irreparable breakdowns in the collaboration and/or lead to poor decision making. A case in point are Lynn[3] and Christine, two adult best friends who participated in one of our studies (Azmitia and Crowley forthcoming). Over time, Lynn became increasingly frustrated by their inability to solve the problem and Christine's tendency to block or ignore her contributions. She began to berate Christine in Vietnamese, gesticulating to the task materials and a sketch that she had made of a potential solution. Christine interrupted her tirade by saying: 'Speak English',[4] and then continued her work without even glancing at the sketch. Lynn angrily withdrew from the collaboration and continued sketching solutions which she no longer shared with Christine. In that session, Christine was not able to solve the problem, but did not ask Lynn for help. When they returned a week later, they alternated between working collaboratively and taking turns, but the quality of their discussion was fairly low relative to that which had preceded their fight (that is, they did not elaborate on each other's views, explain their beliefs, or produce analogies). In their exit interview, Lynn remarked that she would never work with Christine again and was not sure they would remain best friends; in turn, Christine stated that they would probably have been able to solve the problem if Lynn had been willing to pull her own weight in the task. Interestingly, at the beginning of the study they had commented on how much they enjoyed working together on projects.[5] Fortunately, collaboration often proceeds more smoothly and productively than was the case for Christine and Lynn. What characterises these enjoyable, productive partnerships? I now turn to this issue.

## Collaborative Cognitive Development

'None of us is as smart as all of us' (Bennis and Biederman 1997, p. 1). Much of the earlier work on collaborative cognition focused on gathering empirical support for this observation by comparing the work of pairs or small groups to that of individuals. The preponderance of studies, mostly carried out in the 1970s and early 1980s, showed that cognitive development was more likely in the social context (for reviews, see Azmitia and Perlmutter 1989, Rogoff 1998). This is not only true in laboratory studies. Historical analyses have revealed time and time again that groups often accomplish great things. Francis Crick would not have discovered the structure of DNA without James Watson, Maurice Wilkins, Rosalind Franklin and Linus Pauling. It is not that solitary work does not lead to progress, but, as Henry James, a famous American author, remarked:

> Every man works better when he has companions working in the same line and yielding to the stimulus of suggestion, comparison, and emulation. Great things have of course been done by solitary workers; but they have usually been done with double the pains they would have cost if they would have been produced in more genial circumstances. (Farrell 1982, cited in Bennis and Biederman 1997)

Recently, some scholars have questioned whether there is such a thing as solitary activity or independent thought. Even when they originate in solitary moments of reflection, our ideas are heavily influenced by cultural beliefs and artefacts and our prior social interactions (see also John-Steiner 1985, Goodnow 1990, Csikszentmihalyi and Sawyer 1995, Wertsch 1997, Rogoff 1998, Azmitia and Crowley forthcoming). Consequently, as I stated in the opening sentence of this chapter, cognitive development is inherently social.

But how does this social process result in cognitive growth? The microgenetic methodology, which was advocated by Vygotsky (1978) as one of the four levels for studying development, has been used by developmental psychologists from a broad range of theoretical orientations, including neo-Piagetian (for example, Kuhn 1995), information processing (for example, Siegler and Crowley 1991) and Sociocultural (for example, Wertsch et al. 1984), to address this question. This approach involves carrying out fine-grained analyses of changes in dialogues, interactions and problem solving over the course of one or several sessions. Researchers assume that these changes reflect moment-to-moment learning and development occurring within the unobservable confines of people's minds (Kuhn and Phelps 1979, Siegler and Crowley 1991, Klahr and MacWhinney 1998). Microgenetic analyses do not require that participants achieve complete mastery of the task or solve the problem; all that is required is that some change, whether progression or regression, occur (Kuhn and Phelps 1979).

The microgenetic method has also revealed that development is gradual and uneven and that correct and incorrect beliefs and strategies co-exist with each other (Kuhn 1995, Siegler 1996). In both laboratory studies and more naturalistic contexts, developmental change is more likely when there is some discrepancy between partners' knowledge but there is still sufficient overlap to facilitate the creation of shared goals and views of the task (Dunbar 1997). In situations where experts and novices collaborate, however, the novices' progress often depends on the experts' ability to use the novices' errors as signals that they must provide more support and their successes as cues to allow them greater independence (Wood 1980).

Whilst researchers have generally not considered the experts' cognitive development following collaborations with novices, it is likely that the process of carefully considering the task, decomposing it into manageable chunks, and explaining the steps to the novice increases the experts' understanding. As many professors know, the best way to master the ins and outs of a domain is to have to teach it.

Collaborative cognitive development also frequently occurs in situations where partners' abilities are more evenly matched. In this situation, collaborators who are able to establish a shared frame of reference, build on each other's ideas, and feel comfortable challenging each other's understanding and resolving differences of opinion, change cognitively during and following the interaction (for examples and reviews of this research see Kuhn et al. 1988, Faulkner et al. 1998, Rogoff 1998). Collaborators who use analogies to relate information or experiments across contexts are also more likely to make significant progress than teams who rely less on this strategy (Dunbar 1997).

Whilst in general, collaborations between relative equals can be very productive, I suspect that the unevenness of collaborative cognition is more evident in this context than in collaborations between experts and novices because partners are working together to discover knowledge and their work may often test the limits of their understanding (see also Baker-Sennet et al. 1992). In any case, a theory that accurately describes, explains and predicts collaborative cognitive development will need to address the developmental messiness that has been revealed in microgenetic studies. As Watson (1968) stated in the preface of his personal account of the discovery of the structure of DNA:

> Science seldom proceeds in the straightforward logical manner imagined by outsiders. Instead, its steps forward, (and sometimes backward) are often very human events in which personalities and cultural traditions play major roles. (p. xi)

Watson's point underscores the fact that developmental researchers often focus on the cognitive and communicative components of collaborative cognition, such as expertise and elaborations or discussions of ideas, and pay little attention to collaborators' personalities and the affective tone of the interaction (see also Brown et al. 1983). Our focus on the intellectual aspects of collaboration has probably prevented us from identifying the potentially more challenging aspects of working together in what can be a very volatile situation.

I suspect that our overreliance on problems which have one correct solution or can be solved through systematic hypothesis testing of a small set of causal parameters has contributed to this rosy, calm picture of collaborative cognitive development. In these tasks, collaborators can isolate the relevant variables, create critical tests of their hypotheses (that is, tests that would support or disprove their hypotheses), and use the results to justify their points and to monitor their progress and avoid taking wrong turns. When the problems are more open-ended, however, these strategies may be less useful because the evidence does not always 'speak for itself'.

In open-ended or ill-formed problems, collaborators must often define the problem and identify the relevant variables before manipulating them, and also assess whether they have achieved an acceptable solution in a situation where the data may be ambiguous. Monitoring progress becomes more difficult and the work and the collaboration more stressful and affect-laden, particularly when the stakes are high. This is the situation that scientists, policy makers, CEOs and other professionals confront every day: no matter how carefully they plan their actions, implement their plans and monitor their results, progress is difficult to assess and the outcome cannot be predicted easily. Indeed, after a long period of hard work and implementation, the outcomes may be negative – for example, the failure of a programme of research, a policy that hurts the individuals it is meant to help, or a company that goes bankrupt. This is also often the type of problem that we encounter as we participate in our personal relationships – what we must do is not always clear because each course of action has both negative and positive consequences. Indeed, Staudinger (1996) has suggested that recognising that solutions are relative, that people have different perceptions about what the best solution may be, and that some problems simply cannot be solved is an important dimension of wisdom.

In contrast to developmental psychologists, social psychologists have devoted considerable attention to how groups solve ill-formed problems. They have been especially interested in how personality and affective elements of interactions affect the decision-making process and its eventual outcome. The findings of social psychologists have great relevance for developmental psychology because understanding positive and negative group processes and outcomes will help us not only to build better theories of collaborative cognitive development, but also to create effective groups in schools, the workplace, and other institutions of daily living.

Much research in social psychology has focused on the question of why highly competent collaborators often make poor decisions or why minority (but correct) opinions are often discarded in favour of an incorrect view held by the majority. In a classic set of experiments, for example, Asch (1956) showed that minority opinion group members' fear of being rejected or disrespected led them to conform to an incorrect majority opinion even when they had at their disposal considerable evidence that their perspective was correct. Similarly, Janis (1973) proposed the concept of *groupthink* to explain why, across history, groups of very intelligent, competent, individuals have made very poor decisions.

The results of social psychology experiments also remind us that collaborators have multiple goals (for example, solving the problem; avoiding stress, rejection, or embarrassment by voicing a dissenting opinion; gaining acceptance and forming relationships; generating consensus), and that the characteristics of the individual (for example, status, self-presentation, consistency of opinions) can influence the dynamics and outcomes of collaborations. In one of the few child developmental studies which considered the role of social status in collaborative problem solving, Pozzi et al. (1993) obtained results that resembled the groupthink phenomenon. They suggested that one way to encourage groups to consider a wide range of strategies and alternatives is to have them present their ideas to other groups who can then question them and prevent them from adopting a very narrow, incomplete focus. It is also important to teach groups how to decide among competing alternatives, especially when the problem feedback is ambiguous or when they are relative novices in the domain. Knowing how to make these decisions can relieve the tension and frustration that group members often feel when they are being pressured to choose a particular option or are unsure of how to proceed.

## Taking Time Out from Collaboration: Affect Regulation and Collaborative Cognitive Development

Groupthink often emerges when decisions are made under very stressful, emotional, circumstances. Some of us have had the experience of being persuaded by a powerful orator and voting for a proposal we subsequently realised was flawed, or failing to express dissent in an important meeting and then having to live with the group's decision. Janis (1973) proposed that one way to reduce groupthink is to take some time to reconsider decisions that have been reached with quick consensus and little discussion of alternatives. Not that all decisions need to be reconsidered, but collaborators should have some time to reflect by themselves, outside the explicit or implicit pressures of the group.

Taking time out from the collaboration can also allow group members to reflect upon an idea without the pressures or distractions of attending to and contributing to the social discourse. Several of the creative individuals interviewed by Csikszentmihalyi and Sawyer (1995) remarked that they often withdrew from interaction to engage in solitary reflection whenever attending to the voices of others, no matter how stimulating, made it hard for them to think. Some added that although their important creative insights often emerged in these solitary moments, they had had their origins in the social discourse. Moreover, these insights often surfaced when the creative individuals were engaged in other pursuits – for example, gardening, walking, or taking a shower. Staudinger (1996) also found support for the contribution of solitary reflection to cognitive change in her study of the role of social interaction in the development of wisdom. In particular, older adults who were given a few minutes to reflect on the discussion they had had with their partner before the individual post-test obtained higher scores on a wisdom measure than those who did not have this opportunity. Taken together, the results of these studies suggest that knowledge and discoveries may need some time to ferment before achieving their 'bouquet' – the creative insight or the developmental shift (for a more extensive discussion of the fermentation metaphor, see Azmitia 1996).

Csikszentmihalyi and Sawyer's (1995) retrospective interviews and the experimenter-controlled reflective episodes in Staudinger's (1996) study do not allow an unequivocal test of my hypothesis concerning the moment-to-moment dynamics of 'time-outs' from collaboration and their role in cognitive development. I now turn to a review of a small pilot project that had this as one of its goals.

Kevin Crowley, Alden Schmid, Sandy Hodges and I (Crowley, Azmitia, Schmid and Hodges, in preparation) studied adult friends' collaborative cognitive development on an ill-formed problem over time, tracking microgenetic changes in their patterns of collaboration and in their theories about the problem. The task involved designing foam-block towers that would withstand a 5-second simulated earthquake. In each session, partners had 15 minutes to test as many towers as they wished on the earthquake machine. The task is challenging because it does not have a single (or even ideal) solution and the variables that help the towers stand interact, thus making critical tests of hypotheses difficult. Finding a solution is further complicated by the fact that there is some element of luck in whether towers stand or fall. Approximately half of the pairs (5 out of 12) solved the problem; that is, built a tower of the required height that withstood the simulated earthquake.

The most relevant findings for this chapter are the time-outs that took place during the collaborative process (for other findings see Azmitia and Crowley forthcoming). In particular, we examined the antecedents and consequences of episodes in which collaborators disengaged from the interaction for at least 30 seconds. We only included instances in which one of the partners continued to work on the earthquake machine. The other partner either became an observer who made no suggestions or other kinds of contributions to the building (for example, did not place or remove blocks), worked on the task on his or her own (for example, sketched potential designs on one of the notepads we had provided), or went off-task (for example, put his or her head on the table, juggled blocks, looked around, or 'spaced out'). Because Lave and Wenger (1991) have argued convincingly that observing is a form of collaboration, we subsequently excluded onlooker episodes from our corpus of time-out events.

Across the 12 pairs who participated, the mean number of 'time-outs' from collaboration was 4.2 (range 0–8). On average, these episodes lasted anywhere from 30 seconds to a few minutes. In 81% of these instances, the partners re-engaged in the collaboration before the end of the session. We were able to identify the antecedent of 73% of the time-outs. The most frequent precipitating events were (1) the pair appeared to have reached an impasse and was unable to generate new ideas; (2) one partner was consistently ignoring or blocking the other's placements and suggestions; (3) the person who disengaged expressed frustration by making an explicit comment, displaying a negative facial expression, or, in one instance, pelting his partner with the foam blocks.[6]

Recall that we defined time-outs from collaboration as instances in which partners went to parallel work. What were the individuals who were not working on the machine doing during these time-outs? Most frequently (64% of the episodes), they were working out an idea to try out on the machine by drawing different tower formations on the notepads we had provided. Occasionally, their drawings were accompanied by self-talk about potential strengths and weaknesses of their towers. At other times, it appeared that individuals were using these solitary moments to manage negative affect; for example, one person put his head down on the table and pulled at his hair while another counted silently to ten. Taken together, these time-outs not only highlight the importance of these solitary moments for collaboration and cognitive development, but also suggest that these periods of disengagement may be used to regulate negative affect in very challenging circumstances.

Because our study focused on adults, we cannot speak to the child-developmental import of time-outs from collaboration. It is possible that they serve the same function, but that children and adolescents have to learn to monitor their affective state to avoid allowing the frustration to escalate to the point that the disengagement becomes permanent. At least in cultures which emphasise individual work, children, though not necessarily adolescents, may find it harder to resume the collaboration than the adults who participated in our study. Obviously, these speculations must be tested empirically.

## Affect and Collaborative Cognition in the Sociocultural Context

The ways in which collaborative cognition is practised vary not only between cultures, but also within cultures. When children, adolescents, and adults join new groups, they often have to learn new ways of working together and creating shared views. As mentioned, these adjustments of collaborative behaviours depend, at least in part, on the personalities and social status of group members. Some groups are more tolerant of newcomers' ideas than others, and some newcomers are better able to detect and adjust to the group's preferred working style. High-status members also have more 'rights' than low-status members – their ideas carry more weight and the group is more willing to put up with any unpleasant behaviours and idiosyncrasies.[7]

Groups vary in their endorsement of cultural beliefs and practices, but to an extent, the sociocultural context influences collaboration by socialising practices concerning the expression of emotion, disagreement and dissatisfaction. Briggs (1970), for example, found that expressions of anger were discouraged in the Eskimo community she studied; Corsaro (1994) wrote about the premium placed on lively *discussione* (conflict and debate) in his ethnography of an Italian pre-school; and direct challenging of high-ranking members' ideas is unacceptable in Japanese groups (Gjerde, personal communication, January 2000). It would be interesting to study the ramifications of these cultural practices on collaborative cognitive development. For example, would time-outs from collaboration, and especially those that stem from frustration and stress, be less likely in these three cultural communities? If so, would creative insights decrease or be delayed because they now must emerge in the cognitively 'noisy' group context?

Studying collaborative cognitive development in the context of relationships may serve as a first step towards answering these questions because by definition, relationships have a strong affective quality. In cultural communities that allow collaborators to express disagreement, individuals feel more comfortable voicing dissent in the context of a personal or working relationship. This is because when they have a long-standing relationship, individuals are not as motivated to gain respect and acceptance and avoid rejection as they are when they work with strangers and acquaintances. In a relational context, people also know that unresolved conflicts and hurt feelings can be repaired because they will have occasion to interact or work together again. Finally, to the degree that their relationship is positive and bound by a commitment to reciprocity and mutual respect, they are more likely than strangers or acquaintances to justify their views and attempt to reach a compromise, thus enhancing the cognitive potential of collaborations (Nelson and Aboud 1985, Azmitia and Montgomery 1993).

Although work in the US has revealed that people who work with a partner or partners with whom they have a history feel more comfortable expressing dissent, the overall affective quality of interactions that occur in longstanding work or personal relationships is more positive than that which characterises interactions between strangers and acquaintances (Hartup 1996). It would be interesting to know whether members of collaborative relationships are also better able to regulate one another's negative affect and frustration because they can read each other's emotional cues better. Two hypotheses stem from this speculation. First, if relationships allow better affect modulation, there may be less need to take affective time-outs from the collaboration, but the time-outs that are motivated by individuals needing to think through ideas will remain unchanged. The alternative is that these affective time-outs will increase because individuals will read each other's signals better and withdraw from the collaboration before the negative affect becomes too high. Whilst I know of no research that has addressed the first possibility, the second alternative is supported by research that has shown that friends are more likely than acquaintances to drop a conflict that they are having trouble resolving, and more likely than acquaintances to resume the interaction at some later point in time (Krappmann and Oswald 1987, Laursen and Hartup 1989).

It is important to consider that there is a high degree of variation in personal and work relationships. These variations have largely been ignored in current research, and thus I cannot address their import for collaborative cognition at this time. For example, not all friends work well together, and at times, acquaintances outperform friends. The nature of the task also affects the dynamics and outcomes of friends' collaborations, as was made evident by the case of Christine and Lynn. Recall that prior to participating in our study, Christine and Lynn had worked together successfully on a variety of projects. Yet, their collaboration broke down in our ill-formed task. While the time-outs they took from the collaboration may have helped them resume their interaction, they were unable to recreate the quality of discussion they had enjoyed prior to becoming frustrated with their lack of progress and with each other. Perhaps if our study had spanned more sessions, they would have been able to repair their differences and their collaborative cognition. Longitudinal research is needed to map the long-term cognitive and relational significance of time-outs in collaboration.

Researchers have also assumed that friend collaborators are less affected by status and personality variables than teacher–student, parent–child and worker groups (Azmitia and Montgomery 1993, Hartup 1996). This assumption needs to be reconsidered. For example, in the two studies we have carried out on collaborations between friends (Azmitia and Montgomery 1993, Azmitia and Crowley forthcoming), some friend pairs have shown clear status differences in their interaction. Although these differences in status have generally not been reliably associated with immediate post-test performances, it may be that in the long run, friend pairs who exhibit discrepancies in status (that is, one friend is clearly domi-nant over the other) may make less cognitive progress because they are less likely to question and debate their positions. Clearly, much work remains to be done to understand the relational aspects of collaborative cognitive development and the role of affect in these processes and outcomes.

## Summary and Conclusion

This chapter reviewed theory and research on collaborative cognition in its sociocultural context and advanced several proposals concerning the role of negative affect and frustration in collaborative cognitive development. The central point was that although these negative emotions can lead to time-outs from collaboration, these apparent disengagements can some-times have a positive effect on cognitive development because they allow individuals to work out ideas and manage their emotions. Not all time-outs from collaboration stem from negative affect, however. At times, these disengagements occur because the collaborative context has become too 'noisy' and individuals need time to think and puzzle over ideas.

Collaborators were portrayed as active, reflective individuals who select which aspects of the shared knowledge they incorporate in their individual theories. Whilst I did not devote much attention to this point, a challenge that we face in mapping the process of collaborative cognition and its selective appropriation by group members is that a significant amount of shared knowledge is appropriated relatively unconsciously – ideas are remembered because of participants' active engagement in the problem-solving process and not necessarily because they deployed memory strategies to encode the information. As the relatively large literature on flashbulb memories (for reviews, see Winograd and Neisser 1993), state-dependent learning (see Bower 1992, Christianson and Torun 1998) and eyewitness testimony has revealed (Ceci and Bruck 1993), high emotional loading can either enhance or impede spontaneous remembering. In the future, it would be interesting to incorporate some of the theoretical models and tasks from these and other areas of research which have considered affective processes in memory into our developmental accounts of collaborative cognitive development.

## Acknowledgements

The research reported in this chapter was supported by grants from the Social Sciences Division and the Academic Senate of the University of California at Santa Cruz. Nameera Akhtar and Barbara Rogoff provided valuable feedback on an earlier draft of this chapter. Address correspondence to Margarita Azmitia, Psychology Department, University of California, Santa Cruz, CA 95064, USA. Email: azmitia@cats.ucsc.edu

## Notes

1. John Dewey (1916) had made these same points earlier, but his work did not receive as much attention as Piaget's, Vygotsky's, or Mead's.
2. Only some of the following researchers would align themselves with the Sociocultural theoretical framework. I group them together because personal relationships constitute one of the most important social and cultural contexts of cognitive development.
3. Not their real names.
4. Christine was also Vietnamese.
5. Subsequently, Lynn enrolled in one of my courses and told me that although she and Christine had repaired their friendship and often enrolled in the same classes, they still avoided working together.
6. It is important to note that not all expressions of frustration led to disengagement from the collaboration. After 38% of the frustration episodes, the collaboration remained unchanged. For the remaining 62%, in 8% of the cases the partners renegotiated their working style or tried a new design, in 18% of the cases one partner withdrew into an onlooker role, and in 36% of the cases one person went to parallel work. It is the latter that were the focus of our analyses.
7. Not that all high-status members are unpleasant and idiosyncratic.

## References

Ames, G.J. and Murray, F.B. (1982). 'When 2 wrongs make a right: promoting cognitive change by social conflict'. *Developmental Psychology*, 18, 894–7.

Asch, S.E. (1956). 'Studies of independence and conformity: a minority of one against a unanimous majority'. *Psychological Monographs*, 70(9), (whole No. 416).

Azmitia, M. (1996). 'Peer interactive minds: developmental, theoretical, and methodological issues'. In P.B. Baltes and U.M. Staudinger (eds) *Interactive Minds: Lifespan perspectives on the social foundations of cognition* (pp. 133–62). New York: Cambridge University Press.

Azmitia, M. and Crowley, K. (forthcoming). 'The rhythms of scientific thinking: a study of collaboration in an earthquake microworld'. In K. Crowley, C.D. Schunn and T. Okada (eds) *Designing for Science: Implications from professional, instructional, and everyday science*. Mahwah, NJ: Lawrence Erlbaum.

Azmitia, M. and Montgomery, R. (1993). 'Friendship, transactive dialogues, and the development of scientific reasoning'. *Social Development*, 3, 202–21.

Azmitia, M. and Perlmutter, M. (1989). 'Social influences on children's cognition: state of the art and future directions'. In H.W. Reese (ed.) *Advances in Child Development and Behavior* (Vol. 22, pp. 89–114). New York: Academic Press.

Baker-Sennet, J., Matusov, E. and Rogoff, B. (1992). 'Sociocultural processes of creative planning in children's playcrafting'. In P. Light and G. Butterworth (eds) *Context and Cognition: Ways of learning and knowing* (pp. 93–114). New York: Harvester Wheatsheaf.

Bandura, A. (1977). *Social Learning Theory*. Englewood Cliffs, NJ: Prentice Hall.

Bearison, D.J. (1982). 'New directions in studies of social interaction and cognitive growth'. In F. Serafica (ed.) *Social Cognitive Development in Context* (pp. 199–221). New York: Guilford.

Bennis, W. and Biederman, P.W. (1997). *Organizing Genius. The secrets of creative collaboration*. Reading, MA: Addison-Wesley.

Bower, G.H. (1992). 'How might emotions affect learning?' In C. Sven-Ake (ed.) *The Handbook of Emotion and Memory: Research and theory* (pp. 3–31). Hillsdale, NJ: Lawrence Erlbaum.

Briggs, J.L. (1970). *Never in Anger: Portrait of an Eskimo family*. Cambridge, MA: Harvard University Press.

Brown, A.L., Bransford, J.D., Ferrara, R.A. and Campione, J.C. (1983). 'Learning, remembering, and understanding'. In J.H. Flavell and E.M. Markman (eds) *Handbook of Child Psychology* (Vol. 3). New York: Wiley.

Bruner, J.S. (1977). 'Early social interaction and language acquisition'. In H.R. Schaffer (ed.) *Studies in Mother–Infant Interaction* (pp. 271–89). London: Academic Press.

Callanan, M. and Jipson, J. (forthcoming). 'Explanatory conversations and young children's developing scientific literacy'. In K. Crowley, C.D. Schunn and T. Okada (eds) *Designing for Science: Implications from professional, instructional, and everyday science*. Mahwah, NJ: Lawrence Erlbaum.

Ceci, S.J. and Bruck, M. (1993). 'Suggestibility of the child witness: a historical review and synthesis'. *Psychological Bulletin*, 113, 403–69.

Christianson, S.A. and Torun, L. (1998). 'The fate of traumatic memories in childhood and adulthood'. *Developmental Psychology and Psychopathology*, 10, 761–80.

Cole, M. (1996). *Cultural Psychology: The once and future discipline*. Cambridge, MA: Harvard University Press.

Corsaro, W.A. (1994). 'Discussion, debate, and friendship processes: peer discourse in the US and Italian nursery schools'. *Sociology of Education*, 67, 1–26.

Csikszentmihalyi, M. and Sawyer, K. (1995). 'Creative insight: the social dimension of a solitary moment'. In R.J. Sternberg and J.E. Davidson (eds) *The Nature of Insight* (pp. 329–64). Cambridge, MA: MIT Press.

Dewey, J. (1916). *Democracy and Education*. New York: Macmillan.

Doise, W. and Mugny, G. (1979). 'Individual and collective conflicts of centrations and cognitive development'. *European Journal of Social Psychology*, 9, 105–9.

Doise, W. and Mugny, G. (1984). *The Social Development of the Intellect*. Oxford: Pergamon Press.

Dunbar, K. (1995). 'How scientists really reason: scientific reasoning in real-world laboratories'. In R.J. Sternberg and J.E. Davidson (eds) *The Nature of Insight* (pp. 265–396). Cambridge, MA: MIT Press.

Dunbar, K. (1997). 'Conceptual change in science'. In T.B. Ward, S.M. Smith and J. Vaid (eds) *Creative Thought: An investigation of conceptual structures and processes* (pp. 461–94). Washington, DC: American Psychological Association.

Faulkner, D., Littleton, K. and Woodhead, M. (1998). *Learning Relationships in the Classroom*. London: Routledge.

Goodnow, J.J. (1990). 'The socialization of cognition: what's involved?' In J. Stigler, R. Shweder and G. Herdt (eds) *Culture and Human Development* (pp. 259–86). Chicago: University of Chicago Press.

Graf, P., Carstensen, L.L., Weinert, F.E. and Shweder, R.A. (1996). 'Epilogue: reflections and future perspectives'. In P.B. Baltes and U.M. Staudinger (eds) *Interactive Minds: Life-span perspectives on the social foundation of cognition* (pp. 413–40). New York: Cambridge University Press.

Greenfield, P. and Lave, J. (1982). 'Cognitive aspects of informal education'. In D.A. Wagner and H.W. Stevenson (eds) *Cultural Perspectives on Child Development* (pp. 181–207). Oxford: Freeman.

Hartup, W.W. (1996). 'Cooperation, close relationships, and cognitive development'. In W.M. Bukowski, A.F. Newcomb and W.W. Hartup (eds) *The Company they Keep: Friendships and their developmental significance* (pp. 213–37). New York: Cambridge University Press.

Hatano, G. and Inagaki, K. (1991). 'Sharing cognition through collective comprehension activity'. In L.B. Resnick, J.M. Levine and S.D. Teasley (eds) *Perspectives on Socially Shared Cognition* (pp. 331–48). Washington, DC: APA Books.

Hutchins, E. and Paley, L. (1993). 'Constructing meaning from space, gesture, and talk'. Paper presented at the NATO-sponsored workshop Discourse, Tools, and Reasoning: Situated Cognition and Technologically Supported Environments. Lucca, Italy, November.

Janis, I.L. (1973). 'Groupthink'. *Yale Alumni Magazine*.

John-Steiner, V. (1985). *Notebooks of the Mind*. New York: Harper.

Klahr, D. and MacWhinney, B. (1998). 'Information processing'. In D. Kuhn and R.S. Siegler (eds) *Handbook of Child Psychology* (Vol. 2) *Cognition, Perception and Language* (pp. 631–79). New York: Wiley.

Krappmann, L. and Oswald, H. (1987). 'Negotiation strategies and peer conflicts: a follow-up study in natural settings'. Paper presented at the biennial meetings of the Society for Research in Child Development, Baltimore, MD, April.

Kuhn, D. (1995). 'Microgenetic study of change: what has it told us?' *Psychological Science*, 6, 133–9.

Kuhn, D., Amsel, E. and O'Loughlin, M. (1988). *The Development of Scientific Thinking Skills*. New York: Academic Press.

Kuhn, D. and Phelps, E. (1979). 'A methodology for observing development of a formal reasoning strategy'. *New Directions for Child Development*, 5, 45–58.

Laboratory of Comparative Human Cognition (1983). 'Culture and cognitive development'. In P.H. Mussen and W. Kessen (eds) *Handbook of Child Psychology* (Vol. 1) *History, Theory and Methods* (pp. 295–356). New York: Wiley.

Laursen, B. and Hartup, W.W. (1989). 'The dynamics of preschool children's conflicts'. *Merrill-Palmer Quarterly*, 35, 281–97.

Lave, J. and Wenger, E. (1991). *Situated Learning*. Cambridge: Cambridge University Press.

Mead, G.H. (1934). *Mind, Self, and Society*. Chicago: IL: University of Chicago Press.

Nelson, J. and Aboud, F. (1985). 'The resolution of social conflict between friends'. *Child Development*, 56, 1000–17.

Ninio, A. (1973). 'Joint book reading as a multiple vocabulary acquisition device'. *Developmental Psychology*, 19, 445–51.

Perret-Clermont, A.-N. (1980). *Social Interaction and Cognitive Development in Children*. London: Academic Press.

Piaget, J. (1932). *The Moral Judgment of the Child*. Glencoe, IL: Free Press.

Pozzi, S., Healey, L. and Hoyles, L. (1993). 'Learning and interaction in groups with computers: when do ability and gender matter?' *Social Development*, 2, 222–41.

Rogoff, B. (1998). 'Cognition as a collaborative process'. In D. Kuhn and R.S. Siegler (eds) *Handbook of Child Psychology* (Vol. 2) *Cognition, Perception and Language* (pp. 679–744). New York: Wiley.

Rogoff, B. and Toma, C. (1997). 'Shared thinking: community and institutional variations'. *Discourse Processes*, 23, 471–97.

Rogoff, B. and Wertsch, J.V. (eds) (1984). *Children's Learning in the Zone of Proximal Development*. San Francisco, CA: Jossey Bass.

Siegler, R.S. (1996). *Emerging Minds: The process of change in children's thinking*. New York: Oxford University Press.

Siegler, R.S. and Crowley, K. (1991). 'The microgenetic method: a direct means for studying cognitive development'. *American Psychologist*, 46, 606–20.

Staudinger, U. (1996). 'Wisdom and the social-interactive foundation of mind'. In P.B. Baltes and U. Staudinger (eds) *Interactive Minds: Life-span perspectives on the social foundations of cognition* (pp. 276–315). New York: Cambridge University Press.

Suchman, L. (1993). 'Centers of coordination: a case and some themes'. Paper presented at the NATO-sponsored workshop Discourse, Tools, and Reasoning: Situated Cognition and Technologically Supported Environments. Lucca, Italy, November.

Tharp, R. and Gallimore, R. (1988). *Rousing Minds to Life*. New York: Cambridge University Press.

Vygotsky, L.S. (1929). 'The problem of the cultural development of the child'. *Journal of Genetic Psychology*, 36, 415–34.

Vygotsky, L.S. (1978). *Mind and Society*. Cambridge, MA: Harvard University Press.

Watson, J.D. (1968). *The Double Helix: A personal account of the discovery of the structure of DNA*. New York: Atheneum.

Wertsch, J.V. (1997). *Mind in Action*. New York: Oxford University Press.

Wertsch, J.V., Minick, N. and Arns, F. (1984). 'The creation of context in joint problem solving'. In B. Rogoff and J. Lave (eds) *Everyday Cognition: Its development in social context* (pp. 151–71). Cambridge, MA: Harvard University Press.

Winograd, E. and Neisser, U. (1993). *Affect and Accuracy of Recall: Studies of flashbulb memories*. New York: Cambridge University Press.

Wood, D.J. (1980). 'Teaching the young child: some relationships between social interaction, language, and thought'. In D. Olson (ed.) *The Social Foundations of Language and Thought* (pp. 280–98). New York: Norton.

# Part V
# Making Space for Collaborative Learning

# 12
## Up for Debate: CMC as a Support for Collaborative Learning in a Campus University Setting

Vivienne Light, Paul Light, Emma Nesbitt and Stevan Harnad

### Introduction

With institutions putting an ever-increasing emphasis on computer-assisted learning and computer-mediated communication (CMC), place and space for 'face to face' is in danger of being ousted from the timetable. It is increasingly argued that, to survive, all universities will have to cross the 'e-line' into internationally competitive, IT-based online learning (for example, Oblinger 1999). Such a move implies change in the process of learning and in the roles played by both staff and students within universities and other higher education (HE) institutions.

Rosenberg (1999) suggests that the interactive and virtual nature of online education is transforming the traditional role of the teacher into that of 'information and knowledge facilitator' and 'technical integrator'. Riel (1995) has likewise argued that the technology leads to a shift in role for the tutor, from being controller of information to intellectual leader. The tutor's task, these authors suggest, becomes that of structuring challenging conversations among a community of learners rather than channelling expertise and knowledge to the student. The reference to a community of learners points up the sense in which, in such a context, learning is a *communal* rather than simply an individual process. Our interest, in this chapter, is to address some of the ways in which CMC can support a more communal learning experience in a campus-based university setting.

Of course, the successful promotion of collaborative learning experiences depends at least as much on the pedagogic style, approach and assumptions of tutors as it does on the affordances of the teaching/learning medium (Light et al. 2000b). Many of the key social skills needed for nurturing online collaboration are not specific to the CMC environment. Rather 'they are the skills needed by any tutor, facilitator ... involved in any peer learning situation' (Kaye 1991). Some tutors will be better than others in designing and implementing group learning experiences. Harasim et al. (1995) suggest that those who find themselves comfortable with the basic premises of peer learning and small-group work (in the face-to-face situation) will adapt well to the CMC environment.

Moreover, provision of CMC course support resources does not in itself guarantee any sort of transformation of students' learning experiences. Typically the tutor not only has to make the CMC resources available to students but also has to 'sell' their usefulness for supporting communication and collaboration before learners will take advantage of them. Crook (1997) reports on students' use of hypertext lecture notes, which were supported by a bulletin board and email facility designed to facilitate interaction and questioning in relation to the notes. He found that although the students read the notes and regarded them as a valuable resource, none used the bulletin board for discussion and few used the email launcher.

These observations suggest that interactivity rarely occurs spontaneously, even in a well-supported CMC environment. Rather, it usually requires a facilitator to engineer and maintain it. This facilitator is usually the tutor, whose task is to create a context within which there can be shared goals, interests and commitments (Kaye 1991). Inevitably, the direct engagement of tutors is likely to influence the kind of discussion that takes place. Even where tutors are wholly absent from the CMC discussion, the way in which they have framed the activity may be a significant factor influencing the course of discussion. Light et al. (2000a) describe a case in which the tutor was absent from CMC-based discussions taking place in parallel groups of students. The style of contribution was relaxed and linguistically varied. However, there were also instances of 'flaming', when selected participants were personally targeted with offensive messages. Such instances can have a very disruptive effect on the whole group, and prejudice the likelihood of useful learning outcomes.

The relationship between the CMC resource and other available learning resources is important, as is the relation of all learning resources to the curriculum and assessment of the course. The CMC element has to be embedded in the whole course rather than being merely an 'add-on'. This chapter uses linked case studies to explore the ways in which one particular approach to 'CMC in HE' impacted on connections amongst and between students, their tutor and their learning.

## Skywriting

The study reported here shows how one tutor teaching psychology undergraduate students in a campus-based university set about such a task, and reviews the outcomes from both the tutor's and the students' perspective. Earlier research (Light et al. 1997, Light and Light 1999) with the same cohort of students meant that the researchers had data from students who had been in their first year and were now presently in their third, thus providing a relatively rich context for the study.[1]

The tutor in this study developed a form of CMC that he called 'Skywriting' (Harnad 1990, 1995, 1999). He did not invent the 'original, original term' which was 'for writing in the sky, for the aeroplanes', but he appropriated it for scholarly use in 1990, labelling it 'Scholarly Skywriting'. Under this heading he was interested in setting up 'pre-print archives and electronic journals' for academic debate. Following on from this, in 1994, the tutor set up 'Student Skywriting' for collaborative use by any student registered on his courses. The content of student skywriting was intended to be 'intellectual discussion rather than flaming and chit-chat'. From the beginning the tutor saw student skywriting as an adjunct to his teaching rather than a replacement. He hoped its use would encourage sustenance of a collaborative learning environment outside of the classroom.

This chapter reports on the use of student skywriting on three courses; one in the first year and two in the third year. Each course ran for one semester. The first-year course was a lecture- and tutorial-based course for the whole cohort of students. Of the third-year courses, the first was a seminar-based optional course, whilst the second was a lecture-based course for the whole cohort. The seminar course took place in the first semester and the lecture course in the second. Skywriting was an integral part of each course. Contributions from all students were required although they were not directly assessed.

All skywriting messages were posted to a course email list that included all students and the tutor. As well as receiving all messages directly, participants could access them via the Internet, where the tutor archived them using Hypermail at regular intervals. Accessed in this way, the messages could be sorted by author, date or (most usefully) subject thread. Students were encouraged to use a quote/comment procedure. To do this the students would save the text into a text file in a word processor and then select the lines of text they were going to comment on, using '>' quote/indents. URLs contained in messages became active hypertext links.

In guiding the students as to the style and level of contributions expected, the tutor asked the students to write in 'Kid-Sib' mode, by having in mind a 'super-intelligent younger sibling' who was 'brilliant, fervently interested in finding out what you've learnt, but COMPLETELY ignorant about it, and with no patience at all when what you are saying doesn't make sense'. The tutor said that his version of Kid-Sib was but one of many. In one posting he cited late Nobel-Laureate physicist Richard Feynman's version of Kid-Sib: 'Imagine that you are explaining your ideas to your former, smart but ignorant, self at the beginning of your studies.' Underlying the use of Kid-Sib was the premise, as put by one student: 'If you can't explain it in simple terms you probably don't understand it.' Very quickly the students learnt that asking for a Kid-Sib explanation from their tutor was a useful device. For example, one third-year lecture student wrote: 'I'm tying myself in knots over "inverse fallacy", any chance of a kid-sib explanation?'

Apart from academic postings, skywriting was also used to deliver administrative notices, technical tips, advice for exams, and so on. The students were eventually to find it easy to mix the academic with the social, as for example in the posting: 'i.m having problems accessing the hidden comms directory ... what do I do?! Also what's going on with the 3rd year party?'

## A First-Year Lecture Course

The study was conducted at a UK campus-based university. Almost all students were full-time residential students. 'Explaining the Mind'[2] was a first-year lecture course taken by some 80 Psychology Honours students (plus 50 other students) in 1996. A full account of the use made of skywriting on this course is available in Light and Light (1999); a briefer account will be given here to contextualise the account of the same students' use of skywriting in two of their third-year courses.

Skywriting was offered as a supplement to the traditional structure of the course, namely two lectures a week and a fortnightly tutorial in groups of about ten. Students were encouraged to use skywriting to ask questions and to enter into debate with the tutor and fellow students about issues arising in the lectures or tutorials.

Over three-quarters of the students were straight from school, the remainder being mature students, mostly in their thirties. Three-quarters were female. A questionnaire measure of attitudes to, and prior experience with, computers (based on Davis and Cole 1993) was administered to all students on entry to the Psychology programme. There was an overall gender difference in self-reported prior experience (males reporting more), but attitudes to computers were equally positive in both groups. A complete 'round' of tutorials was observed and tape-recorded, from which a measure of the frequency of unsolicited verbal contributions by students was obtained. Male students, though a minority, made on average more than twice as many such contributions as female students.

Turning to the frequency with which the students used the skywriting facility (measured at the halfway point in the 12-week course), only about 40% of the students made multiple contributions in this medium (range 2–12 messages). The female students made just as much use of skywriting as the males, and neither attitude to computers nor the self-reported experience with computers was predictive of extent of use of skywriting.

A measure of learning style, the Revised Approaches to Study Inventory (Tait and Entwhistle 1996) was administered to a subset of 24 students; 12 of whom had contributed actively to the skywriting, and 12 who had not. The active 'skywriters' scored significantly higher on the index of deep approaches to study. Frequency of skywriting contributions also showed a modest but significant positive correlation with assessment outcomes on the course, whereas frequency of face-to-face tutorial contributions did not.

The skywriting contributions themselves tended to be short (c. 100 words) and usually took the form of a question addressed to the course tutor. Almost all were replied to, the result being that almost half the messages on the list were from the tutor. Few student contributions expressed opinions, and few drew any response from fellow students.

Interviews with 19 students (11 active contributors and 8 non-active) highlighted the advantages of skywriting for those students too 'slow off the mark' or too reserved to make much input to the group tutorials. At the same time, the students were very conscious of their peers as audience when using skywriting. Whereas their messages were for the most part questions directed at the tutor, they were clearly concerned that any silly mistakes they might make, or any withering response from the tutor, might 'show them up' in front of their peers. Moreover, they were using other students' messages as a basis for social comparison, gauging how well they themselves were doing relative to their peers.

Though the balance of student opinion at the end of the course was quite favourable to skywriting, the overwhelming majority preferred face-to-face tutorials. The immediacy of response and the continuity of discussion figured prominently amongst the perceived advantages of traditional tutorials.

Reflecting back on this first-year lecture course, the tutor said that he had introduced skywriting very much as an 'enthusiast'. Use of online discussion was not common amongst other tutors in the department, and certainly not amongst the students (Light et al. 1997). The tutor recalled their 'initial resistance ... about computers themselves'. He almost had to 'blackmail' students into posting 'at least one message ... and then a second ... it was a bit like pulling teeth'.

The breakthrough came when he used skywriting to offer a pre-seen exam of 76 questions for the students to answer as practice. This seemed to break the ice. However, it made him realise that if all of the students became very active it could rapidly become overwhelming for him as a tutor. During the course semester the tutor did indeed make a lot of postings, 166 in total.

To make economic sense of his online time answering questions, he thought it a good idea to build a data resource. Thus he developed Frequently Asked Question (FAQ) files which could be archived through hypermail link to other skywriting files: 'so they loop through one another's material'. Thus students could be redirected to a file which already contained the answer to their question. This meant that when answering a question for the first time it was worthwhile to 'grandstand a little bit ... [otherwise] I wouldn't have taken the trouble to answer one student quite that extensively'.

Certainly the students made good use of the tutor's postings. Everyone read them, including those who made no contributions of their own. However, the tutor regretted that he was perceived as the main 'interlocutor'. He wanted skywriting to be more interactive, with student-to-student as well as student-to-tutor exchanges. He hoped this would happen in the later seminar options, where there were relatively few students and where discussion arising from weekly meetings could carry over into skywriting.

The students involved on this course were new to university study and new to skywriting. The tutor was also new to using skywriting in this way with students. The opportunity to return to this same group of students being taught by the same tutor two years later thus afforded a chance to look at how experience impacts on both students' and tutor's use of this type of CMC resource.

### A Third-Year Seminar Course

Fourteen students enrolled for a final-year seminar course entitled 'Sociobiology and cognition'.[3] Students met weekly for seminars and took turns in presenting to the group a synopsis of a book or articles they had read in the preceding week. Following this, the same students then used skywriting to post a summary version of their presentation, taking account of the class discussion. Everyone was invited to comment on it online, using the quote/comment procedure. The tutor also encouraged the students, as in the first year, to post him if something came up during the tutorial session 'and we don't get a chance to cover it to your satisfaction'.

As with the first study, the researchers used a multi-method approach to collect data. They attended three of the seminars. These were each 1 hour

40 minutes long. They were introduced to the students by the tutor and the students were apprised of the nature of the research project. The researchers' names were added to the skywriting course list so they had instant access to all online contributions. The three seminars were audio-taped and observation notes were taken.

At the end of the course the students completed a standard course evaluation questionnaire for the tutor. They were asked to evaluate course content, course organisation and tutor contribution on a scale of 1–5 (strongly agree to strongly disagree). The anonymous responses were made available to the researchers. The researchers then invited students to individual interviews of between 20 and 30 minutes. Of the 14 students, 12 accepted this invitation. They were asked to look back to their first-year use of skywriting and to compare it with their most recent use. All interviews were transcribed and analysed qualitatively.

Initial analysis of the data from the three seminars attended, along with the accompanying skywriting contributions, showed that not all the students contributed to seminar discussions (five making no verbal contribution at all). All of the students contributed to skywriting, although only half of them had done so on the year-one course. As one student reflected, it 'didn't seem to be like a duty or a threat, something you *must* do. Instead it just comes out [that] I *should* do it.'

The students not only felt a commitment to their peers to make contributions but they also felt their contributions should be good: 'I always make sure it's a decent message, and that I've thought about it and planned it out.' The use of skywriting seemed to reinforce relationships: 'I know people better than in my other seminar class' (where skywriting was not used). It created 'a sense of community' within which they could 'get the idea of what everyone else is thinking'. They also appreciated the practical 'efficiency gains' of sharing the reading load, which they all felt was heavy.

The students' contributions showed an effective use of skywriting both as a tool for summarising tutorial discussions and as a tool for critique. A somewhat less formal tone was apparent between student and tutor; for example: 'Sorry, I've had a delay getting back to you via e-mail but right now I have been immersed in lots of reading and very little analysing. Luckily, your points left me doing an awful lot of further thinking, which is a great help!' In what followed, the same student offered opinions, started sentences with, for example, 'I agree ...', 'I admit I'm still not sure ...', 'Why should it matter ...?', and ended with 'Let me get back to you on that one!'

Many of the skywriting ideas were picked up on in the face-to-face seminar sessions and vice versa. Skywriting, as one student put it, 'gets more of a debate going amongst people'. This contrasted with other seminar courses where students aimed to 'score lots of marks because you said what the lecturer wants you to say'. However, it 'had taken the whole course for people to work out how best to use skywriting'.

The students saw the point of the Kid-Sib analogy: 'If you can't explain it in simple terms you probably don't understand it.' When writing messages, only three of the students said they primarily directed them to the tutor; seven others said they were intended for everyone, whilst two students relied equivocally. Altogether, the 14 students contributed 74 messages and the tutor contributed 33. The balance differs from the first year, where the tutor contributed as many messages as the students, but still reflects a high level of participation by the tutor. The students were appreciative of his active role: '[He] keeps us on the right lines because I think sometimes we do go off on a tangent'; '[He] guides us towards the right frame of mind.' However, this did not mean that the tutor was 'chairing' the discussion: 'He gives input but he doesn't really structure the discussions.' In contrast, in face-to-face seminar sessions the tutor definitely took a structuring role in discussion.

All the students found the skywriting postings useful for exam revision and accessed them from the archive. One student would regularly 'download the messages onto a disk then take it home, sift through it and delete all the bits that are rubbish and keep all the good bits' and then 'just print them out and revise from them adding my own comments'. Of the twelve students interviewed, nine owned their own computers, though only three of these were networked.

In contrast with the first year, peer contributions came to be regarded by the students as a valuable resource for learning. 'When you've read an article you've [only] got your own understanding of it. But if you go on the skywriting and read loads of other people's commentaries it puts things together. The fact that it's all grouped into different categories [lets] you see where the course is going and where you are going in your reasoning.' However, there was still some irritation about contributions which took them 'down the wrong road', as this was 'a waste of time'.

Compared to the first year, there was less concern about the public nature of the system: 'If you get things wrong you get things wrong.' One student who was initially worried about everyone reading her comments said at the end: 'I think that's a good thing ... because ... instead of writing a paragraph of useless drivel you actually go away and research.' All agreed that working within a small group, 'you feel more confident' – 'In the first year [there were] so many more people, but with a seminar you do know the people in the group so if you cock it up or say something really stupid nobody really minds.'

However, the social comparison aspect of skywriting was still significant for the students. One commented that other people's errors gave him 'confidence that not everybody else is completely understanding everything'. The students were reticent 'to criticise somebody else' when skywriting. This contrasts with the seminars: 'In class you can back down, you can say fair enough or whatever.'

The third-year students were also much less concerned than they had been two years earlier about being 'shown up' by the tutor's response to their messages. In part, they thought that this was because the tutor had changed his style of response. One student suggested that the tutor had 'toned it down a lot ... In the first year he used to say "No, that's completely wrong" and you'd think, "Oh my God!" Now he says "No, but ..." or "It was a very good try, but ...", so it's useful.' Another student referred to first-year replies from the tutor as a 'bit of a hacksaw ... but [he] now appreciates your ideas and your questions'. The extent to which this is a matter of changing student perceptions or of higher-quality student contributions is hard to judge, but the tutor certainly felt that the change was more in the students than in his own behaviour.

The students perceived skywriting as complementary to face-to-face tutorials. The latter allowed for 'immediate reactions' and immediate explanations, whilst the former gave them a chance to 'have ideas continually ticking over' throughout the week. It seems that working within a smaller group the students were able to evolve a way of working that drew the best from both learning environments. The course evaluation questionnaires gave high ratings for the course and particularly for the tutor. The tutor later described this group as a particularly good one, resulting from: 'self-selection ... These were the ones who were up to it ... they were all top students.' Seven of the students indeed obtained first-class marks on the course.

The seminar topics chosen by the tutor were 'explicitly about controversial things'. He observed that 'because it's socio-biology of cognition which is controversial as well [as] relatively new ... it produced several zealots ... people who ended up being more bullish about socio-biology and cognition than I was'. Towards the end of the course, the tutor felt that they had succeeded in '[bringing] down a few intellectual barriers', with students becoming actively engaged in debate. He felt that skywriting had helped to get away from the 'school ethos' to something 'much more level' between tutor and students.

However, this was only a matter of degree. The students still tended to pit their arguments against the tutor rather than against their peers. Overall, the tutor was still regarded as the expert. The students remained more interested in *his* contributions, in *his* responses and *his* ideas on the ambiguities left over from the class, than in those of their peers. There would undoubtedly have been fewer readers if there had been no tutor contributions; the tutor was the 'catalyst'. There remained a lurking suspicion that peer contributions were 'a bit suspect'. Overall, though, the students were confident users of skywriting and made good use of it for shared learning.

## A Third-Year Lecture Course

'Current Debates'[4] was a compulsory lecture course taken by 80 students in the second semester of the third year, tackling a range of contentious issues in contemporary psychology. Skywriting was again a required, although not an assessed, part of the course. The tutor's aim in using it was 'to increase student contribution' rather than student querying, and 'to elicit more student-on-student comments'.

To this end, the tutor decided to reformat the skywriting structure for this course. The course itself was based around target articles and peer commentaries from the journal *Behavioral and Brain Sciences* (*BBS*). Thus the basic reading material consisted of ten *BBS* target articles (plus peer commentaries and author responses). This material was accessible via the web, although hard copies were available in the library. Each student's task was to 'quote/comment on a few assigned pages out of three of the ten *BBS* article/commentary/response sets'.

For example, in the first assignment seven students were asked to quote/comment on particular parts of the target article, and then seven more were asked to reply to these comments. Four other students were asked to quote/comment on specified *BBS* peer commentaries, with four more students replying. Lastly, two students were asked to quote/comment on the *BBS* author response with two further students replying.

Thus, altogether this assignment called for 26 student contributions. There were ten assignments in all. The smooth running of the assignments depended on the first students getting their commentaries in on time, as without these the following students could not do theirs.

At the first lecture the researchers were once again introduced to the students and were added to the online course list. By now they were familiar faces to many of the students, having spent some time in the department. The researchers attended four of the ten lectures, which were very interactive in style and drew upon the skywriting contributions. At the last lecture attendance was relatively poor, perhaps due to impending examinations, but the 42 students present completed a course evaluation questionnaire. This was completed anonymously and copies were made available to the researchers. Of the 42 students, 37 also returned a (non-anonymous) research questionnaire focusing on the use of skywriting on the course.

The students were asked to evaluate on a numerical scale of 1–5 (strongly agree to strongly disagree) how well skywriting had worked for them: for their understanding of course material, as support for face-to-face learning, for exam preparation, and so on. The questionnaire contained a tick box to indicate a willingness to participate in individual interviews. Twelve were selected, to include all those (five) who had taken the 'Sociobiology' option, plus seven drawn at random from those who had not, but who had attended the first-year lecture course.

The semi-structured interviews lasted about 20 minutes each and the students were encouraged to reflect on how their attitude to skywriting had changed (if at all) since the first year, and the effects (if any) of having had more experience of using it. Further issues of learning were also explored. Again, all interviews were transcribed and subjected to qualitative analysis. Finally the tutor gave an interview of an hour and a half in which he reflected on his use of skywriting with the students in their first and third years. This interview was audiotaped and transcribed. The interview topics arose from observed events from the past year. Additional sources of material were the researchers' observations and notes from course attendance and more informal discussions with the tutor.

In the first lecture when the tutor introduced and explained the procedure, he asked the experienced skywriters amongst them to lead small-group revision sessions on how to use quote/comment for skywriting. This took place in the lecture theatre. However, the tutor received feedback from some students that they were still confused, so he emailed a summary to the course list. He identified the first 26 students (alphabetically), assigned each a specific task in relation to the first target article, and added tips for transferring the text from the web to the email so that it could be quoted/commented on.

The next message from the tutor contained the next assignment plus messages/reminders for those who had not yet done their first assignments. Inevitably many were late, thus holding up the others. The tutor afterwards described the whole procedure as 'grotesquely convoluted'. As the course progressed it became increasingly time-consuming to keep track of who had done what. Towards the end of the semester, with exams nearing, the tutor had to give more reminders about missing assignments. At one point there were 28 overdue contributions. Tutor contributions were relatively few, though some were long where he felt additional input was needed (the longest reply to a student query was about 2000 words).

By monitoring the skywriting contributions closely, the tutor attempted to spot difficulties and to sort matters out earlier rather than later. For example, when some were having difficulty producing quote/comment contributions, he gave them a model for doing so. He consistently emphasised that the task was not to memorise the text but to interact with it. Learning in any medium, he argued, starts with a structure. In a lecture he said: 'With books it is often underlining words, while with emails you can "just sit and absorb"', and 'slot in new learning like a lego block'. Not all of his students found reading off a screen easy, however. Many commented that prolonged reading from the screen hurt their eyes. This was certainly not a new complaint from the students, and is indeed a problem for many computer users.

The students realised from the beginning that, although they would gain tutor approval from being actively involved in skywriting, there were no real marks at stake. Thus the tutor 'sold' skywriting using different tactics. One example was when he replied to a student query in a lecture about how to gain good exam marks. His answer was that for a 'lower second' they should bring in readings from the target article and commentaries; for an 'upper second' they should use the target articles, commentaries and lectures and for a 'first' they should use all of the former sources plus skywriting.

However, the tutor also felt the need to make it clear that they couldn't just depend on skywriting to get them through the course. Indeed, near exam time he put out a warning that it 'would be VERY risky to try the exam having read only the skywriting as not only will it be incomplete, but some of it may well be wrong. So use it to test your knowledge (and to discuss if you like) but DON'T use student summaries as your primary source.'

Overall student evaluation of skywriting in 'Current Debates' was positive. The research questionnaire showed that most students felt it had worked well in a number of ways. It had improved understanding of the course and worked well as a support for the face-to-face sessions. In contrast to the first year, the students reported that they found the contributions of their peers useful: 68% said that skywriting comments on target articles were useful, and 55% said the same of student responses to student commentaries: 'I will be going to the commentaries and ... look what people have said about it as well ... it is good to have it as a resource.'

Notably, the students reported less reliance on skywriting contributions from their tutor than on the (much more numerous) contributions from their peers. This may partly have been because the tutor 'said at the beginning he was trying to avoid commenting ... trying to find a happy medium'. However, one student did comment that 'without the tutor ... I think [participation] would have dropped [to] about 40 or 50% of the class'.

Not surprisingly, given the course structure, students reported a heavy reliance on the web and little reliance on books/printed journals: 'I don't need to [rely on books] which is really good ... [it's a] nightmare trying to find books.' Compared to their first year, these students were feeling altogether more comfortable with CMC. As one student commented: '[We] had to get over that phobia of technology ... now [we] use it a lot.'

The size of the group was seen as a problem, particularly by those who had used skywriting in the seminar option: 'It's so big you can't have that interaction ... people are commenting but they are not just sending questions to each other, whereas last semester we were just sending questions to each other all the time'; 'A small group of eight or ten seems like the ideal size because it's enough people that you are not going to be intimidated by.'

In spite of the positive feedback, the tutor felt that he had not achieved his objective in using skywriting, 'because all they did was their little, microscopic module'. His feeling was that the students had not engaged thoroughly with the material, often 'sounding off with only 20% of the information'. He 'very rarely saw someone that had mastered the material'.

If he ran 'Current Debates' again, rather than trying to force them to do 'a paraphrase, of some material' he would try to get them to 'dig their teeth ... actively into the subject matter', 'to focus them and keep them involved in several more iterations'. What was evident was that what the students gained the most from was 'being more actively involved with the subject matter', rather than 'passively listening to my answering questions ... or producing semi-authoritative summaries', of which others were sometimes mistrustful.

In this way, he believes, skywriting can change the way the students think, not least by keeping the debate alive throughout the week, rather than, as one student put it, 'just turning up on Tuesday'. By using 'a discipline of writing for posterity' the students might be brought to think of these things differently: 'Once they get an insight they get a different vantage point on the same thing. They now listen, they can see their fellow students [as] naive in a way that they are no longer naive.'

## Discussion

Most of the students we have observed in these case studies experienced skywriting only in one first-year and one final-year course. A minority experienced skywriting in three of their courses, but these taken together still made up a small part of their studies. Some of their other courses used email lists, but 'just to say about room changes etcetera'.

The mere fact of *having* to participate in skywriting had evidently helped many students to overcome their fear of computers and technology. 'You are made to do it and then you finally get to do it and now ... it's so much better.' This confidence building was helped by the tutor's willingness to give his students time and to extend their computer skills and knowledge: 'He just sat me down and showed me how to use it and then I went away and it made everything so much quicker.' By the end of the third year most were confident users, 'using the net quite a lot' for their dissertation and project. One student 'actually emailed authors because I couldn't find the articles'.

One effect of using skywriting has been social. 'We've started talking about it outside the lectures, getting people talking, that's what's been nice … the whole atmosphere, it's like a breaking of ice. I felt this year I've just been talking to so many more people within the year … because you read their skywriting comments you are more likely to just say Hi!'; 'You can just speak with people as you wouldn't have done before because you've heard their name, all the sorts of contacts have become a little bit more diverse.' The students were interested in what others have to say and felt encouraged to talk about their skywriting contributions. Much of this interaction took place in the computer room of the department. 'Everybody will sit in the computer room and either do it [skywriting] at the same time or they'll talk about what they are going to do or you have interactions with who's commenting on you.'

Using skywriting they have come to appreciate the benefits of having: 'somebody arguing with you', as it helps 'to crystallise things'. They have also become shrewd judges of whose contributions to look out for. One student described this as 'the filtering effect': 'You pick up on the people who have got the grasp of this subject and you think "Oh!, I'll read her – she's good at this".' Thus they have learnt to take the best from their peers whilst at the same time feeling a commitment to make good contributions themselves. For most on the course, learning has become a less solitary experience: 'Talking amongst ourselves is very important but is only done in relation to [this tutor's] course.'

Both in the first year and the third, the students were interested in each other's contributions, even when some were sceptical of their validity and worth. In part this was because they provided a basis for social comparison, establishing where they stood in the intellectual hierarchy. A corollary of this was an anxiety about being 'shown up'. Such fears seemed to be allayed by time and familiarity with each other. By the third year, as one student put it, 'They know where you are coming from, know that you are not stupid. If you say something that's nonsense, they won't think "This person is dim".' Such confidence was particularly apparent amongst those who had used skywriting in the third-year seminar option.

The tutor felt that, over the three years, skywriting helped to build a relationship between himself and his students: 'There was a kind of a shared intellectual mission sense that I got, and I think it was to a great extent because of skywriting.' In the first year he was skywriting a few hours a day, typically late at night. 'When they were coming fast and furious they were getting answers within 24 hours, within 12 hours some of them and that's when it was the most enjoyable. It was stressful and taxing [but] I also think it was fruitful.' In the third-year course he was less intensively involved, but he felt that skywriting 'brought down a few barriers ... You can be with students for three years and never have one intellectual spark, and I got the feeling that a little bit more of that did happen.' Using skywriting didn't cut down on room visits by students; in fact, the effect was the opposite: 'They come to see me a little bit more than they did without it.'

Skywriting, then, did not make students more independent of their tutor – quite the contrary, in fact. However, as we have seen, skywriting did eventually change the relationship of students with one another, with their tutor and with their learning in quite significant ways. Their experience of learning was less private, as was their engagement with the tutor. Their sense of belonging to 'a learning community' was enhanced. There are indications too that their sense of their discipline as 'process rather than product' was strengthened by the experience. The evidence on this point is by no means clear-cut, but it is perhaps here that the critical potential of 'CMC in HE' really lies.

## Notes

1. http://www.cogsci.soton.ac.uk/~harnad/Hypermail/
2. http://www.cogsci.soton.ac.uk/~harnad/Hypermail/Explaining.Mind97/
3. http://cogsci.soton.ac.uk/~harnad/Hypermail/Cognition.Sociobiology.98/
4. http://cogsci.soton.ac.ul/~harnad/Hypermail/Debates98/

## References

Crook, C. (1997). 'Making hypertext lecture notes more interactive: undergraduate reactions'. *Journal of Computer Assisted Learning*, 13, 236–44.
Davis, N. and Cole, D. (1993). 'Students' IT experience on entry to initial teacher education'. Report to the Association for Information Technology in Teacher Education, Croydon.
Harasim, L., Hiltz, S.R., Teles, L. and Turoff, M. (1995). *Learning Networks: A field guide to teaching and learning online*. Cambridge, MA: MIT Press.
Harnad, S. (1990). 'Scholarly skywriting and the prepublication continuum of scientific inquiry'. *Psychological Science*, 1, 342–3.
Harnad, S. (1995). 'Interactive cognition: exploring the potential of electronic quote/commenting'. In B. Gorayska and J.L. Mey (eds) *Cognitive Technology: In search of a humane interface*. Amsterdam: Elsevier.
Harnad, S. (1999). 'The future of scholarly skywriting'. In A. Scammell (ed.) *i in the sky: Visions of the information future*. London: Aslib.

Kaye, K. (1991). 'Learning together apart'. In A.R. Kaye (ed.) *Collaborative Learning through Computer Conferencing*. London: Springer-Verlag.

Light, P., Colbourn, C. and Light, V. (1997). 'Computer mediated tutorial support for conventional university courses'. *Journal of Computer Assisted Learning*, 13, 228–35.

Light, P. and Light, V. (1999). 'Analysing asynchronous interactions: computer-mediated communication in a conventional undergraduate setting'. In K. Littleton and P. Light (eds) *Learning with Computers: Analysing productive interaction* (pp. 162–79). London: Routledge.

Light, V., Nesbitt, E., Light, P. and Burns, R. (2000a). '"Let's you and me have a little discussion": computer-mediated communication in support of campus-based university courses'. *Studies in Higher Education*, 25(1) 85–96.

Light, V., Nesbitt, E., Light, P. and White, S. (2000b). 'Variety is the spice of life: computer communication in support of campus-based university courses'. *Computers and Education* 34(3/4), 257–68.

Oblinger, D. (1999). 'What's the connection?' *Guardian Higher Education*, 25 May, p. vii.

Riel, M. (1995). 'Cross-classroom collaboration in global learning circles'. In S. Star (ed.) *The Cultures of Computing* Oxford: Blackwell.

Rosenberg, H. (1999). 'Virtuality and interactivity: the changing roles of teachers and students'. *Proceedings of CAL 99: Virtuality in Education. What are the future educational contexts?* Available: http://www.elsevier.nl/homepage/sag/Cal99/output/abs82

Tait, H. and Entwhistle, N. (1996). 'Identifying students at risk through ineffective study strategies'. *Higher Education*, 31, 97–116.

# 13
# Technological Mediation of Synchronous Collaboration: Science and Statistics in SharedARK and KANSAS

*Eileen Scanlon, Tim O'Shea, Randall B. Smith and Richard Joiner*

## Introduction

This chapter discusses the implications of a ten-year series of experiments designed to explore the usefulness of the technological mediation of collaborative problem solving. The components of the technological mediation are access to shared simulations and access to a variety of means of communication with co-workers. These means of communication range from audio contact only to video conferencing with full eye contact. The context for this work is the desire to make the future use of such technologies by distance learners as effective as possible. Over the period in which these experiments have been run, there have been developments in the extent to which such technologies are available and affordable for schools and colleges. A simultaneous trend in science education has led to an increase in the use of simulations and virtual experimentation.

In these preliminary experiments we identified an appropriate problem and task domain for use in testing this innovative new software technology, and explored and developed an appropriate evaluation methodology. The research approach explored in these studies and developed in the further programme of work was exploratory. It consisted of the selection of a hard problem with a counter-intuitive solution which the technology has a potential to illuminate, posed in a form which could be worked on collaboratively. It consists of the selection of a range of methods for studying the effects of interacting with the technology and methods for exploring how the collaboration develops.

This chapter therefore reviews some of a programme of work which aims to describe how the use of information and communication technology alters the experience of learners in these settings. Learners can engage in productive experiences of collaborative learning using a variety of computer systems to support their learning. This programme builds on past work evaluating science-based computer-assisted learning software with both children in schools and adults in other settings (see, for example, Smith et al. 1991, Scanlon et al. 1993b, Taylor et al. 1993). We conduct a variety of naturalistic and laboratory-based studies of collaboration, but the focus in this chapter is the latter. The focus of the programme is to explore the potential of collaborating technologies for distance learning and to match task performance with a number of collaborative conditions. The motivating question for the research is: 'What is different when members of a problem-solving group are physically separated then reconnected via this type of computer and communications technology?'

## Tasks Mediated by Technology

Introducing technology into a setting can have both predictable and unpredictable effects. Properties of the technology such as communication or simulation capacity can be used to plan a problem-solving activity where such properties can offer advantages. However, it is our experience that using technologically mediated collaboration changes the nature of the activity in ways we had not predicted. We discuss these later in the case studies, but first we review findings from other empirical studies of technologically mediated problem solving.

There have been a number of industrially-based studies of technologically mediated collaborative problem solving, mainly focusing on the effect of different communication modalities on task performance. Early studies looking at pairs problem solving with such media as telephone and video and later studies looking at face to face, phone, documents and desktop video telephones (for example, Fish et al. 1992) shared the common view that voice is the most important communication media. A recent paper by Kraut et al. (1996) manipulated video and audio conditions on remote collaboration on a bicycle task but found no differences in success between pairs using different combinations. Reviewing this research, Flor asserts that:

> This result suggests that collaboration is an adaptive process that can take advantage of whatever modes technology makes possible. (Flor 1998, p. 204)

However, while this assertion is plausible there is more to be said about the different support for tasks offered by the different modalities. One key to this is also the collaboration processes required to be supported by the technology. For example, the bicycle task may have required task division rather than discussion and this may influence the effects of particular media combinations.

Flor has studied side-by-side collaboration during programming tasks which were demanding enough to require collaboration. He points to the importance of a shared workspace for collaboration in information tasks. This is one of a number of assertions which are made about the features of a task setting that promote collaborative problem solving in the literature. We have selected a number of these to adopt in the formulation of our tasks, each of which contain a shared simulation as a focus, a joint product of activity and for the participants to sustain co-ordinated activity over a period of time.

A number of other studies of adults' use of video conferencing have been conducted. A human computer interaction approach to studying video conferencing led to a Daly-Jones et al. (1998) report on two experiments which demonstrate significant advantages for video conferencing over audio-only conferencing in the context of a negotiated task using electronically shared data. O'Conail et al. (1993) compared two different video-conferencing systems with different properties with face to face, concluding that the interaction when conducted over high-speed video links was more formal than face to face. O'Malley et al. (1996), describing experiments with a map task, assert that performance and communicative efficiency of high-quality video pairs were more like audio-only pairs than face-to-face co-present pairs, even when a video tunnel allowed participants to use accurate eye contact. Sellen (1992, 1995), experimenting with a specially designed video set up to facilitate turn-taking in multi-party communication became concerned that video-mediated communication did not provide the expected gains in communicative efficiency. The tasks used in these studies reported above varied considerably and range from open-ended discussions through instructions about manipulating objects and constructive tasks like programming. Results from research in this area seems to be dependent on the nature of the tasks used and the quality of the communication channel.

## Case Studies of Synchronous Collaboration

We have been studying synchronous collaboration in the context of adults working on shared simulations. The main technological base has been provided by a number of systems designed by Randall Smith. The Alternate Reality Kit, ARK (Smith 1992), is a system for creating interactive animated simulations implemented in the Smalltalk–80 programming environment.

The Shared Alternate Reality Kit, SharedARK (Smith et al. 1991), and KANSAS, a network shared application space (Smith forthcoming) are prototype technologies for allowing students to work together at a distance from each other on a shared simulation whilst maintaining voice and eye contact. The following are two simulations used to explore the capabilities of the shared space for problem solving; the 'Running in the Rain' experiment and the 'Gameshow' experiment.

## The 'Running in the Rain' Experiment

Our primary purpose in this experiment was to assess the learnability and usability of the SharedARK technology and to identify factors which were important in facilitating collaborative problem solving with this technology. We did this by comparing remote electronically mediated communication during collaborative problem solving with that occurring during physical co-presence. These experiments involved nine pairs of adults working at a simulation of an underspecified problem. Four of the pairs of participants used the video tunnel whilst working together on the simulation, three worked on the simulation as co-present participant pairs, and two pairs worked remotely with only audio contact. We used the problem of whether to run or walk in the rain without an umbrella (De Angelis 1987). (Running means spending less time in the rain, but, on the other hand, since you are running into some rain, you might end up wetter than if you had walked.)

In these experiments two users were in separate rooms with a workstation each, and communicated through a high-fidelity, hands-free audio link and with a camera/monitor device called a video tunnel which enabled both voice and eye contact. After an eight- to ten-minute introduction to the interface and the task, the participants were given a simulation containing a rain cloud, a rain runner and a device to control simulation parameters such as the speed and the direction of the rain and the wetness of the runner. During the introduction they were told that the object of the activity was for them to jointly agree when it is worth running in the rain. They were shown how to make the runner wider and narrower, how to make the runner move and how to switch the rain on and off. Participants were invited to use the simulation to test their ideas, and after 90 minutes they were asked to report on their findings.

A data-capture suite was used to capture video records of the interaction, which were then displayed in a four-way matrix. For pairs this meant capturing each user's screen and their video conferencing record. (For the larger groups a single shared screen was recorded with each individual user's video.) Video cameras were used to record task performance. One camera was used to record task performance. One camera captures the information displayed on screen. This data collection set-up was inspired by the development of the media space at Xerox PARC in the mid-1980s (see Bly et al. 1993), and then developed further in Rank Xerox's research centre in Cambridge where the 'running in the rain' experiments were recorded. This facility was then developed in the Computers and Learning Research Group at the Open University where later experiments described in this chapter took place.

There were four synchronous video signals made up of what was displayed on the two video-tunnel screens and the two simulation screens worked on by the participants. The video protocol was analysed by relating utterances made by participants to both events in working with the simulation and eye contact. Participants' activities and utterances from their verbal protocols were categorised according to the type of activity in which participants were engaged, according to whether it involved the interface (for example, figuring out how to alter the rain runner's speed, or make the rain runner wider), or the task (discussion about running in the rain or social interaction (for example, laughing at jokes). These utterances were then further assigned to subcategories, called meta-level activity, specific activity and recovery, which describe the nature of the activity. For example, meta-level activity might be generating hypotheses, or discussing problem-solving strategies; specific activity might be talk generated in doing the task, and recovery from breakdown might be recovery from interface errors or misunderstandings during a conversation. Features of the dialogue are described in Taylor et al. (1993), the type of augmented problem solving which was facilitated is described in Scanlon et al. (1993b), and the nature of the shared space and its role in establishing successful collaboration is described in Smith et al. (1991).

This analysis revealed some interesting features. Use of the video channel was correlated with activity when participants were not directly manipulating the interface. We found several examples of jokes being cracked across the video channel. There are long periods where the video tunnel was not used at all; for example, when objects are being manipulated or data points collected. However, when the participants were talking about what they observe or suggesting hypotheses or planning experiments, they looked towards their partner through the tunnel. Another difference was that participants who could see each other were terser and less explicit. We hypothesised that a video channel might encourage non-interface specific activity, and indeed meta-level discourse about the task was accompanied by much higher levels of eye contact than was specific talk about the interface. There were also considerable differences in the way that different pairs negotiated their problem solving.

The unique shared space created by the participants using the technology is interesting. The use of overlapping (shared) and non-overlapping work areas seemed to have encouraged task division, but role division was also fluid. Participants can be both face to face through the video tunnel and side by side looking at the SharedARK interface. This would suggest that pairs using the video tunnel might do better in solving the problem. Since being face to face facilitates patterns of mutual gaze, we thought that more productive problem solving might ensue. The use that participants made of the video tunnel coincided with joint assent to certain decisions, particularly at the planning phase. This side-to-side and face-to-face combination was not available to co-present pairs, and seemed to influence how role and task division took place. In the audio-only condition there was more explicit negotiation of task division than in the video condition.

In substance it appeared from this exploratory experiment that the addition of a video channel influenced the users' activity by encouraging interaction about the problem.

Comparing the problem solutions produced by pairs on this task with written problem solutions (see Scanlon et al. 1993a), the study demonstrated that the use of audio links and video tunnels does not attenuate the problem-solving behaviour of pairs working on the task, but in fact enhances it.

### The 'Gameshow' Experiment

This work has informed the design of a series of studies exploring a statistics-based simulation implemented in a new distributed classroom environment designed by Randall Smith at Sun Microsystems called KANSAS. This allows several physically distributed users to move about in a 2D space (called 'KANSAS' because it is very extensive and flat, not because it also stands for KANSAS, a networked shared application space.) Moving together and apart in KANSAS will make and break audio connections. Users each have a window in which they can see their local portion of KANSAS. Each user sees a small local rectangular portion of KANSAS and can scroll his or her viewpoints across the vast surface, causing his or her rectangles to overlap in order to collaborate, or can move away from others to work alone. Our experiment here was conducted on a version of KANSAS which supports up to five simultaneously active users (or, of course, up to five groups of users) and users can be given access to audio or both video and audio links between each of the five locations. Randall Smith has experimented with larger numbers of simultaneous users. We are using Gameshow: the simulation of a well-known statistics problem – the Monty Hall dilemma. We are using this to explore a number of related themes:

- The effect of working with a simulation on concept development in statistics

- The influence of the bandwidth of the communication channels on the collaboration
- The scalability of the collaborative experience
- The usability of the interface design.

We have collected data on six pairs of participants; two groups of three and a group of four using the shared simulation augmented by audio communication. We have also collected data on five pairs who used a video tunnel to provide a video channel of communication, and a further four pairs working with altered video tunnels where there is no eye contact. In this chapter we are focusing on a comparison of audio groups with pairs working with video tunnels where eye contact has been facilitated. We are currently comparing data from pairs working with the video tunnels and pairs working with the altered video tunnels (Scanlon and Joiner, forthcoming).

We are using 'gameshow', a simulation of a well-known statistics problem – the Monty Hall dilemma – originating in a TV gameshow called *Let's Make a Deal*, where the gameshow host encourages contestants to make a choice between three items, and then they are given the opportunity to change their choice. This hard problem caused extensive correspondence between statisticians when discussed in a newspaper (see Hoffman 1999). The groups of participants were asked to explore the problem with the aid of a shared simulated gameshow setting, a shared note-taking tool and a remote human host. They communicate over an audio or video link. The gameshow host displays the consequences of their choices. We have recorded videos of adults working together on the statistics simulation in different physical locations and observed their problem-solving behaviours and the impact of the experience on their understanding of concepts in probability.

To complement this observation, participants were interviewed and given individual pre- and post-test questionnaires. The participants were told:

*You are a game show contestant. You have won through to the final round and your final challenge is to choose one of three doors. Behind one but only one of the doors is a Mercedes. You announce your selection but before you open the door the game show host 'helpfully' opens one of the doors which was not the one you have chosen. It doesn't have a car behind it. What should you do, stick to your original choice or change?*

They were asked individually to make a prediction and to give a reason for that prediction. Then they were introduced to their partners and given a shared simulation to conduct experiments. The time taken on the task ranged from 30 minutes to 90 minutes. After the simulated experiment, students were asked to make a joint statement of their solution and to comment on whether it had changed from their individual statements. Then they completed an individual post-experiment questionnaire to establish what their own opinion was. They were asked to state what they thought was the best strategy for the game contestant to pursue. They also were asked to make a prediction about what was the best strategy to pursue if the problem had four doors and the gameshow host opened two of them.

The participants displayed many misconceptions associated with probabilistic reasoning; for example, that an event occurring at random means that it occurs 50% of the time. They displayed superstitious behaviour with respect to patterns, to turn-taking and to individuals – in one case becoming convinced that one of their group was 'lucky'. Also, some participants, whilst correctly interpreting the probabilities, asserted that changing the choice of doors carries a higher 'emotional risk' of leaving a choice that turns out with hindsight to have been right. As one pair commented:

> It looks to me that you have got more chance changing
> *Yes I wouldn't do that myself though*
> Wouldn't you?
> *No*
> You'd stick
> *I'd stick all the time*

When probed further this behaviour turned out to be due to the perception that, 'You'd feel so bad if you changed and then it won.'

The main observation from our collection of results of different groupings is that learners behave differently when they use systems like KANSAS from the way they behave when they are in the same room, and that the dynamics of groups of learners alter in very distinct ways depending on the number of participants who are simultaneously working together. One key aspect of shared system use that affects behaviour is the clarity and economy of the note-taking methods devised or adopted by the group. Some groups generated chronological and detailed records of every use they made of the simulation. The level of detail was such that they had to scroll in a shared window to view the data although this did present its own problems. Such difficulties meant that groups often agreed on counter-factual summaries of the data that matched their expectations or prejudices, such as: 'It's 50:50 either way.' Larger groups were more likely to record unmanageable amounts of data and to agree incorrect summaries, although in some cases some of the participants were able to provide useful comments. One group of four was exploring the hypothesis that particular letters were lucky:

There's not a pattern forming linked to one particular letter is there?
*Well, that's what I'm thinking, I mean when we tried it on B it didn't work,*
*but when we tried it on A it did work*
It did
**It didn't work every time**
So should we try it on C a few times?

The intervention in bold did point to an inconsistency in the group's thinking, but it still did not lead to the group abandoning an unproductive line of enquiry.

When groups devised simple, highly focused ways of summarising the data that could be viewed in a single window they were much more likely to identify and resolve their mathematical misconceptions. The most elegant summary was a two-by-two matrix of success/fail versus stick/change, where the appropriate cell was updated by one of the participants after each go at the game.

In this experimental situation the learning experience was managed in part by the gameshow host, and this raises another issue related to scalability – the issue of learner support. In this case the learning support demands appear to be much more acute than those found in the conventional classroom (see O'Shea et al. 1997).

This system was designed to allow participants working collaboratively to solve a particular problem. The particular focus here was on trying to understand how students could use a system which allowed them to conduct variable-based practical experiments to help them develop their knowledge and understanding of a statistics topic. Simulations on computers can allow many experiments to be conducted quickly to develop an understanding of statistical topics. We found some success with this method (the majority of students made progress in their understanding of the problem, in addition to the detection of many of the misconceptions about randomness cited above). However, students held widely differing views about how many trials of different strategies were necessary to build up a sensible picture of the outcomes of different strategies. A full account of their attempts is given in Scanlon et al. (1997).

As to the influence on collaborative problem solving due to access to two different communication channels, we are able to compare the behaviour of pairs communicating with an audio channel only or a video channel. The influence of the video channel was less marked than in the previous SharedARK experiment in terms of pattern of discourse. Some pairs using audio were fairly terse, but some were quite discursive. The use of audio-only, however, did require more interchanges clarifying task division – for example, one pair communicating over audio-only about their use of the shared note-taking tool commented:

Sorry, D, am I blitzing you?
*Yeah I didn't realise that, so who is going to ... what shall we do about ... shall we have a procedure for making the notes so we both don't try and type at the same time?*
OK
*Shall I type in?*
You go ahead and type in yes

However, in some pairs, the access to and use of the video channel did lead to a better co-ordination of views between the two participants – what they thought the position was and what they thought would be a good experiment to try. One pair in particular used the video channel to explain their current view of the problem, and were even drawing diagrams to explain what they thought the explanation for the successful strategy was. In addition, this pair's conversations over the video channel had a particularly courteous quality:

Do you want to do any more, or do you think we've ...?
*I'd quite like to try ten more with not changing*
OK. You're best at writing, do you think, it doesn't depend on who chooses does it?
*I don't think so*
It's the policies what count, so do you want to choose and I'll count this time?

## Comparison of the Case Studies

The two systems described here differ in the extent to which the computer-based component and the audio-video component are distinct. In SharedARK they are disjointed, as the audio-video is output to a device completely separated from the computer screen; whilst in KANSAS, the audio-video is integrated with the interface. However, more fundamentally for both systems the video and computational components are separate. For the use of the systems that we have explored this is not an issue, as we have used audio-video only for communication between learners, but the possibilities of integration between video and simulation lead to possibilities for more extended experimentation.

Videoconferencing is an appealing possibility for distance education. Multiple video images can be displayed on a single monitor (for effects, see

Smith forthcoming). For pairs of students the augmented video contact of the video tunnel provided a sense of eye contact . Multiple video sources can be displayed together, but there is no way yet to simulate this improved eye contact for larger groups of users.

Comparing the two simulations, they had some similar features but also some differences. For example, the 'Running in the Rain' simulation required more attention from participants, whilst the 'Gameshow' simulation was more dependent on the successful use of the shared note-taking tool. In addition, in both experiments, as well as acting as an experimental resource, the shared notebook implemented on the screen became a shared focus for discussion (see, for example, Enyedy et al. 1997).

## Conclusions and further work

The motivating question for the research described here was to explore situations in which members of a problem-solving group are physically separated then reconnected via combinations of computer and communications technology. The provision of a simulation which members of the group could explore is a key feature of the systems we describe here. Our finding in general is that distributed problem solving can be supported by appropriate technologies without attenuation, but we have also noticed ways in which the interaction is altered by the technology. If we consider a pair of individuals working together in the same room, the way in which they interact will vary over time, and their proximity will vary. When a technology is the medium of communication between two physically separated individuals, the proximity relations will be altered. They will not be able to touch, but equally they cannot remove themselves from the interaction without breaking it off altogether. They can work side by side, whilst in the video condition be face to face with their partner. So although there may be a loss of quality in the communication via audio or video channels, the proximity relations may be enhanced with an effect on talk about the problem (see Smith et al. 1991 for further discussion of this).

In this case study we see examples of various mechanisms by which it has been proposed that collaborative learning takes place (see, for example, Crook 1994 for a review). We have seen students having access to increased cognitive resources, access to conflicting views as a resource, and opportunities to construct both individual and group products as they proceed with the problem solving. These systems 'which allow users to directly see and hear each other, and allow them to directly act together in a shared world', have fulfilled the initial promise that they were 'easily learned and minimally threatening' (Smith 1992, p. 137).

The key dimensions of variation which have been explored in these experiments are the number of learners working together, whether or not they are physically co-located, and the bandwidth of the communication channels available to them. The bulk of experience reported here is with pairs of participants communicating remotely over audio or video with physically co-located pairs used to draw comparisons. Indeed, the main result of this work is to develop a picture of the shared space created by shared simulations and video communication tools. In both cases, the participants quickly learn to use the simulations and come to terms with the shared audio-video-computer space in which they find themselves. The shared space created by this technology places participants into a kind of enhanced proximity in which it is possible to be simultaneously side by side and face to face. There is still much to be explored about how such workspaces can be designed to maximise the beneficial effects of collaborative problem solving.

We can in these case studies demonstrate particular ways in which participants have used this rich shared resource to augment and facilitate their joint problem solving, which gives us considerable hope that such systems will be developed for distance learners. Sometimes it has been claimed that the nature of the activity change caused by the use of technologically mediated collaboration alters the authenticity or reality of the learner's experience, either positively or negatively. However, the change in the working practices of scientists over the last few years whilst we have been engaged in this research means that communication over networks as part of collaborative working is now a common part of the working practices of modern scientists. Therefore the context of this work, which began as a laboratory investigation of an unfamiliar and futuristic setting for group working, is one which today's students now accept as a reflection of the type of settings they may encounter in their future working. Students and teachers can confidently predict the continuing integration of information and communication technologies with other tools, and educational researchers can expect to build and test virtual learning environments, focusing on identifying the different special properties of such new shared spaces.

## Acknowledgements

The authors gratefully acknowledge the members of the Running in the Rain project team (Josie Taylor and Claire O'Malley) and Gameshow project team (Yibing Li, Richard Joiner and Mark Treglown).

# References

Bly, S., Harrison, S. and Irwin, S. (1993). 'Media Spaces: bringing people together in a video, audio and computing environment'. *Communications of the ACM*, 3628–45.

Crook, C. (1994). *Computers and the Collaborative Experience of Learning*. London: Routledge.

Daly-Jones, O., Monk, A. and Watts, L. (1998). 'Some advantages of video conferencing over high-quality audio conferencing: fluency and awareness of attentional focus'. *International Journal of Human-Computer Studies*, 49, 21–58.

De Angelis, D. (1987). 'Is it really worth running in the rain?' *European Journal of Physics*, 8, 201–2.

Enyedy, N., Vahey, P. and Gifford, B. (1997). 'Active and supportive computer-mediated resources for student-to-student conversations'. In R. Hall, N. Miyake and N. Enyedy (eds) *Proceedings of Computer Support for Collaborative Learning 97*, Toronto, 10–14 December.

Fish, R., Kraut, R., Root, R. and Rice, R. (1992). 'Evaluating video as a technology for information communication'. *Communication of the ACM*, 36, 48–61.

Flor, N. (1998). 'Side by side collaboration: a case study'. *International Journal of Human-Computer Studies*, 49, 210–22.

Hoffman, P. (1999). *The Man Who Loved Only Numbers*. London: Fourth Estate.

Kraut, R.E., Miller, M.D. and Siegel, J. (1996). 'Collaboration in performance of physical tasks: effects on outcome and communication'. *Proceedings of the Computer Supported Cooperative Work Conference, CSCW '96* (pp. 57–66). New York: ACM Press.

O'Conail, B., Whittaker, S. and Wilbur, S. (1993). 'Conversations over video conferences: an evaluation of the spoken aspects of video-mediated communication'. *Human-Computer Interaction*, 8, 389–428.

O'Malley, C., Langton, S., Anderson, A., Doherty-Sneddon, G. and Bruce, V. (1996). 'Comparison of face-to-face and video-mediated interaction'. *Interacting with Computers*, 8, 177–92.

O'Shea, T., Smith, R., Scanlon, E. and Li, Y. (1997). 'Exploring the scaleability of object-oriented environments that support synchronous distributed collaboration'. *Proceedings of EDMEDIA–97*, Calgary.

Scanlon, E. and Joiner, R. (forthcoming). 'Manipulating video communication on a statistics problem solving task'. Internal document. Milton Keynes: Open University.

Scanlon, E., O'Shea, T., Driver, R., Draper, S., Hennessy, S., Hartley, J. R., O'Malley, C. and Twigger, D. (1993a). 'Twenty-nine children, five computers and a teacher'. *Proceedings of the Fifteenth Annual Conference of the Cognitive Science Society*. Boulder, CO: Cognitive Science Society.

Scanlon, E., O'Shea, T., Smith, R., O'Malley, C. and Taylor, J. (1993b). 'Running in the rain – can a shared simulation help to decide?' *Physics Education*, 28, 107–13.

Scanlon, E., O'Shea, T. and Smith, R. (1997). 'Supporting the distributed synchronous learning of probability: learning from an experiment'. In R. Hall, N. Miyake and N. Enyedy (eds) *Proceedings of the Second International Conference on Computer Support for Collaborative Learning, CSCL '97* (pp. 224–30). New York: ACM Press.

Sellen, A.J. (1992). 'Speech patterns in video-mediated conversations'. In P. Bauersfeld, J. Bennet and G. Lynch (eds) *Proceedings of CHI '92* (pp. 49–59). New York: ACM Press.

Sellen, A.J. (1995). 'Remote conversations: the effects of mediating talk with technology'. *Human Computer Interaction*, 10(4), 401–44.

Smith, R.B. (1992). 'A prototype futuristic technology for distance education'. In E. Scanlon and T. O'Shea (eds) *New Developments in Educational Technology* (pp. 131–8). Berlin: Springer-Verlag.

Smith, R.B. (forthcoming) 'KANSAS: a dynamically programmable multi-user virtual reality'. In T. O'Shea and E. Scanlon (eds) *Virtual Learning Environments and the Role of the Teacher.*

Smith, R.B., O'Shea, T., O'Malley, C., Scanlon, E. and Taylor, J. (1991). 'Preliminary experiments with a distributed, multi-media problem-solving environment'. In J.M. Bowers and S.D. Benford (eds) *Studies in Computer Supported Cooperative Work: Theory, practice and design* (pp. 31–48). Amsterdam: North-Holland.

Taylor, J.A., O'Shea, T., Scanlon, E., O'Malley, C. and Smith, R. (1993). 'Discourse and harmony: preliminary findings in a case-study of multi-media collaborative problem solving'. In R. Glanville and G. de Zeeuw (eds) *Interactive Interfaces and Human Networks.* Amsterdam: Thesis Publishers.

# 14

## Collaborating and Learning in a Project of Regional Development Supported by New Information and Communication Technologies

*Pascale Marro Clément and Anne-Nelly Perret-Clermont*

### Introduction

Research in education, if it wants to offer some means for efficiency in the field, requires a double commitment: first, to the understanding of the psychological processes that mediate learning and teaching and that allow for the appropriation by the individuals of new skills and knowledge; and, second, to the 'nesting' of these processes in the complexity of the historical events in which the educational endeavour takes place and in which the learners – but also the wider society – have stakes, and from which learning gets its meaning. This latter reality is not just a 'context' for the learning nor just the 'background' of the scene on which the didactic action takes place: it is the scene itself in which the social actors come to negotiate their offers and their needs, learning being one among others. Learning is not always an aim *per se*, it is very often a mediational activity toward other goals. What are these other needs? And to what extent do they sustain or impeach learning, or more precisely the learning of what the teacher or the programme is trying to transmit?

Methodologically, a double approach is needed to deal with these questions in a continuous back-and-forth movement from the field to the laboratory. If the laboratory is seen as a 'manufacturer' of intellectual 'lenses', and the field as the place where the newly made lenses are tested, the back-and-forth movement between these two areas can be an opportunity both to ameliorate the lenses (or identify the need for other types of lenses) and to deepen the understanding of the educational enterprise under scrutiny.

It is with these types of questions and scopes that our research group accepted an invitation extended by the promoters of the Poschiavo Project to observe their launching of an experience of adult education intended to teach both human ecology and new information and communication technologies to linguistically and geographically isolated inhabitants of an Alpine valley.[1] We will not present here the whole Poschiavo Project nor the entire monographic study carried out to document this experience, via participant observations, study of the archives, transcriptions of video recordings of important decision-making meetings, interviews, and so on. In this chapter we will concentrate on the main hypothesis; that is, that the nature and degree of the collaboration between the teachers and the learners plays a crucial role in the success of the endeavour. Laboratory studies provided us with evidence for making this hypothesis and encouraged the promoters' actions in investing efforts on this line. But the confrontation with the reality of the field has made us, and the actors of the Poschiavo Project, even more aware of the crucial importance of this factor. It has led the promoters of the experience to an in-depth reconsideration of what being a 'teacher' or a 'learner' means in such a context, and to radically change their project.

This chapter describes an opportunity to reflect on the use and meaning of 'collaboration' in such a project. Our approach is a qualitative monographic description of some of the psychosocial processes at work. The description is informed by laboratory work, but is not so much aimed at establishing facts, as at developing theoretical means to understand a little better the complexity of the negotiation between those who want to teach and those who want to gain the experts' knowledge.

## Collaboration and New Technology in Education

In general, new information and communications technologies are part of educational programmes offered by various institutions (for example, primary schools, secondary schools, universities, and also businesses). In order to understand what happens in terms of learning, we have to consider the situation as a whole and examine how the meanings it has for the different actors are shared. From this perspective, we can then analyse the actual processes observed in the field.

From a social constructivist perspective the success of an education and learning activity is linked with the psychosocial processes of collaboration that underlie it (Joiner 1999, Van der Linden et al. forthcoming). For many years, numerous studies (Woods 1980, 1990, Perret 1985, Light and Perret-Clermont 1988, Sirota 1988, Brown et al. 1989, Perret-Clermont and Schubauer-Leoni 1989, Carugati 1990, Elbers 1991, Resnick et al. 1991,

Light and Butterworth 1992, Lave and Wenger 1993, Säljö and Wyndhamn 1993, Foot et al. 1994,) have shown that the subjects who are involved in an educational task interpret it. These interpretations concern the situation, the objectives, the tasks and the status of the partners. They are linked with the respective expectations and representations of the individuals (Gilly 1992) and they affect the learning of individuals (Grossen 1989, Liengme Bessire et al. 1994).

It has been observed that in a learning activity participants have to share the definition of the situation to be successful. Accordingly, the individual is going to develop various ways of 'inhabiting the situation', which not only concern the strategies of resolution of a task but also social strategies of communication (Mercer 1995, Engeström and Middleton 1996).

Process-oriented studies (Slavin 1992, Fonzi and Smorti 1994, Light et al. 1994, Baker 1995, Dillenbourg et al. 1996, Marro Clément 1997, Marro Clément 1999) have shown the great diversity of the processes at work in joint activity towards a mutual goal. These processes of collaboration and negotiation apply to the distribution of the work between peers (task and role), the verbalisations regarding the various ways of resolving a task, the resolution of sociocognitive conflicts, and so on. Are the processes of collaboration of the same nature in educational programmes involving new technologies? Does the presence of technological tools influence the relationship to knowledge or interpersonal relations? What is the role of the mediators in the teacher–learner relationship and in the fulfilment of the activities?

Studies of collaborative learning mediated by computer and studies of distance education give interesting answers to these questions. Perriault (1996) described the nature of distance education in terms of its historical and institutional aspects and of its goals. His approach shows the influence of these various aspects on the activities of the learners and on their attitudes towards information and communication technology (ICT).

The nature of students' attitudes in learning contexts involving new technologies has also come under scrutiny. For example, De Grada and colleagues (1987) conducted comparative studies of Italian high school students' attitudes towards computers in the classical, scientific and technical branches; Galli's (1988) study concerned young adults' attitudes towards new technology in Italian-speaking Switzerland; and Schubauer (1989) observed the kinds of attitudes developers, teachers and pupils are likely to have towards mathematics software. Whether they are really or virtually present, each of the partners (promoter, user, tutor) sees the technological tool according to his or her representations of its role in the planned activity. When a user is in such a context, he or she is confronted not only with a new technology but also with the logic, attitudes and expectations of other individuals (Grossen and Pochon 1988, Perriault 1989).

Other research studies have been concerned with specific features of this educational context. In particular, studies have focused on computer-mediated social interaction (see, for example, the experiments documented by Cohen 1995); on changing expectations on the part of new consumers of distance learning (Perriault 1991, 1993); and on changes in interpersonal relations and educational practice accompanying the introduction of new communication tools into the educational process – tools such as the fax (Dudezert-Delbreil 1994), video conferencing (Duchaine and Bellet 1994), the videophone (De Fornel 1992) and minitel (Toussaint 1992). Other interesting studies have been conducted, at the crossroads between psychology and anthropology, on the 'ecological nest' of technical tools and on the way they are used, often for purposes other than those intended (Perriault 1989; see also the studies presented in Chambat 1992), opening the way for a psychology of the user. The technological tool mediatises the relationship between users and promoters and is transformed through their interactions.

There is much evidence that teachers and learners develop competencies and acquire knowledge through a continual readjustment and sharing of meanings (Schubauer-Leoni 1986, Edwards and Mercer 1989, Adams et al. 1990, Perret and Wirthner 1991, Schubauer-Leoni et al. 1992, Pontecorvo 1993, Cestari 1997, Mercer 1997, Renshaw and Brown 1997, Carugati and Perret-Clermont 1999). This collaborative activity is worked out as the interaction proceeds, but also according to individuals' previous experiences. Can such processes be observed in an educational programme like the Poschiavo Project too?

## Collaboration in a Specific Educational Programme

The question of collaborative learning in an educational programme supported by new information and communication technologies is seen in this chapter at two levels. At the first level, we study the processes of negotiation that took place between the project team and all the users when the latter were confronted with the constraints of the ICT-based programme that they were being offered. At the second level, we analyse the collaboration between adult learners and the evolution of their attitude towards ICT and training.

### The Negotiation between the Project Team and the User Groups

When we arrived in the field, we realised that we could not immediately begin analysing the education processes and the role of new technologies in terms of their impact on learning or on interpersonal relations – we were dealing with groups of adults whose interests and expectations regarding new technologies or the educational programme as a whole were quite different from those of the project team. The processes of negotiation between the project team and the user groups, considered in their economic, political and social context, had to be considered first and foremost.

As in our other recent field studies (Garduno Rubio 1998, Golay Schilter et al. 1999, Muller and Perret-Clermont 1999, Perret and Perret-Clermont forthcoming), before focusing on the learners' psychology we first had to examine the wider context. In this situation of education integrating ICT and concerning a population of adults, what are the characteristics of this encounter between the project team (teachers) and the users (learners)? What do their respective adjustments teach us? What are the conditions for the success of such an enterprise? We chose to analyse the first moment of the encounter between this educational programme and the users since it allows us to observe a group of processes which are crucial to the understanding of the subsequent issues and dynamics of collaboration and learning: the dynamics between the goal-directed activity of the learners and their learning of new information and communication technology.

## Adult Learners' Attitudes Towards ICT and Training

The second objective was to understand the evolution of the user groups' attitudes to ICT and the training of the inhabitants of the valleys (adults who do not necessarily correspond to the usual model of students of classic education studies) between their initial encounter with the Poschiavo Project and the realisation of its objectives.

The dynamics of learning and education take place in a field where cognitive processes (reasoning, acquisition, application of new knowledge, transmission of knowledge, and so on) and social processes (sense of belonging to a group, interactive processes, intersubjectivity, and so on) are closely intertwined. The learners, all the more as they were adults, developed a wide range of competencies. The education concerns these various competencies, some of which were not envisaged at the start by the project team. The training offer changed through contact with the users. We put forward the hypothesis that the individuals concerned constructed together, but also probably individually, different types of activity in order to realise their goals. Do these activities require the acquisition of competencies that had not been planned initially? Are they claimed to be education activities from the actors' point of view? What is the role of technology?

## Implementing an ICT-Based Distance Learning Programme and the Users' Reactions: A New Type of Social Encounter

In the Poschiavo Project, the project team was quickly confronted with the needs of the population. Although consideration of the user groups' reactions and needs was a major component of the pedagogic model advocated by the project team, it went far beyond a mere adjustment of viewpoints. This confrontation and its consequences are interesting from the angle of the social psychology of knowledge dissemination and collaborative learning in the context of education integrating new technologies.

In order to understand the transformation of the Poschiavo Project, we took part in a series of activities. For example, we participated in 20 meetings where the learners (who presented themselves as members of the regional, economic, cultural, or welfare projects) and the teachers (who were members of the project team and were to become responsible for the supervision and follow-up of these projects) were gathered. It was important to know the history of the project, its social and institutional insertion and its support network in order to understand its development and the expectations of learners and other social actors of the valleys concerned. We therefore analysed the available sources: various written documents, audio-visual material, and articles published in the press.

### The Initial Plans of the Poschiavo Project

The name of Poschiavo came to mean 'Italian-speaking valleys of the canton of Graubünden that are distant from the administrative, linguistic and cultural centres of Switzerland'.

The Poschiavo Project was initiated by D. Schürch (Schürch 1996, 1999), director of the Istituto Svizzero di Pedagogia per la Formazione Professionale (ISPFP) of Lugano. The ISPFP is responsible for the training of teachers for the professional schools the canton of Ticino and of the Italian-speaking valleys of the canton of Graubünden, and it works with the professional school of the Poschiavo valley. Within this collaboration, problems linked with distance, and thus with the training of teachers and students, emerged. In order to overcome these problems the ISPFP tried to encourage communication and information exchanges between the professional schools of Lugano and Poschiavo as well as the development of joint education programmes. A working group of the ISPFP (called the 'operative group') was set up. This group's task was to think about the potential offered by ICT. It was set up to define the main objectives of the educational programme (which was to become the Poschiavo Project). These main objectives were the training and familiarisation of the population with new technologies and with the possibilities of access to information that they offer, the introduction of the most modern technologies in a global and coherent way in order to develop isolated regions that are far from the centres of knowledge, and developing a region by making it ICT accessible and literate.

The training in ICT was designed with the goal of achieving long-term autonomy for the region, in terms of training. The plan was first to train a limited number of inhabitants of the valleys in new information and communication technologies. These people would then constitute a group of 'experts' called 'practice assistants'. Once trained, these 'practice assistants' would serve as tutors for the participating population and, in doing so, they would disseminate the technological knowledge into the valleys – thus the region would not be dependent on Lugano for the delivery of its new technology training.

The central concept of the programme was the concept of 'human ecology' which brings together the environmental, economic, social and cultural aspects of the development possibilities of a region, including ICT. It is a multidisciplinary approach to relations between humans and the environment, and between the environment and technology (Del Don and Schürch 1998). In that sense, new information and communication technologies must be available to an entire region in order to promote its development with respect to the human, environmental and cultural aspects of the region. This concept was chosen by the operative group, which developed the idea of offering distance courses on human ecology to certain categories of the population of these valleys.

In the long term, the effects of the overall programme had to go far beyond the mere experimentation of ICT. The aim of the training programme was not only to introduce a population to new technologies through the training in human ecology, but also to create a new image of these isolated valleys, an image that combined modernity and cultural heritage. This programme, offering distance courses on human ecology, was then presented to the authorities and to the people in charge of the professional teacher-training in the valleys.

## From Confrontation to Co-construction

From the first consultations onwards, the potential users showed a definite interest in the project, which they comprehended in terms of their specific socioeconomic history. In accordance with the dynamics that already existed within the communities of the valleys, the idea of a possible opening up through ICT was adopted from the outset. Indeed, despite the actual geographical and linguistic[2] barriers, it transpires (history shows it) that the inhabitants did not await the advent of new technologies to establish links with the outside world and preserve their cultural heritage. Seen from the outside, for example, Poschiavo gives the impression of already adapting to new technological developments. It can be observed in the types of local shops: hi-fi equipment and electronics, upmarket watchmaker's or organic food. In addition, the inhabitants claimed an ecological, cultural and community life consciousness that did not exactly correspond to the gaps assumed by the designers of the project.

The project team had to adapt their initial proposal (distance courses on human ecology) by taking the population's suggestions into account. The inhabitants wished to use the new technologies to support what was already established in the different sectors of the community (economy, education, culture and the tourist industry). These negotiations led to the creation of another distance learning programme, in which human and technical resources of the Poschiavo Project were utilised in the creation of regional development projects (Project Groups – PGs) that were conducted by the inhabitants themselves. The Poschiavo Project provided the infrastructure from which it was possible to realise many different projects. In that sense, the Poschiavo Project became the 'home' of many PGs. This was a complete change to the initial programme.

The new programme was designed to be achieved in a number of stages. During the first stage of the project, the project team, based in Lugano, was in charge of training the 13 practice assistants responsible for the PGs (for more details, see Johnson and Schürch 1995). The inhabitants of the valleys were then invited to make project tenders. According to a certain number of criteria defined in terms of principles of human ecology, various projects were selected by the operative group to take part in the project and benefit from the human and technological resources made available by the programme. The second stage of the project was the realisation, through networking, of the objectives of the various PGs. In addition to their specific goals, the PGs had to develop websites that would be a part of the main website of the Poschiavo Project.[3] The third stage of the Poschiavo Project, which was still under way at the time of writing, was aimed at continuing the activation of the distance contact network and allowing the inhabitants of the different valleys to become independent of the infrastructure offered by the project team.

From this invitation to tender, 21 PGs (about 120 people), distributed in various sectors of activity, were accepted. Each PG developed a specific programme of activity and had at its disposal people (the practice assistants and the members of the operative group) with distinct and complementary knowledge and skills.

## A Model of Education with ICT Closely Linked to Community Needs: A New Form of Collaboration

As a consequence, the model resulting from the collaboration between Lugano and those remote valleys of Eastern Switzerland was not a model of distance learning in the classic sense of the word. This was no longer a top-down offer of education from a group of teachers to a group of learners. The user groups did not so much wish to receive a general training in new education and communication technologies; rather, they wanted scientific and technical support for the shaping and realisation of development projects that concerned the community. The Poschiavo inhabitants demanded a network of activities initiated by the users in a bottom-up fashion.

We could observe the creation of a negotiation that resulted in rethinking the initial educational model. This creation was made possible, on the one hand, by the promoters' desire to develop a concept of distance learning closely linked with a human, economic and social reality; and, on the other, by the user groups' expression of a number of needs relating to technology and the development of their community. Thus the framework of the Poschiavo Project, as it had been initially designed, was considerably modified, and more radically than could have been predicted from our reading of the literature. From a relatively fixed framework it turned into a framework that was specific and 'structured' enough to allow the promoters to help/support/train the inhabitants, but was also 'flexible' enough to enable each group of users to exploit it in its own way. The roles and tasks were redefined: the task, initially defined as the possibility of taking a distance course in human ecology, turned into a task of realising a project with the help of ICT; the 'learners' turned into 'entrepreneurs' (in the sense of Aumont and Mesnier 1992) and the 'tutors' into 'coaches'.

This phase of transformation of the Poschiavo Project was the story of a negotiation between an 'education offer' and the inhabitants' needs. This negotiation led to a departure from a classic distance learning model to more of a support model for the users actively engaged in endogenous economic, cultural, social and technological developments. Insofar as we were interested in collaborative learning and in the use of ICT in different educational contexts, the psychosocial processes of negotiation observed at this initial stage showed us how technology finds its 'nest' ('nest' in the sense defined by Perriault 1989). And, reciprocally, it alerted us to the active role of the learners who, in the programme, look where to 'nestle' in order to achieve their objectives. This new form of collaboration between the learners and the teachers was essentially based on the opportunity for both to co-construct a learning situation which satisfied both their expectations and their needs. The processes of negotiation and of reinterpretation led, insofar as the different partners were aware of them, to modifications of the interaction framework and thus of the activities that would take place in it.

## Adult Learners' Attitudes Towards ICT and Training and Their Ongoing Activities Within the Community

During the activities planned by the PGs, we observed a richness and an amazing complexity in the diversity of the functioning of these PGs, the established communication networks, the use of the resources offered by the device, the acquired competencies in terms of mastering the technologies, and so on. What could be learned from all the elements of this complexity? Some of the processes that could be observed included:

- learning to collaborate and supervise a project
- learning to surround oneself with competent people
- learning to use ICT.

To observe the development of the projects and how the PGs were integrating the technological training, we carried out 24 interviews (eight PGs at each of three different stages of the realisation processes) with project actors during the different phases of realisation and in the different areas of the Poschiavo Project: culture, the economy and the tourist industry, training and administration. The results of these, together with other information (gathered from participants in all official meetings, along with analyses of official documents or video conferences of the different meetings), permitted the documentation of the experiences of each PG, paying particular attention to the dynamics between the goal-directed activity of the PGs and their learning of new information and communication technologies.

### The Various Project Groups

We noticed that participation in the Poschiavo Project led to the development of very different skills because of the diversity of the PGs. Let us illustrate this diversity by presenting a few representative projects.

*PG1: Poschiavo–Una Vallata Alpina: the writing of a book*

The PG1 was made up of four people. Its aim was to publish a book about the valley, using photographs of everyday life and selected texts. In addition to the 'paper' version of the book, the participants planned to make a CD version of the material.

*PG2: Economia online and the marketing of local products*

PG2 was made up of four people. Its main objective was to develop an Internet site with the co-operation of an association of shopkeepers to sell typical products of the valley.

*PG3: Informazione, aggiornamento e consulenza a distanza in ambito sanitario: the continuing education of doctors and nurses*

PG3 was made up of five people (doctors, nurses and the administrator of the hospital). It was in charge of the organisation of the training and the continual professional development of all the employees in the hospital. Its main objective was to organise video conferences for the continuing professional development of doctors and nurses in this institution.

*PG4: Il centro artiganale preindustriale – Dal punt da la Rasiga in Aino: restoring a mill*

PG4 was made up of four participants. The main objective of this group was to restore a pre-industrial craft centre, in order to safeguard a historical and architectural 'jewel' of the region. Besides the technical part of the renovation, the group intended to investigate the historical, technical, anthropological and educational aspects of this site. The information gained from this investigation would enhance the experience of visiting the site, and it would also be published on a website so that people could make 'virtual' visits.

*PG5: Biblioteca – Una finestra sul mondo: management in a library*

PG5, comprising five people working at the library of Poschiavo, pursued different goals with a view of openness to the world thanks to new technologies. Its main objectives were to use new technologies to manage its library activities, to communicate with other libraries through networking, and to organise activities within the school.

## What do these Case Studies Reveal? A Process of Enhancing Learning via Entrepreneurship

*Learning to collaborate and to supervise a project*

At the beginning of the Poschiavo Project, the PGs differed from each other according to whether they existed already as a group, which was then grafted on to the Poschiavo Project, or whether they were formed on the occasion of the invitation to tender, in order to benefit from the support offered.

The first type of PG had already developed methods of working: the members knew each other and they already had experience of various forms of communication and collaboration before the implementation of the education programme. Their attitude was thus one of revision and/or improvement of these skills within the 'possibilities and constraints' imposed by the new framework. We noticed, for example, that PG1, *Una Vallata Alpina*, which was a group that had been established before the programme, made the most of the opportunity offered by the general programme.

> Probably, we are in a somewhat particular situation ... our project began before the beginning of the Poschiavo Project ... it started differently ... if we had to start from scratch, with the real Poschiavo Project, I imagine that it would be very different from what it is now ...[4]

PG1 used the programme as a motivating framework (meeting deadlines, for example), and to solve a number of communication problems linked with distance. The participants also saw in it an opportunity for self-promotion:

> ... because we saw that the Poschiavo Project was becoming known outside too ... and also a new way of carrying information, also promotional, if we want ...

In other PGs which were formed at the start of the programme, the participants declared that they developed a number of new skills. In PG2, *Economia online*, for example, the members said that they had to develop new skills that were linked not only to ICT but also to the achievement of the group's objective as a whole; that is to say, the sharing of resources regarding the products, the construction of a collaborative strategy in terms of advertising and distribution, the organisation of the work and the planning of the tasks to be performed, and so on:[5]

> Everything started with the Poschiavo Project, before, nothing of all that existed.

> It was difficult to know how to develop four goals that had to be integrated in a global project. It was discussed, we put themes and we worked them out. We had to take account of various factors such as economy, geography, ecology ... it was constructed slowly, often by chance, by comparing with the others.

*Learning to surround oneself with competent people*

Contrary to what was envisaged in the promoters' model, some PGs did not directly take part in all the phases of the project. Whether it was at the level of specific skills or the mastery of new technology, many PG members did not learn to master ICT but 'hired' practice assistants or experts from the field for specific activities! This was a surprise to the designers of the Poschiavo Project. It was responsible for familiarising the inhabitants of the valley with ICT, who, once familiarised, 'externalised' the costs of learning to master ICT. A clever strategy indeed!

For instance, PG5, *Una finestra sul mondo*, or PG1, *Una Vallata Alpina*, systematically contacted the practice assistant when aspects linked with the implementation of technology and with the resolution of problems regarding the instructions coming from the project team were concerned:

> The practice assistant was the one who was most often confronted with the computer because he has been trained in ICT.

> It was our practice assistant who made the links on the web site, we just gave the text.

In addition, for PG1, *Una Vallata Alpina*, the participants said that they worked in a delegation mode. The group collaborated with various specialists in the field – graphic designer, advertising executive, marketing organiser:

> Marco is our companion and colleague who lives in French-speaking Switzerland. He ... works for an advertising agency, he is experienced in the field ... he met us ... he will have to perform certain tasks such as dealing with ... all that regards printing ...

> The graphic designer from Lugano developed a concept for the book and, afterwards, for the web page ...

*Learning to use ICT*

And what about the effect of the introduction of ICT on the participants' attitudes towards ICT? The diversity of the actors' needs with regard to the use of the network or to the work on the network (creation of web pages and/or CDs, preparations for the video conferences) led to very different attitudes towards new technologies. Interviews and observations revealed that the participants used ICT for a number of different functions.

One function of ICT was covering the distance that separated the inhabitants from their potential interlocutors:

> ... and also with the two others who are not always here ... so, it is better to send the things and then to phone each other from time to time too ...

> ... to meet, instead of phoning each other, we send an e-mail ...

Another function of ICT was as 'a specific tool of communication'. For some PGs (PG3, *Informazione, aggiornamento e consulenza a distenza in ambito sanitario*, or PG4, *Dal punt da la Rasiga in Aino*, for example), the technological tool was immediately considered in this context. Thus, the individuals developed a reflection not only on the advantages and limits of technology but also on the organisation of the communicational and educational content that it carried (selection of information, mastery of the hypertext, and so on), the interlocutors at whom it was aimed, and the general context in which it was integrated.

To illustrate an aspect of this function, we refer here to the video-conference experience made in PG3. From the start, the participants developed a critical reflection on the way to integrate the video conference, which seemed to offer a more conservative educational approach than the approach they were used to:

> I have been working at the Nursing School for six years. They changed all the methods for the courses. Now there is a lot of group work in the school programme ... the video conference would be a step backwards.

> ... we should study the problems of how group work can be organised and how subtler technologies could be used in conjunction with different teaching methods ...

This short example illustrates another attitude towards technology: not as a constraint to adopt blindly but as a communication tool whose advantages and limits must be understood so that its use may be optimised in a specific educational context.

## Beyond Learning and Entrepreneurship: the Fun of a New Game?

Finally, we noticed the existence of an attitude that went beyond the specific objectives of each project. This attitude was one of curiosity and attraction to the novelty of the new technology itself, regardless of its functionality. Indeed, many participants were surprised by the possibilities of the technologies, which they tried to explore and use in a creative way. Communication by e-mail between members of a family from one room in the house to another, the use of databases to classify recipes, and 'surfing' the web to find information necessary for school work were a few examples of this type of attitude from which a range of skills developed.

## Conclusions

In this kind of ICT educational project – perhaps even more so than in other educational contexts – we have explored two main challenges that the promoters ('teachers') have had to face, and we have reflected on what can be learned about the necessary collaboration between experts and novices in such a venture.

The first main challenge concerned the negotiation of the teaching offer. We have seen that the valley, although attracted by the idea of being helped in its 'modernisation' via ICT (at a time when ICT was perceived sometimes as a threat and sometimes as an almost magic key for the future), and in spite of having accepted the project, initially considered the training to be inadequate for its needs.

The second challenge for the teachers was to discover that adult learners are quite different from young learners. Schoolchildren are used to receiving knowledge offered to them top-down by acknowledged adult experts. They develop strategies to make sense of it and do their 'job' as students: to learn and to show that they have learned. But adults engaged in daily responsibilities and work, who are only part-time, occasional learners, have quite different attitudes towards learning. Of course, sometimes they just want to learn for the pleasure of learning, of discovering new technologies, or of reflecting on the equilibrium between the ecological, social, cultural and economical characteristics of their environment. But more often they view themselves not as learners but as entrepreneurs who need new knowledge to achieve their goals. This has at least two consequences: they have precise expectations that cannot always be fulfilled (for instance, when the teachers and/or the technology cannot cope, or when they have no expectations regarding the expert or the technology on offer); and they are likely to find routes other than 'learning' to reach their goals (for example, we have seen them hire the appropriate expert rather than learning themselves to use the computer). Teaching is a complex process: learners are not just learners. But this does not prevent them from becoming caught up in the fun of learning or being surprised by the hidden possibilities of ICT.

## Acknowledgements

This research was conducted thanks to the Priority Program 'Switzerland tomorrow' of the Swiss National Science Foundation (subsidy no. 500479) at A.-N. Perret-Clermont, J.-F. Perret and L.-O. Pochon's request. We thank these latter two colleagues warmly for their contribution to the work that we present here and of which they are also part-authors.
We warmly thank R. Joiner for his comments and helpful reading of this chapter, and M. Dubois for her help in the translation work.

## Notes

1. Our gratitude goes to the Poschiavo Project Foundation; the Istituto Svizzero di Pedagogia per la Formazione Professionale (ISPFP, Lugano); D. Schürch, who is the promoter of the project and the director of the ISPFP Lugano; his colleagues; as well as the inhabitants of the Poschiavo valley; and more particularly Danilo Nussio, for their invitation to join them on the field and share with them its social (and technical!) as well as intellectual life. The observations and reflections that are presented here, for which we alone take responsibility, would not have been possible without their help.
2. The administrative language of the other Alpine valleys is not Italian, but Rumantsch or German.
3. The address of the site of the Poschiavo Project is:
   http://www.ispfp.ch/ricerca
4. These extracts are taken from interviews conducted with the participants in the PGs during the different phases of the project.
5. This observation ties up with those we made in other studies on dyads and small groups of young adults or of children taking part in problem-solving tasks (with or without computers) (Marro Clément 1997, 1999, Grossen et al. 1998, Golay Schilter et al. 1999).

## References

Adams, D., Carlson, H. and Hamm, M. (1990). *Co-operative Learning and Educational Media*. Englewood Cliffs, NJ: Educational Technology Publications.
Aumont, B. and Mesnier, P.-M. (1992). *L'acte d'apprendre*. Paris: Presses Universitaires de France.
Baker, M. (1995). 'Negotiation in collaborative problem-solving dialogues'. In R.-J. Beun, M. Baker and M. Reiner (eds) *Dialogue and Instruction: Modeling interaction in intelligent tutoring systems* (pp. 39–55). Berlin: Springer Verlag.
Brown, J.S., Collins, A. and Duguid, P. (1989). 'Situated cognition and the culture of learning'. *Educational Researcher*, 18, 32–42.
Carugati, F. (1990). 'From social cognition to social representation in the study of intelligence'. In G. Duveen and B. Lloyd (eds) *Social Representations and the Development of Knowledge* (pp. 126–43). Cambridge: Cambridge University Press.
Carugati, F., and Perret-Clermont, A.-N. (1999). 'La prospettiva psico-sociale: intersoggettività e contratto didattico'. In C. Pontecorvo (ed.) *Manuale di psicologia dell'educazione* (pp. 41–66). Bologna: Il Mulino.
Cestari, M.L. (1997). *Communication in Mathematics Classrooms: A dialogical approach*. University of Oslo: Faculty of Education.
Chambat, P. (ed.) (1992). *Communication et lien social*. Paris: Editions Descartes.

Cohen, R. (ed.) (1995). *La communication télématique internationale*. Paris: Retz (Pédagogie en Europe).

De Fornel, M. (1992). 'Le visiophone, un artefact interactionnel'. In P. Chambat (ed.) *Communication et lien social*. Paris: Editions Descartes.

De Grada, E. (ed.) (1987). 'La rappresentazione del computer in gruppi diversi della popolazione italiana'. *Rassegna di Psicologia*, 4, 5–24.

Del Don, C. and Schürch, D. (1998). 'Poschiavo Project: first outcomes of the implementation of a regional development schema based on IT and human-ecological principles'. *European Distance Education Network*, vol. 1 (24–6 June), 48–52.

Dillenbourg, P., Baker, M., Blaye, A. and O'Malley, C. (1996). 'The evolution of research on collaborative learning'. In E. Spada and P. Reiman (eds) *Learning in Humans and Machines* (pp. 189–211). Oxford: Elsevier.

Duchaine, J. and Bellet, J.-C. (1994). 'Les vidéotransmissions interactives du CNED – Centre national d'enseignement à distance'. *Sciences et techniques éducatives*, 1, 237–59.

Dudezert-Delbreil, M.-J. (1994). 'Usage du télécopieur: une nouvelle relation pédagogique dans l'enseignement à distance'. *Sciences et techniques éducatives*, 1, 261–71.

Edwards, D. and Mercer, N. (1989). 'Reconstructing context: the conventionalization of classroom knowledge'. *Discourse Processes*, 12, 91–104.

Elbers, E. (1991). 'The development of competence and its social context'. *Educational Psychology*, 3(2), 73–94.

Engeström, V. and Middleton, D. (1996). *Cognition and Communication at Work*. Cambridge: Cambridge University Press.

Fonzi, A. and Smorti, A. (1994). 'Narrative and logical strategies in sociocognitive interaction between children'. *International Journal of Behavioral Development*, 17(2), 383–95.

Foot, H.C., Howe, C.J., Anderson, A., Tolmie, A. and Warden, D. (eds) (1994). *Group and Interactive Learning*. Southampton/Boston, MA: Computational Mechanics Publishers.

Galli, E. (1988). *Giovani e computer: attitudine e cultura nella percezione giovanile delle nuove tecnologie: studio sociologico regionale*. Lugano: Banca della Svizzera Italiana.

Garduno Rubio, T. (1998). 'Action interaction et réflexion dans la conception et la réalisation d'une expérience pédagogique: l'Ecole Paidos à Mexico'. *Dossiers de psychologie*, 51, Université de Neuchâtel.

Gilly, M. (1992). 'Institutional roles, partners' representations and attitudes in educational interactions'. In E. de Corte, A. Lodewijns, R. Rummentia and P. Span (eds) *Learning and Instruction* (pp. 229–38). Oxford: Leuven University Press.

Golay Schilter, D., Perret, J.-F., Perret-Clermont, A.-N. and de Guglielmo, F. (1999). 'Sociocognitive interactions in a computerised industrial task. Are they productive for learning?' In K. Littleton and P. Light (eds) *Learning with Computers. Analysing productive interaction* (pp. 118–43). London: Routledge.

Grossen, M. (1989). 'Le contrat implicite entre l'expérimentateur et l'enfant en situation de test'. *Revue suisse de Psychologie*, 48(3), 179–89.

Grossen, M., Liengme-Bessire, M.-J. and Perret-Clermont, A.-N. (1998). 'Construction de l'interaction et dynamique socio-cognitive'. In M. Grossen and B. Py (eds) *Pratiques sociales et médiations symboliques*. Berne: Peter Lang.

Grossen, M. and Pochon, L.-O. (1988). 'Rapport sur l'utilisation du nano-réseau à l'école primaire'. *Cahiers de psychologie*, 27, Université de Neuchâtel.

Johnson, S. and Schürch, D. (1995). *La formation à distance*. Berne: Peter Lang.

Joiner, R. (1999). 'The negotiation of intersubjectivity in children's computer-based collaborative problem solving'. Paper presented at the symposium Intersubjectivity and Collaborative Learning: Multidisciplinary Perspective, 8th AERLI Conference, Göteborg.

Lave, J. and Wenger, E. (1993). *Situated Learning: Legitimate peripheral participation.* Cambridge/New York: Cambridge University Press.

Liengme Bessire, M.-J., Grossen, M., Iannaccone, A. and Perret-Clermont, A.-N. (1994). 'Social comparison of expertise: interactional patterns and dynamics of instruction'. In H.C. Foot, C.J. Howe, A. Anderson, A. Tolmie and D. Warden (eds) *Group and Interactive Learning.* Southampton: Computational Mechanics Publishers.

Light, P. and Butterworth, G. (1992). *Context and Cognition: Ways of learning.* New York/London: Harvester Wheatsheaf.

Light, P., Littleton, K., Messer, D. and Joiner, R. (1994). 'Social and communicative processes in computer-based problem solving'. *European Journal of Psychology of Education,* 9, 93–110.

Light, P. and Perret-Clermont, A.-N. (1988). 'Social contexts in learning and testing'. In J.A. Sloboda (ed.) *Cognition and Social Worlds* (pp. 99–112). Oxford: Oxford Sciences Publications, Oxford University Press.

Marro Clément, P. (1997). 'Résoudre à deux un problème de fabrication assistée par ordinateur: analyse interlocutoire d'une séquence de travail'. *Document de recherche du projet 'Apprendre un métier technique aujourd'hui',* 11. Neuchâtel: Université de Neuchâtel, Séminaire de Psychologie.

Marro Clément, P. (1999). 'Deux enfants, un problème technique, une solution: analyse interlocutoire de la construction interactive d'un raisonnement' *Verbum,* 21(2), 175–89.

Mercer, N. (1995). *The Guided Construction of Knowledge: Talk among teachers and learners.* Clevedon, England: Multilingual Matters.

Mercer, N. (1997). 'Socio-cultural perspectives and the study of classroom discourse'. In C. Coll and D. Edwards (eds) *Teaching, Learning and Classroom Discourse. Approach to the study of eductional discourse* (pp. 13–21). Madrid: Graficas Rogar.

Muller, N. and Perret-Clermont, A.-N. (1999). 'Negotiating identities and meanings in the transmission of knowledge: analysis of interactions in the context of a knowledge exchange network'. In J. Bliss, R. Säljö and P. Light (eds) *Learning Sites. Social and Technological Resources for Learning* (pp. 47–61). Oxford: Pergamon.

Perret, J.-F. (1985). *Comprendre l'écriture des nombres.* Bern: Peter Lang, Collection Exploration.

Perret, J.-F. and Perret-Clermont, A.-N. (forthcoming). *Apprendre un metier technique aujourd'hui.*

Perret, J.-F. and Wirthner, M. (1991). 'Pourquoi l'élève se douterait-il qu'une question peut en cacher une autre?' In J. Weiss (ed.) *L'évaluation, problème de communication* (pp. 137–47). Cousset (Fribourg): Delval.

Perret-Clermont, A.-N. and Schubauer-Leoni, M.L. (eds) (1989). 'Social factors in learning and instruction'. *International Journal of Educational Research,* 13(6), 573–684.

Perriault, J. (1989). *La logique de l'usage. Essai sur les machines à communiquer.* Paris: Flammarion.

Perriault, J. (1991). *Deux études de cas sur l'intégration de l'enseignement à distance dans des politiques de développement régional.* Strasbourg: Council of Europe.

Perriault, J. (1993). 'Le savoir à distance'. In *Le travail du XXI$^e$ siècle.* Paris: Dunod.

Perriault, J. (1996). *La communication du savoir à distance.* Paris: L'Harmattan.

Pontecorvo, C. (1993). 'Discourse and shared reasoning'. *Cognition and Instruction,* 11(3–4), 189–96.

Renshaw, P.D. and Brown, R.A.J. (1997). 'Learning partnerships: the role of teacher in a community of learners'. In L. Logan and J. Sachs (eds) *Meeting the Challenges of*

*Primary Schools.* London: Routledge.

Resnick, L.B., Levine, J.M. and Teasly, S.D. (eds) (1991). *Perspectives on Socially Shared Cognition.* Washington, DC: American Psychological Association.

Säljö, R. and Wyndhamn, J. (1993). 'Solving everyday problems in the formal setting: an empirical study of the school as context for thought'. In S. Chaiklin and J. Lave (eds) *Understanding Practice. Perspectives on activity and context* (pp. 327–42). Cambridge: Cambridge University Press.

Schubauer, R. (1989). 'Des logiciels en usage'. *Interactions didactiques*, 10. Universities of Geneva and Neuchâtel.

Schubauer-Leoni, M.-L. (1986). 'Le contrat didactique: un cadre interprétatif pour comprendre les savoirs manifestés par les élèves en mathématique'. *European Journal of Psychology of Education*, 1(2), 139–53.

Schubauer-Leoni, M.-L., Perret-Clermont, A.-N. and Grossen, M. (1992). 'The construction of adult intersubjectivity in psychological research and in school'. In M. Von Cranach, W. Doise and G. Mugny (eds) *Social Representation and the Social Bases of Knowledge.* Bern: Huber.

Schürch, D. (1996). 'Progetto Poschiavo: une utopie pour la Suisse de demain?' *Panorama*, 38, 3–5.

Schürch, D. (1999). 'Verso una pedagogia dello sviluppo territoriale: il caso Poschiavo'. In P.L. Amietta (ed.) *I Luoghi dell'apprendimento.* Paris: Franco Angeli.

Sirota, R. (1988). *L'école primaire au quotidien.* Paris: Presses Universitaires de France.

Slavin, R.E. (1992). 'When and why does cooperative learning increase achievement? Theoretical and empirical perspectives'. In R. Hertz-Lazarowitz and N. Miller (eds) *Interaction in Cooperative Groups* (pp. 145–74). Cambridge: Cambridge University Press.

Toussaint, Y. (1992). 'Historique des usages de la télématique'. In P. Chambat (ed.) *Communication et lien social.* Paris: Editions Descartes.

Van der Linden, J.L., Erkens, G., Schmidt, H. and Renshaw, P. (forthcoming). 'Collaborative learning'. In P.R.J. Simons, J.L Van der Linden and T. Duffy (eds) *New Learning.* Dordrecht: Kluwer Academic Publishers.

Woods, P. (ed.) (1980). *Pupil Strategies: Explorations in the sociology of the school.* London: Croom Helm.

Woods, P. (1990). *Teacher Skills and Strategies.* London/New York: The Falmer Press.

# 15
# Rethinking Collaborative Learning: An Overview

*Karen Littleton*

Over the last three decades much research has converged around the question of when and how opportunities for peer interaction facilitate the development of understanding and learning. Whilst acknowledging the valuable insights afforded by this work, the contributors to this volume recognise that to date 'the research agenda on the processes of collaborating has been rather narrow in its focus' (Crook, p. 166). In inviting us to 'rethink collaborative learning' the authors have begun to sketch out a broad and challenging new research agenda for psychologists, educationalists and instructional designers alike. In this synopsis I will use the voices of the contributors to summarise the key themes and issues emerging from their contributions, and present the key facets of this exciting new research agenda. Unless otherwise specified, references to contributors refer to their contributions in this volume.

## The Ecology of Collaboration

Much of the work designed to understand the processes of productive interaction has involved detailed microgenetic analyses of brief, time-limited, localised sessions of talk and joint activity. Such analyses frequently neglect the crucial evolutionary and temporal dimensions of collaborative group work, effectively reducing collaborations to atemporal 'inventories of utterances' (Crook 1994, p. 150). There is, therefore, a need for careful analyses of discourse which focus on the continual, subtle, evolutionary processes of negotiation and renegotiation of meaning. However, there is also a pressing need for analyses which consider the particular historical, institutional and cultural contexts of collaborative activity. Throughout the volume, there has been a clear recognition that discourse in any socially defined setting is nested within the wider socio-cultural context (Valsiner 1997) and that the groups of children we study do not undertake their joint work in a vacuum. We therefore need 'to attend to the wider context within which collaborative activity occurs' (Howe et al., p. 97).

As Crook makes clear, 'understanding contexts for collaborative learning involves more than understanding how the immediate joint activity is resourced'. This is a point echoed by Howe et al. who comment on the 'undue emphasis on factors that are specific to the collaborative experience'. Noting that 'there will always be more to peer collaboration than the collaborative activity itself', Howe et al. emphasise that 'we cannot hope to progress by focusing on collaboration alone'. Learners' collaborative interactions are framed by, and therefore can only ever be fully understood within, their specific cultural niches. The challenge, then, is for interactions to be understood with specific reference to the broader social, institutional, cultural and historical contexts within which they are positioned. Different contexts will afford different opportunities for, and place different constraints upon, interaction. In the case of collaborative interactions in school, for example, 'children's interpretations of experience, the meanings they attach to their learning – will, in part, be determined by their involvement with schools and other institutions of their society ... schools have their own body of cultural knowledge, and their own ways of communicating and legitimising knowledge' (Mercer 1992, p. 31).

Understanding collaborative interactions in their broader context is undeniably difficult and poses a considerable challenge for the researcher. Crook, however, argues that one way of meeting this challenge is to adopt a strongly ecological approach to the analysis of collaborative activity. This entails taking the material environment 'in which collaborations get organised – the tide in which we swim – as the starting point for analysis' (p. 161). Such an approach not only requires us to characterise the cultural niches within which collaborative activity is orchestrated, it demands that we register the systemic nature of such activity and understand how collaborating implicates artefacts or technologies (Crook, p. 169). Several of the contributors to this volume are particularly concerned to establish the ways in which signs, artefacts, tools and technologies are implicated in collaborative activity. Counteracting the prevailing 'tendency to decouple the collaborators' talk from the material circumstances in which it is embedded' (Crook, p. 168), these researchers have started to explore the 'mediated' character of social interaction.

## Mediated Activity and the Processes of Joint Meaning Making

The concept of mediation is central to 'situated' approaches to understanding cognitive activity. It is a concept which refers to the fact that our relationship with the outside world is always mediated by signs and artefacts (Säljö 1996, 1999). The choice of which artefact to use alters the structure of our work activity (Scribner and Cole 1981) and fundamentally transforms the cognitive and communicative requirements of our actions (Säljö 1996, p. 90). A sociocultural view of learning 'sees thinking and action as inseparable' (Murphy, p. 157), the implication being that when studying collaborative learning the appropriate unit of analysis becomes 'people in action using tools of some kind' (Säljö 1999). The mediational means thus forms part of the actions in situated practice.

The need for analyses that are sensitive to the mediated nature of collaborative activity is clearly highlighted in Scanlon et al.'s work on the technological mediation of undergraduates' collaborative problem solving. It is further underscored by Joiner et al.'s study of scientific reasoning in children. Here the use of a computer, as opposed to physical apparatus, changed the nature and type of collaborative activity observed, and affected the development of scientific reasoning. These findings are in accord with a number of other striking illustrations of the ways in which computers and computer software structure and reorganise the social processes of problem solving and teaching and learning (Järvelä 1995, Fitzpatrick 1996, Golay Schilter et al. 1999, Keogh et al. 2000). Recent work on gendered responses to ICT (Light and Littleton 1999), however, also reminds us that we never experience artefacts in isolation, but only in connection with a contextual whole: 'artefacts acquire cultural meaning prior to serving as a focal point for co-ordinated activity' (Crook, p. 176).

The importance of understanding the dynamic processes of meaning making is highlighted in the contribution from Murphy, whose work in primary schools focuses on learners' and teachers' constructions of the meaning of educational tasks. Whilst meaning is not a tangible or fixed commodity, in practice it is often assumed that educational 'tasks are given' (Murphy, p. 155). Murphy, however, advances a position that sees tasks as being constructed through a process of interpretation and reinterpretation, emerging as a result of action and interaction. The implication is that our analyses of collaborative activity need to problematise the processes of intersubjectivity, negotiation and co-construction involved in the joint creation of meaning. This involves a recognition that meaning may change dramatically over time, may differ between peers, and may be at odds with that intended by the tutor or teacher. Murphy also reminds us that whilst 'meanings are "in the mind" they have their origins and significance in the culture in which they are created' (Bruner 1996, p. 3, cited on p. 139). She thus argues that 'children's understandings of values, rules and common representations of school ... will influence their interactions with each other and their ability to negotiate and develop shared reference' (p. 140). Murphy's work illustrates the problems that ensue if meanings are assumed and not established. It also establishes that teachers have a pivotal role to play in mediating 'between the learner's personal meanings and the culturally established meanings' (p. 141). Furthermore, it reveals that gender-related ways of being 'reveal the different views of salience that girls and boys may bring to the same activity – views that influence the tasks they perceive and the solutions they judge to be appropriate given the same circumstances'. Thus, episodes of collaborative activity are not just about the construction and negotiation of understanding, they are fundamentally about the subtle processes involved in the moment-to-moment negotiation of identity.

## Identity, Affect and Motivation

This notion of identity as 'a moment in action as children situate themselves in relational activities with others' (Murphy, p. 156) reminds us that the processes of thinking and identity construction go hand in hand:

> to think or to reason well in a situation is, by definition, to take on the forms as well as the substance of a community of reasoners and thus to join that community. Much of discourse, and thus [much] of cognition serves to situate an individual with respect to others, to establish a social role or identity. (Resnick et al. 1997, p. 9)

It also throws into stark relief the limitations of approaches to collaborative activity which focus solely on cognitive skill. Moreover, it demonstrates that it no longer makes sense to say that we need to study the social and emotional *dimensions* of learning as if such dimensions were analytically separate and distinct from the activity of learning itself. What is needed is a situated, social/emotional approach to understanding cognition. If there were any doubt concerning the need for such an approach, then Murphy's work in primary science classrooms would soon dispel it. Her analyses of Lee carefully reconciling his position as a member of a community of boys with his desire for academic success, shed valuable light on his approach to the ongoing collaborative activity and illustrate how a consideration of identity work should be integral to our analyses of collaboration.

In reading Murphy's analyses we are also reminded that, 'even the imaginary gaze of critical peers is a major threat to children's social identities and significantly affects how they learn to position themselves in subjects. Positions that can constrain their future learning' (p. 157). Similar issues of personal identity, self-presentation and social comparison were also of paramount importance to the undergraduate students studied by Light et al. Students clearly felt exposed putting their ideas or questions into writing, and the permanent visibility of their contributions within the computer conference was a source of anxiety for many. Students were concerned that they might be criticised, or be 'shown up' in front of their peers. The notion of personal criticism was clearly not distinguished from criticism of ideas. The students were also intensely interested in and sensitive to their own ability and the quality of their work relative to their peers. Messages posted to the conference were often used as a source of informal 'feedback' or a means of gauging 'what level everyone is on'. Such social comparison is unsurprising. From a very early age learners are highly skilled at making sense of educational contexts and activities. They construct and participate in discourses about ability and effort (Bird 1994) and are motivated to understand what it means to be a learner and what it means to do and succeed at educational tasks. The social climate of comparison, competition, success, failure and issues of relative status in the classroom rapidly becomes established within the early years of schooling (Crocker and Cheesman 1988) and remains with students throughout their educational careers.

Further criticisms of purely cognitive accounts of group work come from Crook, who notes that 'conceptions of collaborative learning that foreground cognitive skill fail to represent collaboration as something that is motivated' (p. 163). Elaborating on this, he argues that 'the quality of a collaborative endeavour may depend just as much on the participants' enthusiasm for engagement, as it does on their harmony of knowledge, or their experience of resolving cognitive conflict'. We must be mindful, however, that, on the one hand, the motivating experience of collaboration is often realised following little effort on our part; and, on the other, that the quality of affect is not an easy or an inevitable consequence of the contract for joint activity.

## Individual Reflection, Skills and Competencies

Many of the accounts of productive group work developed in the literature rest fundamentally on learners practising various forms of verbally explicit reasoning in talk. Yet productive communication is possible via channels other than talk. For example, Morgan and colleagues and MacDonald and

Miell discuss this possibility in relation to the processes of collaborative music making, arguing that 'dialogue' can occur through the music the children play with each other.

The focus on explicit reasoning in talk seems to have arisen at least in part from the way some analysts have chosen to study collaborative endeavour – in short, self-contained sessions. Researchers who study collaborative work in the context of authentic extended activity, however, remind us of the need to interpret and understand the role of periods of apparent *in*activity as well as observable activity.

The issue of individual reflection is raised in the contribution by Howe et al. who 'point to a learning process which accords a more substantial role to individual reflection and sense making than Vygotsky would have envisaged'. The importance of reflection for the development of understanding has previously been highlighted by Azmitia (1996, p. 155), who questioned whether our fascination with peer interactive minds may have led us to underestimate the contribution of solitary work and reflection to cognitive development and learning, or at least to fail to acknowledge that development and learning may require both. In this volume Azmitia develops this stance, portraying collaborators as 'active, reflective individuals who select which aspects of the shared knowledge they incorporate in their individual theories'. She also extends her discussion of 'time out' from collaboration to highlight that in some circumstances apparent disengagement can have a positive effect on cognitive development.

This finding is echoed in a recent qualitative study of an extended period of collaborative group work undertaken by Golay-Schilter et al. (1999). These researchers invite us to question our assumptions about learners who appear to be 'being left out'. In their work, the negative connotations associated with 'being left out' are replaced with the notion of a learner who is 'at a distance'. Golay Schilter and colleagues argue that in some cases distance can facilitate a 'meta-view' of the action taking place. In their study, a student who does not have to act (albeit through lack of power) appears to 'develop a meta-cognitive space for reflecting upon what is happening' (1999, p. 133). Whilst this student did not have sufficient social weight to impose his point of view, through the persistence of his comments his contributions came to play an essential role in the solution of the task. As Golay Schilter and colleagues make clear, this notion of distance as opposed to marginalisation only emerged through a detailed analysis of the session of work as a whole. That is to say, it was only by studying the evolution of the collaborative activity over time that this characterisation of the learner emerged. In highlighting this example of productive apparent inactivity I do not wish to deny that isolation and disengagement *are* experienced by some, perhaps many, students who are being expected to work collaboratively. Rather, the purpose is to illustrate how, in this instance, the careful study of the evolution of joint activity revealed the fruits of quiet critical reflection.

Contributions from Messer and Pine and Ding and Flynn also put the spotlight firmly on the individual members of pairs or groups. Drawing on the work of Karmiloff-Smith, Messer and Pine argue that 'representational levels may influence the individuals' ability both to discuss the phenom- enon and to make use of the discussion of others. As a result, collaboration and peer interaction may not have *uniform* influences across all individ- uals; instead, their effectiveness may depend on the levels of an individual's representation' (p. 33).

The issue of 'the relationship between the development of children's collaborative abilities and some of their more general cognitive skills' (p. 3) is rehearsed in Ding and Flynn's contribution. They conclude that 'the direction of effect between successful collaborative learning and the under- lying skills may not be straightforward' (p. 16). They also comment that 'the possession of certain cognitive abilities will contribute to a successful learning situation. However, researchers such as Gauvain and Rogoff (1989) have suggested that the experience of working in a collaborative situation encourages the development of metacognitive abilities'.

These contributions clearly underscore the inherent tension in this volume between a developmental psychological tradition, which tends to focus on the developing individual, and a situated approach to learning that emphasises learning as a collective activity in a cultural context.

## Making Space for Collaboration: Designing Collaborative Learning Environments

The contributions to this volume 'shift the agenda away from peer collab- oration in comparison with non-collaborative methods and onto strategies for optimising collaboration itself' (Howe et al., p. 98). Thus, underpinning many of the contributors' interests in understanding productive interac- tion is the idea that through the study of collaborative interactions we can come to understand how better to support learners' joint endeavours.

Throughout this volume we have seen many different visions of how to support and sustain effective collaboration between learners. Some, such as Wegerif, argue that children should be encouraged and enabled to practise certain forms of 'reasoning in talk'. The groundrules of exploratory talk he outlines do not directly teach children to think. Rather, he believes that 'they serve to open up and maintain an intersubjective space of creative diversity in which alternative solutions to problems are generated and allowed to develop and compete as ideas without threatening either group solidarity or individual ego identity' (p. 134). It is in an attempt to create such intersubjective spaces of creative diversity that he outlines a classroom-based intervention programme designed to transform his proposal (and that of his colleagues) into educational practice.

However, the ecological approach advanced by Crook suggests a different approach. Seen in these terms, researchers should 'probe how local space can be designed to "work", that is to be richer in collaborative opportunities' (p. 174) and investigate 'how the circumstances for a potential collaboration are made more optimal, how they are designed and engineered, with expectations that putative collaborators can more readily fall into them to productive effect' (p. 167). In recognising that collaborations are situated activities the implication is that they 'must be precipitated out of the larger social systems – the larger communities to which collaborators belong' (p. 177).

Murphy's emphasis on the construction of educational tasks challenges us to consider how such tasks resource collaboration between learners. Clearly, the simplistic use of everyday settings and applications are problematic not least because 'they assume a ubiquitous view of relevance ... trivialise the complex processes involved in meaning making ... [and] fall far short of the authenticity that a sociocultural approach considers essential to engage children and support learning' (Murphy, p. 156). Mindful of the current political landscape, Murphy questions 'whether there is potential to reconceptualise approaches to [science] education in ways that recognise the cultural process of meaning making. In the English education system this appears unlikely. Currently, there is a retreat to simplistic models of mind that is reflected in formal assessment procedures based on the bell curve conception of human ability and, the introduction of nationally prescribed pedagogic approaches that limit the time and organisational possibilities for science learning' (p. 158).

Several of the contributors point to the role of computer technology in supporting collaborative endeavour and many of these discussions are bound up with challenging existing conceptions of the processes of teaching and learning. For example, in discussing the use of websites with undergraduate students, Crook comments that perhaps their future use could 'move away from "delivery" models (repositories for handouts, lecture overheads or assignment details) towards a more community-oriented model (celebrating the corporate discussions and products of the learning group)' (p. 175). This notion of providing effective support for a collaborative community of enquiry in higher education is developed by Light et al., who note that in CMC environments 'the tutor's task becomes that of structuring challenging conversations among a community of learners rather than channelling expertise or knowledge to the student

(p. 199). What is being aspired to here is 'a move away from the "school ethos" to something much more level between tutor and student' (p. 209), a move which should bring with it a sense of an academic discipline as process rather than product.

So, whilst Marro Clément and Perret-Clermont document the challenges associated with tutoring their somewhat entrepreneurial adult learners, students in UK higher education appear to be very much accustomed to having the tutor or teacher in control of what they do in educational contexts. Despite being given the opportunity to engage in peer discussion in an innovative computer environment, the students in Light et al.'s study nevertheless waited in expectation of the 'proper answer' from the lecturer. Computers undoubtedly have the potential to reorganise learning interactions in a variety of significant ways, but experience suggests that established social institutions have a remarkable capacity for 'neutralising' the effects of new developments, technological or otherwise. The established culture of learning can impact significantly on the prospects for new computer-mediated communication initiatives and existing practices will offer resistance to the 'bolting on' of new forms of educational technology (Crook and Light 1999). Computer technology does undoubtedly have the capacity to free students from the constraints of time and place, but we must remember too that participating in activities situated in a specific time and place does not necessarily constrain human activity.

Running alongside the pleas to engineer and design collaborative space is the recognition that 'collaborative learning may also crystallise out of learning communities: occurring as rather informal and improvised occasions. Such collaboration is not something that is prompted through the official demands of some curriculum (or the stage directions of some researcher)' (Crook, p. 169). Crook's observation reminds us that many opportunities for collaborative learning are fortuitous, they simply emerge as a consequence of being part of a particular community of learners.

An interest in such informal contexts for collaboration emerges in several of the contributions. For example, Light et al. draw our attention to the nature of informal interactions taking place in a computer room and Tolmie and colleagues address the issue of pedestrian training. This focus on informal contexts for collaboration is perhaps not surprising given 'that we are essentially dealing with processes which originate and have a natural ecology within informal learning contexts' (p. 101). Moreover, there is some suggestion that 'finding ways of marrying formal and informal learning practices might well be the key to the reinvention of educational systems' (p. 101). This suggests that 'what needs to happen in the end is a re-direction of the energy that accompanies playful collaboration into collaborations that arise in school settings' (Crook 1999, p. 106). A 'central challenge for educational practice becomes the creation of continuities between existing concerns and new ones that we are asking them to reason about together in classrooms' (Crook 1999, p. 105). The contributions reviewed here make it clear that this is just one of the many challenges involved in 'rethinking collaborative learning' and it is important that new research is undertaken to meet these challenges. Psychologists, educators and instructional designers do not exist in isolation from the social contexts they study. We too are 'situated' in particular institutional, cultural and historical contexts and it is in such contexts that we actively create our subject. Theories and research on the nature of collaborative learning have the potential to shape the environments in which children develop and learn. Thus, in an era of 'standardised assessment tests' and the like, designed to drive up educational standards by highlighting individual success and failure, there is considerable merit in drawing attention to the fundamentally social and relational bases of such achievements.

## References

Azmitia, M. (1996). 'Peer interactive minds: developmental, theoretical, and methodological issues'. In P.B. Baltes and U.M. Staudinger (eds) *Interactive Minds: Lifespan perspectives on the social foundations of cognition* (pp. 133–62). New York: Cambridge University Press.

Bird, L. (1994). 'Creating the capable body: discourses about ability and effort in primary and secondary school studies'. In B. Mayall (ed.) *Children's Childhoods: Observed and experienced*. London: Falmer Press.

Bruner, J. (1996). *The Culture of Education*. Cambridge, MA: Harvard University Press.

Crocker, T. and Cheesman, R. (1988). 'The ability of young children to rank themselves for academic ability'. *Educational Studies*, 14(1), 105–10.

Crook, C. (1994). *Computers and the Collaborative Experience of Learning*. London: Routledge.

Crook, C. (1999). 'Computers in the community of classrooms'. In Littleton, K. and Light, P. (eds) *Learning with Computers: Analysing productive interaction* (pp. 102–17). London: Routledge.

Crook, C. and Light, P. (1999). 'Information technology and the culture of student learning'. In J. Bliss, P. Light and R. Säljö (eds) *Learning Sites: Social and technological contexts for learning*. Oxford: Pergamon.

Fitzpatrick, H. (1996). 'Peer collaboration and the computer'. Unpublished PhD thesis, University of Manchester.

Gauvain, M. and Rogoff, B. (1989). 'Collaborative problem solving and children's planning skills'. *Developmental Psychology*, 25, pp. 131–51.

Golay-Schilter, D., Perret, J.-F., Perret-Clermont, A.-N. and De Guglielmo, F. (1999). 'Socio-cognitive interactions in a computerised industrial task: are they productive for learning?' In K. Littleton and P. Light (eds) *Learning with Computers: Analysing productive interaction* (pp. 118–43). London: Routledge.

Järvelä, S. (1995). 'The cognitive apprenticeship model in a technologically rich learning environment: interpreting the learning interaction'. *Learning and Instruction*, 5(3), pp. 237–59.

Keogh, T., Barnes, P., Joiner, R. and Littleton, K. (2000). 'Gender, pair composition and computer versus paper presentations of an English language task'. *Educational Psychology*, 20(1), 33–44.

Light, P. and Littleton, K. (1999). *Social Processes in Children's Learning*. Cambridge: Cambridge University Press.

Mercer, N. (1992). 'Culture, context and the construction of knowledge in the classroom'. In P. Light and G. Butterworth (eds) *Context and Cognition: Ways of learning and knowing* (pp. 28–47). Hemel Hempstead: Harvester Wheatsheaf.

Resnick, L., Pontecorvo, C. and Säljö, R. (1997). 'Discourse, tools and reasoning'. In L. Resnick, R. Säljö, C. Pontecorvo and B. Burge (eds) *Discourse, Tools and Reasoning: Essays on situated cognition*. Berlin/New York: Springer Verlag.

Säljö, R. (1996). 'Mental and physical artefacts in cognitive processes'. In H. Spada and P. Reiman (eds) *Learning in Humans and Machines* (pp. 83–96). Oxford: Pergamon.

Säljö, R. (1999). 'Mental and physical artefacts in cognitive processes'. In K. Littleton and P. Light (eds). *Learning with Computers: Analysing productive interaction* (pp. 144–61). London: Routledge.

Scribner, S. and Cole, M. (1981). *The Psychology of Literacy*. Cambridge, MA: Harvard University Press.

Valsiner, J. (1997). 'Bounded indeterminacy in discourse processes'. In C. Coll and D. Edwards (eds) *Teaching, Learning and Classroom Discourse*. Madrid: Fundación Infancia y Aprendizaje.

# Index

*Compiled by Sue Carlton*

## DATE DUE

| | | |
|---|---|---|
| | | |
| | | |
| | | |
| | | |
| | | |
| | | |
| | | |
| | | |
| | | |
| | | |
| | | |
| | | |
| | | |
| | | |

GAYLORD     #3522PI     Printed in USA